1991

MEDIAEVAL PHILOSOPHICAL TEXTS IN TRANSLATION
No. 27

James H. Robb, L.S.M., Ph.D., Editor

St. Thomas Aquinas, O.P.

QUESTIONS ON THE SOUL

[*Quaestiones de Anima*]

Translated from the Latin
With an Introduction

by

JAMES H. ROBB
Professor of Philosophy
Marquette University

MARQUETTE UNIVERSITY PRESS
MILWAUKEE, WISCONSIN 53233

Printed in the United States of America

ISBN 0-87462-226-3

Library of Congress Catalogue Card Number: 84-061636

DEDICATION

The Questions on the Soul of St. Thomas Aquinas treats human beings as incarnate spirits, spiritual beings who, incarnate in the world of space and time, are constantly transcending the limits of nature through knowledge, love and friendship. And so I dedicate this volume to my friends and to my students, who are also friends, since it is from them that I have over the years learned and continue to learn that if through wisdom we can be united to God in friendship, then it is also true that through deep and continuing friendships we may make progress in our pursuit of wisdom.

PREFACE

Whenever one finishes a work of scholarship and looks back on the long hours devoted to completing the project, one becomes aware that the result is not wholly one's own. A great debt is owed to others. There are some debts that one can repay in life, but in one's intellectual development there are, happily, many debts that one can only acknowledge, and never repay. First I wish to pay tribute to the late Dr. Anton C. Pegis. It was he who first encouraged me to work on St. Thomas' philosophical anthropology and especially on St. Thomas' *Questions on the Soul;* over the years, first as his student and later as colleague, I learned more from him than from anyone else about how to read St. Thomas.

I wish to thank also Maria Carl, my graduate assistant, who checked all the textual references, a demanding and unrewarding task. Dr. Robert Engbring, director of the Marquette University Press, and Mrs. Lois Carlson, his assistant, have been of unfailing help and encouragement. Over the years they have worked tirelessly to help our Press to achieve distinction.

There is one other person to whom I owe much more than I can even express. This is the Rev. William E. Dooley, S.J. of our Philosophy Department. When I was about to begin the final revision of my translation, Fr. Dooley offered to read my text and to make suggestions for corrections and improvements. I know of no one more qualified to do this. His mastery of Latin and Greek, his splendid competence in both ancient and mediaeval philosophy, his command of English, all make him to be an unsparing and superlative critic. He read every line of my translation and made hundreds of suggestions for improving both the correctness and the clarity of the text, as well as for achieving felicity of expression. I have adopted nearly all of his suggestions, and I shall probably regret that I did not adopt them all. I am listed as translator, and although I must take responsibility for the final text, I consider Fr. Dooley to be my co-translator. With his usual generosity he also volunteered to compile an *Glossary of Terms,* and I am sure that many will find this index to be one of the most useful sections of this book. Those who use this edition will have as much reason as I do to be grateful to all that Fr. Dooley has so generously done.

TABLE OF CONTENTS

TRANSLATOR'S INTRODUCTION

Textual Matters

A. Authenticity

No one has ever questioned the authenticity of the *Quaestiones De Anima*. [1] This work is attributed to St. Thomas in numerous 13th and early 14th century sources, such as The Stationers' List at the University of Paris, the catalogues of Ptolemy of Lucca, Bernard of Guido, Bartholomew of Capua, Nicolas Trivet, John of Colonna and William of Thoco, as well as similar lists. Detailed information on these sources can be found in three standard works which contain collected information on the writings of St. Thomas: A. Michelitsch, *Thomas-Schriften;* Mandonnet, *Des Ecrits Authentiques de S. Thomas d'Aquin;* Grabmann, *Die Werke des Hl. Thomas von Aquin* (3rd ed.) The best and most recent treatment of St. Thomas' writings is that of James A. Weisheipl, O.P., *Friar Thomas d'Aquino, His Life, Thought, and Work.* New York, 1974. As a supplement he has "A Brief Catalogue of Authentic Works," pp. 355-405. His "brief catalogue" is a summary version, updated, of what Fr. Weisheipl calls the most authoritative study of St. Thomas' works, that of I.T. Eschmann, O.P., "A Catalogue of St. Thomas's Works: Bibliographical Notes," in E. Gilson, *The Christian Philosophy of St. Thomas Aquinas* (New York, Random House, 1956), 381-439.

B. The Title

The title of this work in most editions of the disputed questions of St. Thomas is *Quaestio Disputata de Anima* or *Quaestio Unica de Anima.* [2] It is divided into twenty-one articles.

There is no justification, however, either in the manuscripts or in the incunabula for such a title. To the 13th and 14th century scribes and to the editors of this work before 1500 this work was not a *quaestio unica,* divided into twenty-one articles, but rather a series of twenty-one disputed questions on the soul. There is no doubt, of course, that the use of the word *articulus* as the designation of a question is perfectly legitimate, but not in the *De Anima.* The evidence for calling this work the *Quaestiones De Anima* is overwhelming. In fact, in the manuscript tradition, in the early catalogues and lists, and in the incunabula this work is never referred to by any other name.

In the face of this unanimous evidence, it seems that the work should be called simply *Quaestiones De Anima,* and the divisions should be referred to as *Quaestio Prima, Quaestio Secunda* and so on. St. Thomas himself testifies frequently to the correctness of this usage; for example, in the first sentence of the *Responsio* of Question 2 he writes: *Ad evidentiam hujus quaestionis considerandum est . . .* And in the first sentence of the Response of Question 3 he states, *Dicendum quod ista quaestio aliqualiter dependet a superiori.*

C. Date and Place of Composition of the *De Anima*

The exact dates when St. Thomas held his series of disputed questions *On the Soul* as well as the time when he put these questions into final literary form is unknown. And obviously since disputed questions were public academic acts, the question of the place of disputation and of editing and publishing is closely related to their chronology. There is however a considerable body of evidence which strongly supports the conclusion that these questions were disputed in Paris in the Spring of 1269.

As is well known, these disputations were conducted jointly by the master and his advanced students and were held publicly. Later on, after the public dispute had been held, the master frequently wrote out in complete and determinate form the substance of these public exercises. It is generally agreed that none of St. Thomas' series of disputed questions is a reportation. They are all formal written accounts of discussions at which St. Thomas presided and they have been put into their final form directly by St. Thomas himself. One must keep in mind in the discussion which follows the difference between holding a disputation, writing an account of it, and finally the editing of the questions and their publication in the form in which they now exist. [3] This is not to suggest that the evidence on these points is so abundant that all stages of the process can be clearly distinguished. Still, this caution should put one on his guard against drawing too general or sweeping a conclusion from a single, specific fact, and it should suggest to him that he assess the evidence in its totality. For example, there is manuscript evidence that the disputed questions, *De Spiritualibus Creaturis,* were held in Italy. [4] There is internal evidence, reference to the river Seine, in a number of manuscripts which suggests that they were disputed in Paris. Without pretending to settle this controversial question here and now, let me suggest the following possibility. Perhaps they were disputed in Italy, shortly before St. Thomas left rather abruptly for Paris at the end of 1268; in Paris he may then have edited the text before putting it into the hands of the Parisian stationers for publication. This would account for the fact that not all manuscripts contain the name of the Seine. But in the hypothesis we have suggested, it would have been very natural for St. Thomas to have inserted the name of the Seine in place of the name of the Italian river he had used in his first draft of the disputation.

The answer to the question of the time and place of composition of the *De Anima* is closely related to the problems concerning the time and place of the composition of the other disputed questions. The problem of the dating of the disputed questions must be treated as a whole. It is a fact that five distinct, well-organized groups of disputed questions emerge from the manuscript tradition. (Since one of these published groups is explicitly divided into two series, we may say that there are really six sets of questions.) These five groups are: *De Veritate, De Potentia Dei, De Spiritualibus Creaturis, De Anima et De Virtutibus,* and *De Malo.* Can it be determined where and when these series were disputed? [5] The problem of place and time are closely linked, for since the dates of St. Thomas' life, including his various periods of teaching in Paris and in Italy, are quite firmly established, to locate a series as belonging to Paris, for example, is tantamount to locating it in time, at least within a general period; there is the further problem of determining the relative, if not the exact, chronology of these particular works. It is therefore necessary to exploit the catalogues and the manuscript tradition to see what evidence is available for assigning various series of questions to a particular time or place.

Three important catalogues agree substantially with the semi-official List of the Parisian Stationers. The order of the disputed questions in the Stationers' List is as follows:

> *De Veritate*
> *De Potentia*
> *De Spiritualibus Creaturis*
> *De Anima et De Virtutibus*
> *De Malo*

The three catalogues referred to break the series of disputed questions into three groups, each group assigned to a geographical location.

These are the catalogues of Prague, of Bartholomew of Capua, and Nicholas Trivet. Their order is as follows:

De Veritate	Paris
De Potentia et ultra	Italy
De Virtutibus et ultra	Paris

In light of this evidence, it seems safe to assign the *De Potentia* to Italy and the *De Virtutibus* to Paris. But what is the meaning of the oft recurring phrase *"et ultra"*? The meaning of the phrase itself is clear. The authors of these catalogues had at their disposal editions or lists of the disputed questions of St. Thomas that were so well known that all the authors of the catalogues had to do was to mention one question, the initial or principal question of a group, and all their readers would know which questions were being referred to. The real difficulty, since we cannot be absolutely sure which edition or list these authors used, is to decide which questions are included under a particular *"et ultra."*

There may be some help in a very early manuscript which indicates that St. Thomas' total series of disputed questions were arranged in a set order and numbered. This is the Vatican manuscript, *Vat. lat.* 786; this is, as far as I know, the earliest manuscript which contains all of St. Thomas' disputed questions. [6] This manuscript contains the questions in the following order: *De Veritate, De Potentia Dei, De Spiritualibus Creaturis, De Anima, De Virtutibus, De Unione Verbi, De Malo.* This manuscript is the work of a number of scribes, but at the "incipits" and "explicits" of each question and at the tops of the folios appears, in a hand as early as that of the scribes who wrote the text (if not actually the hand of one of them), a consecutive series of numbers, ranging from one to sixty-three. For example, on folio 276ᵛ at the very top of the folio is written, *"Quaestiones de anima* xli", and at the beginning of the text there is the following notation: *"Quaestio est de anima* •xli•*"* The following order of the works can be established as follows:

qq. 1-29	*De Veritate*
qq. 30-39	*De Potentia Dei*
q. 40	*De Spiritualibus Creaturis*
q. 41	*De Anima*
qq. 42-46	*De Virtutibus*
q. 47	*De Unione Verbi Incarnati*
qq. 48-63	*De Malo*

The list of this Vatican manuscript agrees perfectly with the list of the Parisian stationers who possessed the *exemplaria* of St. Thomas' disputed questions. It also agreees with the Catalogue of Stams. One serious objection can be made to its order, however. If one accepts very literally the testimony of Bartholomew of Capua, Nicholas Trivet and the Prague Catalogue, then on the basis of the Vatican manuscript list, the places where the questions were disputed would be as follows:

Paris:	*De Veritate*
Italy:	*De Potentia et ultra*
	ultra: De Spiritualibus Creaturis
	De Anima
Paris:	*De Virtutibus et ultra*
	ultra: De Unione Verbi
	De Malo

There are, however, serious objections to assigning the *De Anima* to Italy. These I shall take up later. There are some general objections to the above scheme. Since the *De Anima* and the *De Virtutibus* are linked in the Parisian stationers' lists with the *De Anima* preceding the *De Virtutibus,* and since the University exemplar which contains the De Anima also contains the *De Virtutibus* and the *De Unione Verbi,* it seems reasonable to group these three series of questions together. The result is the following:

Paris:	*De Veritate*
Italy:	*De Potentia, De Spiritualibus Creaturis*
Paris:	*De Anima, De Virtutibus, De Unione Verbi,* and *De Malo.*

The first *"et ultra"* of the catalogues, then, would refer to the *De Spiritualibus Creaturis* and the second *"et ultra"* to the *De Anima,* and *De Unione Verbi* and the *De Malo.*

The findings thus far are not conclusive, however; more direct evidence is needed to corroborate our present tentative hypothesis. Fortunately, this evidence, although not abundant, is available.

There are notes in two manuscripts which state that the *De Spiritualibus Creaturis* was disputed in Italy. One of these notes is from a Munich manuscript *(Cl. 3287).*[7] On folio 115ᵛ, at which point the *De Spiritualibus Creaturis* begins, at the beginning of the question is this notation in the same handwriting as that of the copyist, *"Hic incipiunt questiones fratris Thome de Aquino disputate in Ytalia."* Another hand, but dating from the same period, i.e. the end of the 13th century, has added a further precision, *"De spiritualibus creaturis."* The validity of this notation has been called in question by Mandonnet,[8] but it is confirmed by another manuscript, this time one from Spain. Beltran de Heredia reports that a Spanish manuscript, which is now preserved in Portugal *(Lisbon, Bibl. Nac. cod. 262)* and which dates from the beginning of the 14th century, contains the *De Anima,* the *De Virtutibus,* and the *De Malo,* in that order. It also contains (fol. 135-151) the *De Spiritualibus Creaturis,* and once again this question is preceded by the notation, *"Hic incipiunt questiones fratris T. de Aquino disputate in Italia."*[9]

There is likewise manuscript evidence that the *De Anima* was disputed in Paris. Glorieux calls attention to a manuscript of Klosterneuburg *(Stiftsbibl. 274)* which has at the end of the *Quaestiones De Anima* the following colophon: *"Expliciunt questiones de anima determinate parisius a fratre Thoma de aquino de ordine fratrum predicatorum."*[10] This manuscript evidence is further strengthened by a manuscript which Axters described, three years after Glorieux had done his work, *Ms. Angers, 418,* a manuscript which dates from the 14th century. This manuscript contains only a fragment of the *De Anima,* breaking off in the middle of the reply to the third objection of Question 2, but its incipit (fol 160ʳ) reads: *"Questiones sancti Thome de aquino disputate parisius de anima. Questio est de anima humana utrum . . ."* The fact that Thomas is referred to as a saint means that the incipit dates from later than 1323, but this notation is still an early witness to the place where the questions were disputed.

Glorieux marshalls a number of other arguments in favor of the Parisian composition of the *De Anima.* In summary form they are the following:

1. Its length: the *De Anima* with its twenty-one questions would fit very neatly into the period from January to June 1269, that section of the academic year during which St. Thomas taught after returning to Paris from Italy.

2. If the *De Anima* were disputed immediately upon his return from Italy, its appearance preceding the *De Virtutibus* in the stationers' lists is explained.

3. St. Thomas had been sent to Paris by the Minister General of his order so that he might combat vigorously the Averroistic teachings of some Parisian masters. That being so, it is likely that he would launch immediately into a series of questions directed at the main errors of Averroism; and as Marcel Chossat points out, the essential and central error of Latin Averroism, as it appeared to the ecclesiastical authorities in Paris at this period, can be seen in the first two propositions condemned in Paris by Stephen Tempier, bishop of Paris, in December of 1270. These two propositions were:

> 1) That the intellect is one and numerically the same for all men.
> 2) That the proposition, "Man understands" is false or improper. [11]

Hence it is against these errors that St. Thomas would probably direct his first series of public disputations, and in the *De Anima* the questions which begin the series are a positive answer to both of the condemned Averroistic positions.

4. The comparison of parallel texts in the *Quodlibets* and the *De Anima* also confirms Glorieux's thesis that the *De Anima* was disputed in the first half of the year 1269.

To Gloriuex's arguments we can suggest several additions:

5. The extreme unlikelihood that St. Thomas would dispute twice on the same topic in the same place and before the same audience; this would have happened if he had disputed the questions *De Spiritualibus Creaturis* and *De Anima* in the same locale. The fact, therefore, that there is very strong evidence for assigning the *De Spiritualibus Creaturis* to Italy and very little evidence for attributing it to Paris lends support to the thesis that the *De Anima* was disputed in Paris.

6. Another text, albeit a minor one, which seems to indicate that St. Thomas disputed the above mentioned two series of questions before two different audiences is that he takes the trouble to point out in each series the fact that Augustine is not the author of the *De Spiritu et Anima,* something he would not need to have done if his auditors were the same.

Summary of the evidence for dating the *De Anima*

It is quite true that the multiplication of "probables" does not result in scientific certitude; still, the direct testimony of some of the early manuscripts, plus the reasonableness of the other arguments in favor of Paris as the place where the *Quaestiones De Anima* were disputed, makes a very strong case for Glorieux's conclusion that the *De Anima* was disputed and written in Paris, during St. Thomas' second sojourn there as a teacher. The evidence is strong, but not so conclusive, that these questions were disputed during the second half of the school year, 1268-1269. In other words, the dating of the *De Anima* by Glorieux, done by him in 1932, still seems to be the most satisfactory answer to the problem. More recent evidence only serves to confirm his conclusions.

One slight change seems to be in order in Glorieux's general chronology of the disputed questions of St. Thomas. As it was suggested above, Axters has discovered in examining the manuscripts of the disputed questions of St. Thomas which are preserved in the libraries of France and Belgium that the *De Unione Verbi Incarnati* follows, with great regularity, the *De Virtutibus.* Since two of the five manuscripts he describes are from the 13th century and the other three from the beginning of the 14th, he concludes that, from the beginning, or as least from a very early date, the *De Unione* was incorporated into the collection of the questions on the virtues. This would account for the fact that the Parisian stationers do not mention the *De Unione* in their lists. On the strength of this evidence it might be better to place the five questions of the *De Unione* after the De Virtutibus and before the *De Malo,* rather than after the *De Malo* as Glorieux has done.

The final chronological arrangement would therefore be the following:

I.	Paris (1256-1259)	*De Veritate*
II.	Italy (1259-1268)	*De Potentia Dei*
		De Spiritualibus Creaturis
III.	Paris (1269-1272)	*De Anima*
		De Virtutibus
		De Unione Verbi Incarnati
		De Malo

D. Text Used

For this translation I have used the text of the *Quaestiones De Anima* that I edited and that was published in 1968 by the Pontifical Institute of Mediaeval Studies in Toronto: *St. Thomas Aquinas, Quaestiones de Anima,* A newly Established Edition of the Latin Text with an Introduction and Notes.

This text, which was not intended to be a critical edition, is rather a corrected edition, designed to serve students of mediaeval philosophy until such time as the Leonine Commission publishes its definitive work. There were, and still are, reasons for making such a corrected edition available. The *Quaestiones De Anima* of St. Thomas have never been properly, let alone critically, edited.

The earliest known printed edition is the Venice edition of 1472, attributed to Franciscus Renner. [12] Like most early printed books it contains no information about the manuscripts on which its text is based; but it can be safely presumed that, again like most printed editions of the 15th and 16th centuries, it was based either on a single manuscript or on a collation made from a very few manuscripts. These same remarks apply to the other three incunabula which contain the *De Anima,* the Venice edition of 1478 or earlier, the Strassburg edition and the Cologne edition, both of 1500.

The next important fact in the history of the editions of the *De Anima* is the preparation of the Piana or Roman text. The Council of Trent had borne witness to the importance of Thomas Aquinas as a theologian; Pius V, who was engaged in carrying out the various recommendations of the Council, and who proclaimed Thomas Aquinas as a doctor of the Church, desired to have at the disposal of the teachers of the Church an authentic edition of the complete works of St. Thomas. The need for an authentic text, according to the editors of the Piana edition themselves, was particularly urgent, for various texts of St. Thomas were being circulated in which the doctrine and the phraseology had been deliberately changed to suit the ideas of certain Protestant reformers. Accordingly, in 1570 and 1571, at the command of Pope St. Pius V, an edition of St. Thomas' *Opera Omnia* was published at Rome.

In evaluating this text two facts must be kept in mind, its purpose and the speed with which it was published. With regard to the first point the Roman editors of 1570 did not intend to produce what would be called today an *editio critica;* they wanted merely an edition that contained genuine texts of St. Thomas, texts which had not been deliberately falsified or altered. As to the second point, it is obvious, when one considers that seventeen folio volumes were issued in a little over a year, that no attempt was made to prepare new editions of all the various treatises. The editors simply took existing, printed versions of the various works and reprinted them, in much the same way as Migne produced his *Patrologia Latina.* This means that the value of each work in the Piana edition has to be individually assessed. If the edition that the Roman editors chose to reprint happened to have been carefully done by its original editor, and if again it happened that the manuscript (or manuscripts) on which the original printed text was based were a good one, then the Piana text (*per accidens,* largely) would be good. That is to say that the editorial and critical quality of the various parts of the Piana edition is extremely uneven and each treatise needs to be individually evaluated.

Because of the fact that the Piana edition was the first complete edition of the works of St. Thomas and because of its semi-official status, this edition has formed the basis for most of the subsequent editions of the works of St. Thomas. The various editors of later editions of the *Opera Omnia* frankly state that their editions purpose to be copies of, or at most, slightly emended or augmented copies of the Roman exemplar. True, the editors of the Antwerp edition of 1612 and the Paris edition of 1660 claim to have had recourse to ancient manuscripts (this was the invariable editorial claim at that time), but their use of manuscripts, if any, was directed at the mere correction of obvious errors or misprints, and nothing like a genuine reediting of the text was attempted.

To come down to more recent times, the Parma editors of 1852-1872 likewise made no effort to produce a genuinely critical text, at least so far as the *Quaestiones Disputatae* are concerned. For the edition of the *Opera Omnia* published in Paris by Vivès (1871-1882) some use was made of the manuscript tradition, particularly for major works such as the *Summa Theologiae* and the *Summa Contra Gentiles,* and the editors list the manuscripts upon which their text is established. In the volumes which contain the *Quaestiones Disputatae,* however, and in particular for the *De Anima,* the traditional text is largely unchanged. Most of the textual notes printed at the bottom of the pages are simply copied from the Parma edition; there are, however, a few new references to a *Codex B* and to a *Codex Victorinus.*

In editions which contain only the disputed questions the story is the same. The text of the *De Anima* printed in all of them is basically that of the Piana edition with a few obvious corrections.

In brief, the only text available until my new edition was printed is one which stems originally from the Piana edition of 1579; this in turn merely reprinted an earlier text that was probably based on one manuscript, or at best on a few manuscripts, and which therefore ignored the riches of the wide and diversified manuscript tradition of this work.

In preparing my edition I decided to proceed as follows: Since St. Thomas' *Quaestiones De Anima* is a Parisian work, and since the overwhelming number of manuscripts follow in general the manuscripts which contain *pecia* indications, that is, the tradition of the Parisian exemplars, I decided to use as the basis for my text a manuscript whose place of origin is the University of Paris, and which contains a complete set of *pecia* indications. This manuscript is one from Oxford, *Balliol College 49.* It is of Parisian origin; it is a carefully written manuscript; there are no corrections by any later hand; it is relatively free from errors; there are few omissions or homoioteleuta; it is legible and complete. It dates from the end of the 13th or the first years of the 14th century, and is thus possibly as early as any manuscript which I have examined. Where this manuscript needed correction, I made use of other manuscripts from the same Parisian tradition. There is another small family of manuscripts which differs in some respects from the Parisian exemplar tradition. I made use of these also, and recorded all important variants. My text, then, represents a corrected version of what was historically the most widely diffused and the most standard and authoritative version of St. Thomas' text as it existed in mediaeval times. It has, therefore, an historical as well as a purely doctrinal importance.

E. On the Translation

In preparing this translation of St. Thomas' *Questions on the Soul,* I have assumed that the majority of readers will be graduate students and other serious students of St. Thomas. I have also assumed that many of the readers will have some knowledge of Latin. As a result I decided that my translation, like Aristotle's golden mean, should be located midway between a bald, literal translation and a fully idiomatic version.

In translating a work that represents a thinker's most developed doctrine on a topic, one is confronted with a text that is both profound and nuanced. As a result one cannot achieve complete consistency in translating key terms, but I have sought as much consistency as possible while respecting the shades of St. Thomas' thought. Also I have tried, whenever the English language makes this possible, to use English terms that would suggest to the person who knows some Latin what Latin term was being translated. Let me give a few examples.

St. Thomas, who is not invariably consistent himself in the use of terms, usually is quite precise in distinguing the terms "different" and "diverse." Normally "different" indicates a lack of identity in kind; these differences can be either essential or accidental. "Diverse," on the other hand, indicates a lack of identity on the existential level. For example, a human being is different from a horse; they have different specific natures. An individual horse is also diverse from a given human being; one is simply not the other. Two individual human beings, on the other hand, are not different specifically, but they are nevertheless diverse. Consequently, I have always used some form of the words "different" or "diverse" to translate the appropriate Latin terms.

Another example is the use of "intellectual" or "intelligible." Sometimes St. Thomas will use "intelligible" where "intellectual" would read more easily in English. However, I have once again normally retained in English the term which is closest to the Latin. In translating *intelligibilia,* I usually use "intelligible objects" except where the context is neo-Platonic; then I have used "intelligibles."

Esse poses, as always in St. Thomas, some special problems. I have had to make judgments. Sometimes I translate *esse* simply as "being" as Anton Pegis frequently did. But at times I have translated *esse* in a more explicitly existential sense, when I felt that the meaning of the passage required this.

The word *sensus* also poses problems, and I am not sure that I have always been consistent. It sometimes means the sense powers in general, as opposed to intellectual powers, for example; sometimes it means a single sense power, but not a specified one. I could multiply examples, but since Fr. Dooley has prepared an *Index Verborum,* this is not necessary.

One other thing I have done that deserves a word of explanation. I have tried as much as possible to maintain the word order of the Latin text, especially when the order might indicate emphasis on St. Thomas' part. That is, if St. Thomas begins a sentence with a dependent clause, I have also tried to do so, but here, of course, the natural flow of the English language has sometimes dictated a change.

Notes to Introduction

1. Whenever the title *De Anima* is used in the introduction, in the notes or references without further qualification, the work referred to is St. Thomas' *Quaestiones De Anima*. Other treatises on the soul will always be cited with an explicit reference to the author.

2. In the Vivès edition, for example, the title is given as *"Quaestio Unica De Anima."* Cf. Vol. 14, p. 61.

3. F. Stegmüller in the introduction to his *Repertorium, vol. I*, pp. xi-xii, points out many possible forms in which a series of lectures on Peter Lombard's *Sentences* may be found. It is unlikely that disputed questions would be found in quite as many divergent forms and varying stages of completeness as commentaries on the *Sentences;* still, many of these various degrees of literary completeness do exist in the manuscripts of disputed questions.

4. Two manuscripts, one of Munich (Clm. 3827) and one of Lisbon *(Bibl. nac. 262),* attribute it to Italy. Cf. Grabmann, *Die Werke,* pp. 304-305.

5. Etienne Axters, *"Pour L'Etat des Manuscrits des Questions Disputées de Saint Thomas d'Aquin,"* in *Divus Thomas* (Piacenza), 38 (1935), pp. 129-159, esp. p. 155.

6. A. Pelzer, *Codices Vaticani Latini,* Tomus II, Pars Prior, Codices 679-1134, 1931, In Bibliotheca Vaticana, pp. 114-115.

7. M. Grabmann, *Die Werke,* pp. 304-305.

8. P. Mandonnet, *Bulletin Thomiste,* 1 (1924), p. 59.

9. B. de Heredia, *"Cronica de Movimiento Tomista,"* in *La Ciencia Tomista,* 37 (1928), p. 67 ff. Cf. also P. Glorieux, *"Les Questions disputées,"* p. 13.

10. P. Glorieux, *"Les Questions Disputées de S. Thomas et leur suite chronologique,"* in *Recherches de Théologie ancienne et mediévale,* 4 (1932), pp. 5-33, especially p. 23.

11. Marcel Chossat, *"Saint Thomas d'Aquin et Siger de Brabant,"* in *Revue de Philosophie,* 24 (1914), pp. 552-575 and 25 (1914), pp. 25-52. Cf. especially p. 565.

12. The reader who is interested can find full documentation on the matters discussed in this section in the Latin edition of St. Thomas' *Quaestiones De Anima.*

LITERARY and DOCTRINAL MATTERS

A. Literary Form

In St. Thomas' day the holding of public disputations was one of the principal scholastic acts of a master in theology at the University of Paris. Because a professor, in setting up a series of disputations, was not forced to follow a prescribed order, as happened when he was commenting on the *Sentences,* he could be freely creative. Furthermore he was at liberty to develop his handling of the questions in great detail. The number of objections raised and discussed was often very large, and the master's treatment of the main issue raised in the question was often very extended. Normally we can say that if St. Thomas raises an issue in one of his series of disputed questions, he will give the matter his most detailed treatment.

What still awaits the work of students of St. Thomas is a detailed investigation of his literary sources, not merely in the sense of identifying and studying the texts which he had read and of which he made use, for a great deal of this work has been done; but rather to search for models that he may have used in organizing his thoughts from the point of view of literary form. I believe I have identified one such model, the model for Question One of the *Quaestiones de Anima.* This text is the work of an obscure Greek bishop, Nemesius of Emesa.

Of Nemesius practically nothing more is known than that he is the probable author of a treatise on man called in Latin *De Natura Hominis* (Περὶ φύσεως ἀνθρώπον) and that he flourished at the beginning of the 5th century. This treatise was translated into Latin in the eleventh century by N. Alfanus, Archbishop of Salerno (1058-1085). A second translation of this work was made in 1159 by Burgundio of Pisa, a twelfth century jurist.[1] It is this second translation which seems to have had the greatest currency in the Middle Ages. Burgundio thought that the work had been written by Gregory of Nyssa and attributed it to him in the dedicatory letter which he addressed to the Emperor Frederick.[2]

The *De Natura Hominis* of Nemesius thus came to the writers of the thirteenth century under the not insignificant authority of St. Gregory of Nyssa, and it was consequently used a great deal. In fact, the bulk of St. Thomas' references to Gregorius Nyssenus which have to do with the soul or with man are to this treatise by Nemesius, rather than to the *De Hominis Opificio* which is a geniune work of Gregory.[3] Ordinarily St. Thomas does not refer to this work by any title; he simply states, "as Gregory of Nyssa say," or some such phrase. His quotations, however, make it clear that he is referring to the work of Nemesius and also indicate that he knew the entire work in the translation of Burgundio of Pisa.

This is not the place to examine Nemesius' treatise in detail. Let us reduce his arguments to compact form. The problem as set forth in Chapter 1 is to explain man in his unity; he proposes to do this by first examining the nature of the soul and secondly by discussing its relation to the human body.

In Chapters 2 and 3 Nemesius does the following things: 1) He states the position of the materialists. 2) He states the position of those who hold that the soul is not a body; the two chief exponents here are Plato and Aristotle. 3) He refutes in brief the materialists by invoking a third position, that of Ammonius Saccas. 4) He next refutes the materialists in detail. 5) He then rejects Aristotle's view of the soul as entelechy, understanding by entelechy a form which is non-subsistent, a non-separable, material form. 6) He concludes that the soul is an incorporeal, immortal substance. 7) He then rejects the position of Plato because it does not account for the unity of the human being. 8) Finally, he adopts as his own the position of Ammonius Saccas which seems to preserve both the soul's self-subsistence and its intimate relation to and function in the human body. In doing so, he locates man on the confines of two worlds, the rational and the irrational.

There are remarkable similaries, not in doctrine, but in literary form, between Question 1 of St. Thomas' *De Anima* and the text just summarized. St. Thomas begins his Response, after a preliminary definition of a *hoc aliquid,* by stating the position of the ancient materialists. He then proceeds to attack their doctrines. It is interesting to note the basis of his opposition to them. If their explanation is correct, he remarks, the human soul would be no different from any other material form. This is the point of attack which Nemesius used against Aristotle after having reduced the Aristotelian position to a form of materialism. St. Thomas evidently agrees that this is one of the crucial issues in this discussion. He disagrees, of course, with any interpretation which would attribute such a doctrine to Aristotle; this is one of the chief points of disagreement between him and the

Averroists. In other words, he attacks the same interpretation of Aristotle that Nemesius did; only Nemesius thought this was the correct interpretation of Aristotle, whereas St. Thomas thinks it is incorrect.

It is interesting to note also that it is St. Thomas' intention to show that the materialists fail to account for the functioning of the soul on all levels of animated beings. Nemesius had posed the problem in the same terms in Chapter 1.

St. Thomas' next step is to group together those philosophers who held that the soul was not a body. Like Nemesius, he assigns both Aristotle and Plato to this group. As we have seen, however, he disagrees with Nemesius on the interpretation of Aristotle. In fact, in distinguishing between Plato and Aristotle, he criticizes Plato, rather than Aristotle. Furthermore he censures Plato, as Nemesius had done, on the grounds that Plato had attributed to the soul too radical an independence from the body.

The historical positions having been set down, St. Thomas next proceeds to develop a more extended argumentation against the position of the materialists. The argument is based upon the order to be discovered among natural forms and upon the progressive transcendence of form over matter that one discovers by examining the hierarchy of being.

Finally, St. Thomas locates the soul, as Nemesius had done, on the border line between two worlds, the corporeal and the incorporeal; in Nemesius' terms, between the irrational and the rational. Like Nemesius, St. Thomas explain the unity of the human being not by an appeal to Plato, nor in terms of a soul which is nothing more than a material form, but by adopting a new position. This is not to suggest that the solutions at which St. Thomas and Nemesius arrived are the same, or even very similar. Essentially, however, their objectives are the same: to avoid, on the one hand, the Platonic doctrine of the soul which would undermine the unity of the human being in an effort to exalt the spirituality of the soul, and, on the other hand, to keep clear of any doctrine which maintains that the soul is a body or a merely corporeal form. Each in his own way tries to preserve the two-fold notion of the soul as a subsistent, immaterial, intellectual being which is intimately united to a human body. Which effort is the more successful is not a literary, but a doctrinal, question.

On the strength of this brief comparison, however, it is not possible to state categorically that St. Thomas deliberately modelled Question 1 of his *De Amina* upon Chapters 2 and 3 of Nemesius' *De Natura Hominis*. However, in view of the fact that St. Thomas was extremely familiar with this entire work, and in view of his frequent use of its as source of information on the history of the problem of the soul's nature, it seems extremely likely that its literary form exerted a direct influence upon him when in 1269 he formulated and developed his own doctrine in this unique question on the human soul, Whether the human soul can be both a form and an entity.

B. Unity of the *Quaestiones De Anima*

Two questions arise as soon as one considers the doctrinal organization of St. Thomas' series of disputed questions: 1) Do all the series of St. Thomas' disputed questions, taken as a whole, constitute one work, inspired and motivated by a single controlling purpose? That is, can one find in them an underlying principle of organization that runs through the entire series, dictating their sequence, date of composition and their content? 2) Is each well-defined series of questions, e.g. the *De Veritate* or the *De Anima,* one work, unified and controlled by a single principle of organization? Most scholars would today answer "No" to the first question; most would agree that it is profitable to try to answer the second question.

It is always hazardous for an historian, in the absence of any clear-cut statement from the author himself, to attempt to assign the purpose for which an author wrote, or to select what he thinks the author's principle of organization is. In many of his major works St. Thomas inserts explicit statements which explain both the order of the matter he is to present, his reasons for selecting a given order, and information as to why he includes certain topics and omits others.

Unfortunately he inserted no such explanation at the beginning of any of his series of disputed questions. Consequently, the student of St. Thomas will have to conduct his own search to see if there is a principle of doctrinal unity or a principle of unity of historical purpose, or both, which control the organization of the *De Anima.*

Even a superficial glance at the questions which comprise this series suggests their doctrinal unity. The very statement of the questions indicates this. All of them, except Questions 4 and 5, contain the word "soul." However, Questions 4 and 5 also deal with the soul; Question 4 really asks whether it is necessary to posit an agent intellect in the soul, and Question 5 asks in effect whether the agent intellect is one and separate, or whether it is *something in the soul.* The *De Anima,* then, is a series of questions on the human soul, and since for St. Thomas the human soul is the formal, specifying principle of a human being, one might say that it is a group of questions on what it means to be a human being.

St. Thomas had completed the First Part of his *Summa Theologiae,* which contains the questions on the nature and creation of man, before he returned to Paris in 1269, probably even as early as 1267; consequently his so-called "Treatise on Man" is anterior to the *Quaestiones de Anima*. His explanatory statements which are found in the *Summa* might, therefore, be carefully examined as guides for understanding his procedures in this area of his thought. In his little "Prologue" to Question 75 of the *Summa* he delineates with sweeping strokes his general plan. After treating both wholly spiritual and wholly corporeal beings, he says, one must turn to the study of man, who is composed of both spiritual and corporeal substance. The study of man has two chief subdivisions: 1) his nature, and 2) his production in being. Now a theologian, he continues, (and one must always remember that it was as a theologian that St. Thomas wrote his disputed questions) is interested in the nature of a human being only insofar as it is related to the soul. Consequently, a consideration of the soul comes first. There are a few more precisions to be made. The theologian is interested in three things about the soul: namely, its essence, its powers, and its operations. One last distinction. The study of the nature or essence of the soul falls naturally into two parts: 1) a study of the soul as it is in itself, and 2) a study of the union of the soul to the body.

An examination of the *Quaestiones de Anima* reveals that by and large its doctrinal organization runs parallel to that of the *Summa*. St. Thomas treats first the nature of the soul, both in itself and as united to the body as the form of the body; next, the powers of the soul; and lastly, the operations of the soul. Equally obvious, however, is the fact that the *De Anima* is not so complete as the section on man in the *Summa*. There are no questions dealing with the appetitive powers; nor is there a well-developed section on the intellectual operations of the soul while it is joined to the body, as is true of the *Summa*. All this means, of course, is that the *De Anima* is not a *Summa;* it makes no pretense of being a completely organized totality of doctrine about either the soul or about being human.

The question of the *De Anima*'s unity of historical purpose is, in some ways, less important than its doctrinal unity, and yet very important also. Often if one can establish the purpose for which a treatise was written, one has a key that will help him understand the doctrine more precisely and profoundly.

We know that St. Thomas normally wrote with a keen and active interest in the problems of his own time, and the year 1269, the year he returned to Paris, was a lively year. The historical milieu in which St. Thomas worked during his second teaching period in Paris has been the object of study for many scholars in the last 25 years. The entry of the Aristotelian *corpus* of writings into the University of Paris, the history of the various schools of interpretation of Aristotle which developed, the influence of the Greek and Arabian commentators, the history of the frequent interventions of ecclesiastical authorities on matters of doctrine being taught in the University, all these questions have been and continue to be the object of detailed research.

In the Spring of 1269 the University of Paris was seething over the question of the interpretation of Aristotle. The great doctrinal condemnation of 1270 was not far off and although the Parisian masters must have been well aware that certain doctrines were dangerous, danger did not breed caution, and extremely unorthodox philosophical positions were taught both publicly and privately at Paris at about this time. Possibly no single topic was so much mooted as that of "man" himself. The constitution of a human being, and particularly the nature of the human soul, the freedom of will, the status of the separated soul, these were all crucial philosophical and theological issues at Paris at the end of the 1260's and the beginning of the 1270's. One has only to look at the list of propositions condemned by Stephen Tempier, bishop of Paris, on December 10, 1270, to realize this. Nine of the thirteen propositions condemened have to do with problems about man and his freedom. Five of the propositions deal with questions that will be raised explicitly by St. Thomas in his *De Anima.*

These episcopal censures were aimed principally at a group of men who are today commonly called "Latin Averroists." They are given this name because they insisted that Averroes' interpretation of Aristotle was to be followed on all points. St. Thomas was well aware of the value of much of Averroes' commentaries on Aristotle, and used them constantly; but he took issue with the Averroists on certain topics, on their tendency to follow their master slavishly. He did not want Aristotle to be identified with philosophy. He was therefore eager to separate Aristotle from some of his interpreters, lest Aristotle be condemned afresh as some of his disciples were soon to be. He makes this point explicitly in both the first paragraph and the last paragraph of his *De Unitate Intellectus contra Averroistas,* where he makes it clear that his avowed purpose is to refute an Averroistic error.

It would be incredible for an historian to suppose that St. Thomas could have disputed twenty-one times on the human soul in the University of Paris in 1269 with a detachment from his milieu so complete that the currently debated Averroistic position on what it meant to be human did not influence the selection, organization or presentation of these twenty-one academic disputations. In fact, his preoccupation with Latin Averroism may well account for the fact that the four questions on the unicity and separateness of both possible and agent intellects are given the place of prominence they have in the *De Anima.*

Furthermore, perhaps at the time when he was holding these

disputations (between January and June of 1269), at least before they were completed and edited, he was probably already planning for his vigorous *De Unitate Intellectus;* hence, there was no need for impassioned and polemical style in the *De Anima.* He could present, rather, a calm and positive answer to the question of nature of the human soul and the constitution of the human person; this would explain the sharply contrasting styles and tones of these two works, which though different in literary form and intent, do much to complement each other. Many facts, then, confirm the general conclusion that the *De Anima,* though not expressly or deliberately a work of controversy, was written by an author fully alert to one of the chief doctrinal problems of his age: the nature of a human being, the nature of the soul. It is not, therefore, directed solely against the Averroists, but against anyone who held what St. Thomas considered to be faulty doctrines on man or the soul. Once again, however, this time on the question of the unity of historical purpose of the *De Anima,* one must limit himself to a modest conclusion: The *De Anima* seems to be an elaborate and positive expression of St. Thomas' teaching on certain key points in his doctrine on the nature of the soul and on the constitution of a human being, selected, developed and articulated with a full awareness of the Averroistic controversies which were agitating the University of Paris at the time when they were written.

C. The Human Being as an Incarnate Spirit

Early in 1269 notice was given in the schools of the faculty of theology at the University of Paris that Frater Thomas Aquinas would hold a disputation on the human soul. The topic he chose would have interested many, for the problem was one with which the thirteenth century was deeply concerned, and it was moreover formulated in a unique and unusual way. St. Thomas had decided to initiate his new series of disputed questions on the soul by asking: "Whether the human soul can be both a form and an entity?" He was proposing to give an answer to the dilemma which his master, Albert the Great, had recognized but had found himself unable to resolve to his complete satisfaction: If the soul is a subsistent being, how can it be the substantial form of the body? If it is the form of matter, how can it possibly be self-subsistent? Albert had despaired of completely reconciling these two aspects of the soul, declaring: "When I consider the soul in itself, I agree with Plato; but when I consider it with respect to the form of life which it gives to its body, I agree with Aristotle."[4] The reconciliation of Plato and Aristotle at which so many thinkers have aimed was still unresolved.

It looks as if St. Thomas, by his way of stating the question, a way which was new for him, is suggesting that a reconciliation of these two seemingly opposed views of the human soul is possible. He is suggesting that the doctrine on the soul which was most dear to Platonists, the soul's subsistence and immortality, and the doctrine which was most authentically Aristotelian, that the soul is a form of the body, are not two opposed answers to two separate questions, but rather two parts of a single answer to a single problem. The conclusion of Question 1 seems to corroborate this. St. Thomas locates the human soul (that is to say, the human person) on the confines of two worlds, that of bodies and that of the pure intelligences, and he does so because he holds that it is a subsistent form of matter.

Thus he is entitled to say to the Platonists: True, the human soul is a subsistent, intellectual substance, but it is the lowest of such substances. To the Aristotelians he can say: Granted that the soul is the form of a natural, organic body, granted even that it is a material form, it is, however, the highest of all such natural forms. The question can be put in a slightly different fashion: Are the lowest of spiritual substances and the highest of bodily forms two distinct realities? Or do these names point to two complementary characteristics of a single being, the human soul?

In developing his answer, St. Thomas had accepted certain fundamental Aristotelian principles. He had learned from Aristotle's *De Anima* that a human being is substantially one and that the source of a human being's unity is the same as that of any other material composite, its substantial form — in this instance, since we have to do with a living being, its soul. But there is more. He insists that it is Aristotle's position, and a position that he accepts, that there can be one and only one substantial form for a being. This principle will carry St. Thomas very far, for it will enable him to say in the face of those who hold for a plurality of forms that in a human being, "through its substantial form, which is the human soul, this individual is not only a human being, but animal, living, body, substance and being."[5]

St. Thomas is going to develop his enquiry about the soul, not by starting from some preconceived definition of what it is to be human. The bedrock upon which he is to erect the carefully articulated doctrine is for him an evident fact, simple and immediate like all evident facts, but so fundamental that to deny its implications would means yielding the very possibility of success in this investigation. It is the fact *that a human being understands and is aware that he understands.* His most forceful expression of this conviction that any true anthropology must be an effort to understand the full implications of the fact that we possess intellectual understanding is found in his *De Unitate*

Intellectus: "For it is evident that this singular human being understands; for we would never ask questions about the intellect unless we had intellectual understanding; nor when we seek to learn about the intellect, are we enquiring about any other principle than that by which we understand." [6]

To delineate the nature and being of the human soul without doing violence to this fact is St. Thomas' goal. He must strive to see and to make clear to us how the intellect, that is, the intellective soul, is part of an individual human being, for only if the intellect is truly part of a human being, can a human being be said to possess genuine intellectual understanding. To do this St. Thomas considers that he must establish three conclusions: 1) that the intellective soul is the substantial form of a human being; 2) that this soul is a subsistent, intellectual form, but of such a lowly type that a need for union with a body is rooted deep within its very nature, and 3) that consequently it can neither be separate in existence from the body nor one in number for all human beings.

Question 1 can be seen as a map for understanding St. Thomas' view of the human being as an incarnate spirit. It presents in broad lines the whole of his doctrine; Questions 2 and 3 add a number of clarifications and precisions. One can then read all the others texts of St. Thomas on what it means to be a human being as enriching, both in detail and in depth, what he says in this unique question.

The Objections of Question 1 make it clear that St. Thomas' answer to the questions will not be an easy one. They also serve to show where St. Thomas must locate his own solution. The 18 arguments fall broadly into two main groups: 1) Those arguments which maintain that if the soul is subsistent, it cannot be the form of its body. This group includes the first 10 arguments. 2) Those which insist that if the soul is a bodily form, it cannot be subsistent. In other words, the first series of arguments would be brought forward by men whom we shall call, for the sake of convenience, "Separatists." These men insist that the soul is a subsistent being, complete in nature and independent of its body. The second type of argument would be adduced by men whom we shall refer to as "Materialists." By materialists, however, in this context, we do not mean simply those men who said that the soul is a body; we include also those who taught that the human intellective soul is merely a material form and who would consequently deny its self-subsistence.

An examination of several of these arguments may help us to see some of the difficulties which St. Thomas faces. The first argument points out that if the soul is an entity, a concrete individual, it must 1) be subsistent, and 2) be complete in the line of existential act. Now, goes the argument, whatever accrues to any being after it is complete in the order of existence can do so only accidentally. The consequence is embarrassing: If the soul is an entity, the human body can be united to it only accidentally. Faced with the prospect of declaring that a human being has only accidental unity, the opponent prefers to conclude that if the human soul is an entity, it cannot be the body's substantial form.

The proportion that should prevail between matter and form is the basis of another argument. If the soul is an entity, existing through itself—that is, if it is a subsistent form—, then, since it has no contrary nor is it composed of contraries, it must be incorruptible. The human body, on the other hand, is by nature corruptible. It seems to be clear that there can be no proportion between an incorruptible soul and a corruptible body. Therefore, if the soul is a subsistent, individual substance, it cannot be the form of a human body.

Arguments 13 to 18, diversified as they seem at first reading, have a basic unity. All of them derive their cogency from the principle that a being has one, and only one, act of existence. The necessity of this unity in the order of existential act controls the development of all these arguments and also St. Thomas' answers to them. The difficulty can be put in several forms: How can there be a single act of existing for a being which is composed of corporeal and incorporeal elements, or which is composed, to put it another way, of the incorruptible and simple and the corruptible and composite?

Those who pose the arguments against St. Thomas' position have not played merely a negative role. They stress what is essentially involved in the notion of a concrete individual, an entity, insisting that an entity be both subsistent and complete and perfect in being. They have pointed out, moreover, the mutual relationships that must prevail between a form and its matter, the dependence of each upon the other, and the part each must play in the ultimate perfecting of the other. Thirdly, they have stressed the unity of existential act that is at the root of the metaphysical explanation of a being. Finally they have hinted that in solving this question one must respect the parallelism that obtains between the order of operation, through which a limited being achieves its perfection, and the order of existential act, from which the operations flow.

There are only two *Sed contra*'s in the first question; each of them consists of two parts since two characteristics of the human soul, its self-subsistence and its role as form of matter, are at stake. The first treats the problem on the level of nature and existence; the second stresses the level of operation.

We are now ready for St. Thomas' development of his own doctrine, the Response of Question 1. The formulations of the two *Sed contra*'s make it clear that the conclusion which he expects to sustain is that the human soul is both a form and an entity. By *human soul* St. Thomas means the rational or intellective soul; we know this to be so because the fact that he is trying to account for is the intellectual knowledge of a human being. In fact, through his *Questions on the Soul* he uses *human soul, intellective soul, rational soul,* and even *possible intellect* as equivalent terms. The form referred to in these questions is the form of matter, the Aristotelian form of composite, material substances, not a separated form in the sense of a Separate Substance. The meaning of entity needs to be made more precise and he begins his Response by explaining what he means by entity.

Strictly speaking, he tells us, and without qualification, a *hoc aliquid,* an entity, is an individual in the genus of substance. From among the many Aristotelian characteristics of such an individual substance, St. Thomas selects two as being primary and essential: 1) that it be self-subsistent; that is, that it does not subsist in another as in a subject; rather, it subsists in itself; 2) that it be complete in a given species and genus.

These precisions on the meaning of entity serve as an introduction to St. Thomas' discussion of the materialists, for the materialists would deny to the soul both of these characteristics of an entity. As examples, St. Thomas chooses Empedocles and Galen. In asserting that the soul is neither complete in species nor subsistent, Galen and Empedocles (as St. Thomas understands them) are affirming that the soul is merely a corruptible form like any other material form. To assert this, however, is tantamount to denying that there is any difference between intellectual knowing and sense knowledge.

St. Thomas holds that the crass materialistic view is inadequate to account even for sensation, for the activity of sensation consists in receiving species apart from matter. In other words, already on the level of sense life there is a cognitive operation which is characterized by a certain degree of immateriality.

St. Thomas now turns to the human soul. If the soul of a human being is nothing more than a mixture or a harmony that arises from material elements, it can never be the principle by which a human being's intellectual knowing is explained. Why not? The rational soul, through which a human being achieves a knowledge of universals, has an operation which is wholly immaterial. This is the operation of abstraction. Abstraction consists in the separation of species not only from matter (this happens also in sense cognition) but even from all the individuating conditions of matter. This is an operation which is wholly intellectual, and this amounts to saying that it is wholly immaterial.[7] No combination of matter, however complex or refined, can ever become immaterial. And since operation proceeds according to the nature of that which operates, no soul which is by nature material can ever operate on the level of the immaterial.

St. Thomas makes this same point with even greater emphasis and in more detail in Question 2, where he is discussing the possible intellect and the need for asserting that it is wholly immaterial. We can now return to Question 1, where he sets down his first conclusions: 1) The intellective soul operates through itself, that is, without making us of a bodily organ in the action of understanding; 2) and since anything operates insofar as it is in act, the intellective soul must necessarily possess an existential act that is essentially independent of its body. From St. Thomas' point of view there are two unacceptable consequences of adopting a materialistic position: 1) Either there is no intellectual understanding at all, or 2) if there is, it is not performed through the agency of a power that belongs to the human being himself. He insists that both of these consequences are contrary to the facts.

The second of these two conclusions poses another question whose answer we must await. Is not that conclusion equally applicable to the position of the Latin Averroists? Even more important, if by a human being we mean *this composite being,* soul and body, does not this consequence even follow from the Platonic position? Will St. Thomas consider the Platonists and the Averroists as being equally responsible for locating the operation of intellectual understanding somewhere outside of the composite being, a human being? The answer will be quick in coming for St. Thomas now turns to the position of those who hold for the self-subsistence of the human soul, and one of these philosophers is Plato.

Very early in the history of philosophy, according to St. Thomas, the immateriality of the operation of intellection was recognized. Both Aristotle and Plato realized that in its operations the human intellective soul is independent from the conditions of matter. They concluded, therefore, that the intellective part of the soul is a self-subsistent being. Aristotle declared that our intellect is an incorruptible substance. Plato held the soul to be immortal and self-subsistent because it is self-moving, taking self-movement in a broad sense; the soul is said to move itself because it operates through itself.

Had Plato stopped there, St. Thomas continues, no one would quarrel with his position; but he went further and taught that not only did the soul exist in its own right, but it even contained in itself the complete nature of the human species. The soul is the human being. In this spiritual, subsistent soul Plato located the entire specific nature of being human and defined a human being as a soul using a body; the relation of soul and body, therefore, was that of a sailor to his ship, or that of a human being to his garments. St. Thomas is unwilling to accept this form of "spiritualism." If Plato's definition is correct, a human being can be said to understand, but by "human being" we no longer mean the human composite of soul and body. In order to save the proposition "A human being understands," the unity of the human composite has had to be sacrificed. St. Thomas is unwilling in his turn to make this sacrifice.

The second form of separatism, Latin Averroism, is also unacceptable to St. Thomas. According to this doctrine the intellect is separate in existence from the body and one for all human beings. The consequence of this is that a human being does not understand, but rather a separate substance does. In a limited sense the unity of the composite is saved, but what a composite it is! It is a composite which can no longer claim to be capable of intellectual operations. If the Averroists are correct, the fact that *this human being* understands is made impossible, so actually the unity preserved is not that of an intellectual being.

St. Thomas is now reaching the point where he must make a crucial doctrinal decision. He has already indicated in his brief remarks on Plato that he is unwilling to go as far as Plato did in the direction of complete self-subsistence. Along with the materialists he will say that the soul is the form of matter.[8] This will preserve the unity of the human being both in being and in operation. In company with the separatists, he will hold that in its intellectual operations, which are wholly immaterial, the soul is somehow separate from the matter whose form it is.

Having stated the position of Plato, St. Thomas is ready to demonstrate that the soul is the form of the human body. In brief his argument is this: That by which the body lives is the soul. Now, for living things the act by which they live is the act by which they exist. Therefore, the soul is that by which the human body actually exists. But, he continues, that by which anything has existence is its form. The conclusion is inescapable: the human soul is the form of the human body. He next wishes to speak of the nature of the human soul. In the *Sed contra*'s St. Thomas had said that form is the specifying principle of being; it is form that places a particular being in its proper species. He now puts this principle to work. A human being is formally constituted a human being insofar as he is rational. It is, therefore, the rational or intellective soul that is the form of a human being. How can this be verified? By our primary evident fact. It is a human being as performing rational actions that we are attempting to understand and explain. St. Thomas will now use these conclusions to criticize the separatists.

If Plato is correct, St. Thomas declares, and the soul is in the body as a sailor is in a ship (that is, as its governor), it will not confer species on the body or on its parts; it will not make the parts to be specifically human. The opposite appears to be true; for when the soul departs from the body, the various parts lose their properly human character and cannot be called by their former names except in an equivocal sense. The eye of a corpse is no more a human eye than a painted or a sculptured one. He has another argument against Plato. If Plato is correct, the union of soul and body would be accidental. Under this supposition, death, which signifies the separation of soul and body, would not be a substantial corruption. This is obviously false.

St. Thomas' argument against Averroism can also be stated succinctly. No material form can be separate in existence from the matter which it informs. Now the intellective soul is the form of the human body. Therefore it is not separate in existence from its body. Nor can the possible intellect be one for all human beings since every form must have certain determinate matter. It must be the form of *this* matter or of *that,* not of matter in general. What is dominating St. Thomas' mind is that brute fact of which we have spoken: This human being understands. If one respects this fact, he is bound to explain the intellectual operations of a human being as arising from an intrinsic, efficient principle. He is not satisfied with the doctrine of the *continuatio,* that linkage between a human being and the separate possible intellect. An operation, he says, is attributed to a substance; and we cannot attribute an operation to a particular substance if the operation is actually carried on by another substance, diverse from the first. Consequently, if the possible intellect is separate in existence from this human being or from that human being, it is impossible that the action of understanding be attributed to this individual human being or to that one. St. Thomas has learned much about intellection from Aristotle and Averroes but he has his own position. This becomes clear when he speaks of the objects of human intellectual knowledge.

St. Thomas argues that our knowledge begins with sensible data, with species or forms present in our imaginations. Intelligible species, through which we know intellectually, when they are present in the phantasms existing in the imagination, are intelligible only in potency. But if a person is a knowing subject only when the intelligible species are understood in act, then it follows that if we are to understand, the intellect must be a power of the human soul. Let us summarize a bit. The soul of a human being, i.e., his substantial form, and therefore the ultimate source of his proper operations, has an operation all its own, one which does not depend upon the body — at least insofar as the origin and the exercise of the act are concerned. Furthermore, to see that the soul has an operation through itself alone is to realize that the soul exists through itself; for the operation of a being is proportioned to its mode of existence. Finally, if one admits this, as St Thomas does, one must conclude that the rational soul, which is a human being's only substantial form, is an entity, a concrete individual; that is, it is a subsistent being in its own right. Let us now examine how St. Thomas integrates these two features of the human soul, its role as form and its being a concrete individual, into two parts of a single answer to a single question.

When St. Thomas wrote the First Part of his *Summa Theologiae,* shortly before returning to Paris from Italy, he treated the same problem in two separate questions: 1) Whether the human soul is a subsistent reality, and 2) Whether an intellective principle is united to a body as its form. That he changes this approach when he came to hold the series of disputed questions on the soul ought to be, and is, significant. It would seem that he wishes to insist that the two problems are so intimately related that neither can be adequately treated apart from the other.

Before looking at his final conclusions in Question 1, we might look again at the *Sed contra*'s. He argues that the rational soul is the form of the human body. Furthermore, since it has an independent, immaterial operation — the action of understanding — the soul is self-subsisting. But is this operation *totally* independent of the body? This is answered in the second *sed contra*. The answer is "No." The operation of understanding is independent of the body only with respect to the active principle from which the operation flows as from an efficient cause. From the side of the objects which specify the knowing intellect, the soul requires phantasms which do not exist apart from a body.

St. Thomas then goes on to say that the ultimate perfection of the human soul consists in knowing truth, and this act is accomplished by the intellect. What is now at stake is the very nature of this intellectual substance; for in pointing to that in which its final perfection consists, he is indicating the soul's nature, for every nature achieves its full self-realization when it attains its proper end. God is self-subsistent truth; human beings, however, attain truth through operation. Now since each being acts according to its grade of being, the way in which an intellectual substance attains truth will be a clear indication of the grade of being and of the grade of intellectuality it possesses.

For St. Thomas, the human intellect is the lowest of all intellects, so lowly in fact that it cannot achieve its ultimate perfection of knowing the truth without help from a body. To become perfect in knowing truth it needs to be united to an organic body. Why? Because it understands through the medium of phantasms which do not exist apart from bodies. He is now ready for his conclusion. He declares

it is necessary for a human soul that it be joined to its body to achieve
its proper perfection and further that it be an entity, a concrete individual substance. The soul is self-subsistent, but it does not possess
in itself the full perfection of the human species. Rather it subsists
in order to perfect the human species through its being the form of
matter. To put this in a slightly different way: The human soul is
a subsistent reality whose nature it is actively to perfect the human
species by being the form of the body; its work as form of matter
actively ministers to the full self-realization of its subsistent being.
The soul is an individual substance which from its very substantiality,
that is, from the most intimate recesses of its being, strives to achieve
the perfection of the human species, not in itself alone, but *for* itself,
in another, namely, in the human composite of which it is the form.

St. Thomas is thinking in terms of a hierarchy of beings, and
particularly of knowing beings. At one end of the scale of being is
God, pure subsistent being, totally actual, totally immaterial; at the
other end is prime matter, wholly potential, wholly material. In
between God and prime matter are many levels of materiality and
immateriality. All knowing beings in some sense transcend the
material, and in this context to say that there is a higher degree of
transcendence of form over matter is to say that each form is progres-
sively less bound to the conditions of matter in its operations than
are forms which are lower than it.

In Question 1 St. Thomas examines the various beings in the
world, beginning with the inorganic, and finally comes to the human
being, whose soul is the highest of those forms which can be called
material forms. Like the pure intelligences above them, human souls
are capable of universal knowledge; they can know all that is or could
be. They fall short of the perfection of the separate substances,
however, in that the human intellect, even as intellect, must acquire
its intellectual, immaterial knowledge from that lower type of
knowledge which arises through the sense powers of the human soul.
The cooperation of sense powers is needed if a human soul is to complete its intellectual work. The human soul *by nature* exists to acquire
its immaterial cognition from material things. The soul needs to be
united to matter; it requires an organic body which it nevertheless
transcends. St. Thomas then concludes: "In this way, therefore, a
human soul insofar as it is united to its body as its form still possesses
an act of existence which is elevated above the body and does not
depend on it; clearly then this soul is constituted on the boundary
line between corporeal and separate substances."

What St. Thomas is doing is proposing a reconciliation between
a spiritualistic Platonism and a materialistic brand of Aristotelianism.
If the human soul is, at one and the same time, and in its totality

of being, both the lowest of intellectual beings and the highest of material forms, the partisans of each of the above positions need not fear that the characteristic of the soul upon which they place the emphasis need be abandoned. St. Thomas has on many occasions balanced against each other these two complementary notions on the soul. One of his clearest texts on this is Question 2 of his series of disputed *Questions on Spiritual Creatures,* where he considers whether or not a spiritual substance is able to be joined to a body as its form.[9]

In this text he argues, as he has done frequently, that the human soul is the most perfect of all forms of matter. His evidence is that it has an operation which utterly transcends matter, its operation of understanding. He points out, too, that though the human soul transcends matter, it is in intimate contact with the matter and communicates its own existence to matter, to its body, the noblest of all bodies, and from this union of soul and body, just as from any union of form and matter, there comes into existence a single being. What is unique in the doctrine of St. Thomas in the 13th century is his insistence on the intimacy of this union of form and matter. His reason is not hard to find.

Unlike St. Augustine, who in good Platonic fashion, sees the end of this union to be the good of the body, which the soul guides and protects, St. Thomas holds that the body exists for the good of the soul. Now intellect, as intellect, does not need a body; intellect in itself is wholly independent of matter. Therefore, if the intellective soul needs to be joined to a body, the reason is not that it is an intellect, but that it is a certain type of intellect, a lowly and weakened one. What is the principal sign of this lowliness? The presence of sense powers in the human soul. It is not because the soul is joined to a body that it has sense powers; rather, because it possesses by nature sense powers, it needs to be joined to a body.

The human soul, then, the lowest of all intellectual substances, has the weakest power of understanding; this is clear from the fact that it cannot, by knowing a universal, come to know those singulars to which the universal form extends. Consequently, in order that its knowledge be made perfect, that is, that it know singulars as well as universals, it needs to acquire its knowledge of truth from singulars themselves. It is absolutely necessary therefore that the soul be joined to a body. The crucial point to focus on is that the soul's being the form of matter is an answer to an urgent and essential need on the part of the soul, the very completion of its inferior intellectual nature through union with a body that will perfect the soul in the soul's very intellectuality.

This can be summed up as follows: The proper operation of the soul, intellection, is wholly independent of matter with respect to the efficient cause or principle from which it flows; yet the proportioned objects of human intellection are not pure intelligibles. They are rather those intelligible forms which exist in material things. Consequently, if the soul is to attain the proper and adequate objects of its intellectual operations, it needs powers which bring it into contact with material objects. In short, it needs sense powers. But sense powers cannot operate without organs; hence the soul needs to be joined to a body which provides the bodily organs through which these sense powers can function. The body, then, is absolutely necessary to the soul if the soul is to achieve its ultimate perfection, the secure possession of truth.

SUMMARY

There is today an ever-present temptation to look on the thirteenth century as the age of Thomas Aquinas, and in the light of subsequent events that perspective is, up to a point, defensible. St. Thomas himself, however, would probably have looked upon his own century as an Aristotelian one. From the twelfth century onward, with ever increasing momentum, a flood of Aristotelian writings and commentaries poured into the intellectual centers of the Latin West.

Then, early in the century had come the condemnations of Aristotle and prohibitions directed against the use of his works, both by the local church authorities in Paris and by papal sanction. The purpose of Pope Gregory IX seems to have been merely to forbid the reading of Aristotle's works until such time as competent scholars had examined them and purged them of possible doctrinal errors; for this purpose he appointed a special commission. Meanwhile, the University of Paris, interpreting the papal prohibitions in not too rigorous a sense, had made compulsory by 1255 the reading of nearly all of Aristotle's works in the faculty of arts.

At about the same time, as part of the papal program for the gradual rehabilitation of Aristotle, the task of providing new and accurate translations of Aristotle directly from the Greek had been undertaken by William of Moerbeke. St. Thomas and St. Albert, moreover, had begun their prolonged series of commentaries on the Aristotelian treatises.

Along with this intense literary activity of preparing translations and commentaries, and allied to it, came another development, the transformation of philosophical teachings under the pressure of Peripateticism. Into an age which doctrinally owed more to Plato, via St. Augustine and his followers, than to any other non-Christian thinker of antiquity, came the works of a philosopher who had been unsparing in his criticism of the major tenets of Platonism. This would be enough to put Platonists on the defensive. But this new "Philosopher" did not come unattended. He came accompanied by the commentaries of Arabian philosophers (among others) who had emphasized in the doctrine of Aristotle a number of positions or implications which certainly would cause sharp clashes with Christian thought. Among these doctrines were the eternity of the world, of motion, matter and species, a rigorous criticism of the Platonic theory of ideas (which involved an implied criticism of the divine ideas and of illumination), the denial of providence and of personal immortality for human beings.

Some of the sharpest disagreements between Platonists and Aristotelians centered on the meaning of what it is to be human. The Platonic view of being human, as it was known to the thinkers of the thirteenth century, seemed to fit, with very little adjusting, into the Christian scheme of things. Along with the other works of Aristotle came his *De Anima,* which in spite of the well-known ambiguities of certain passages, presents a total and clear-cut view of the constitution of a human being and of the nature of the soul. However, the question was not long in arising: Is a human being, as presented in the *De Anima,* a Christian person, or can he, at least, be Christianized? This question was to be a persistent one.

Seven hundred years earlier the same basic problem of the opposition between Plato and Aristotle on the nature of the human soul and of a human being had been faced by another Christian thinker, of whom we have spoken: Nemesius, bishop of Emesa, and his conclusion had been that the positions of Plato and Aristotle were irreconcilable. His treatise, known to many in the thirteenth century as the *De Natura Hominis* of Gregory of Nyssa, was a permanent reminder of the fundamental disagreement between Plato and Aristotle on the nature of being human. He was of value also because he had set down the basic criticisms that a Christian was bound to adduce against these two men: — that Plato seemed to preserve the spirituality and immortality of the soul at the expense of the unity of the human being, and that Aristotle seemed to account for the unity of the person, but at the cost of the soul's self-subsistence and incorruptibility.

The personal experiences of Nemesius should have made him an invaluable witness to one more fact, namely, that if one wishes to use the classic Greek positions as the foundation for a Christian anthropology, one must as least stay within either one or the other of the two main traditions, or else abandon both of them in order to develop a new position. This lesson will be lost, however, on many thirteenth century figures, who will at least try to combine Aristotelian elements with a basically Platonic orientation of doctrine. Two brilliant efforts, both of which are highly instructive, are those of St. Albert the Great and of St. Bonaventure.[10] Illuminating as their efforts were, neither succeeded in making the soul's role as form of matter (its Aristotelian characteristic) an essential characteristic of the soul. This serves to emphasize the originality in the thirteenth century of the doctrine of St. Albert's most famous student, St. Thomas Aquinas.

St. Thomas began his reading of Aristotle, like nearly everyone else in his day, by seeking help from the great commentators, and especially the Arabian commentators, Avicenna and Averroes. However, St. Thomas soon decided that if Aristotle were to be of use to Christian thinkers, he must first of all be firmly disengaged from his commentators, and especially Averroes. Even a rapid reading of the chapters dealing with the human soul in the Second Book of the *Summa Contra Gentiles,* and those dealing with the end of man in the Third Book, makes it evident that St. Thomas has come to an important decision: — If the Platonic doctrines on the nature of man and of the soul are to be critized in the name of Aristotle, it must be done in the name of an Aristotle who has been separated from his Arabian interpreters. St. Thomas saw his role to be that of showing how authentically Aristotelian doctrines were perfectly compatible with the Christian view of what it means to be human.

His *Quaestiones de Anima* reveal to what extent St. Thomas succeeded in this task. These questions emphasize in a marked degree St. Thomas' two main preoccupations with regard to the doctrine of the soul's nature: 1) to develop what he considered to be a thoroughly Aristotelian answer to an Aristotelian problem, namely, the constitution of the human being in terms of form and matter, in order to criticize the prevalent Platonism of his time, and 2) to do so in the name of an Aristotle who had been purged both of any traces of pure materialism or of any tinges of Averroistic separatism. In the first three questions of his *Questions on the Soul* he accomplishes these tasks to his own satisfaction. Especially satisfying to him, in view of the Averroistic controversies going on in Paris at the time these questions were disputed, must have been the embarrassing position in which his doctrine leaves the Latin Averroists. St. Thomas has insisted that if one looks at the Averroistic human being and focuses his eyes, not on the material composite, but on the intellect, then this human being becomes a Platonic man. Nothing would be more unacceptable to an Averroist than to have it pointed out to him that his brand of Aristotelianism is reducible to Platonism. On the other hand, if what the Averroists mean by a human being is simply this material composite (and not the intellect), then their position is open to all the charges that have been levelled against the materialists.

So much for St. Thomas' refusals. What is his positive doctrine?

As against the separatism of either Plato or Averroes, Thomas Aquinas has insisted that the human intellective soul is by nature the form of the body. Against the materialists he avers that the form of a human being is a subsistent concrete individual since it has an operation that is wholly immaterial, that is, the act of intellection. Furtherfore, the self-subsisting soul, whose existential act is an intellectual one, communicates this existential actuality to the matter it informs. It does this for the sake of two goods, one accidental, the other substantial.

What are these goods? The body, which is to the soul as matter is to form, must be united to the soul for the sake of a good which is substantial, namely, that a human being be constituted that is complete in its specific nature. It must also be united to the soul for the sake of an accidental perfection. This accidental perfection is in the line of operation, that operation which is proper to human beings, namely, intellectual cognition. This is an operation which the human soul can bring to perfection only through the use of sense powers which operate through bodily organs.

It is to relieve its own native poverty, then, that the soul communicates its own *esse,* its own existential act, to its body. By nature the lowest of intellectual creatures, the human soul must seek in union with matter the means of its perfection, those intelligibles which are proportioned to such a lowly intellect, those intelligibles immersed in matter.

There is one point which St. Thomas does not make fully explicit in the first three questions; it has to do with the existential actuality of the soul. He is explicit in stating that there is but one existential act for the entire human composite. "It is necessary, if the soul is the form of its body, that there be one existential act common to the soul and the body, and that this existential act belongs to the composite." [11] He is equally explicit that this existential act primarily belongs to the soul. "Although a soul has a complete act of existence, it does not follow that its body is accidentally united to it: both because that identical act of existence which belongs to the soul is communicated to its body in order that there might be one act of existence for the whole composite . . ." [12] No less emphatic is he that this existential act is of such nobility that the body cannot share in it totally. Eminently communicable, the existence which the soul confers on the body utterly exceeds the capacity of matter. This point St. Thomas makes again and again.

There is one question, however, which St. Thomas does not raise within the limits of the questions we have been studying, although he sets the stage for its being asked and provides the materials for its solution. The question is this: What kind of existential act does a human being possess through his intellective soul? Or to put it another way: What is the existential act which the soul confers on the human body?

The questions originates within St. Thomas' discussion with the separatists. He asserted that that by which the body lives is the soul; but he continues: The "to exist" of living things is a "to live." Is the "to exist" which the soul confers on the body *only* a "to live"? This would seem to provide no distinction between the intellective soul of a human being and any other kind of soul. St. Thomas had insisted, while speaking of the materialists, that the human soul is by nature intellectual since it has operations that are wholly immaterial. This would seem to indicate that the "to exist" which the human soul communicates to its body is an *intelligere,* not simply a *vivere,* a "to understand" rather than simply a "to live." Are we drawing unwarranted conclusions, or has St. Thomas drawn a similar conclusion, not in the *Questions on the Soul,* but elsewhere? Fortunately, he has.

In his series of *Questions on Spiritual Creatures,* written shortly before the *De Anima,* in a question dealing with the problem: Whether the powers of the soul are the same as the essence of the soul, the following argument is proposed: The soul is immediately united to the body as its form, and as form it confers some act on the body. This act cannot be *existence,* for even those beings which have no soul exist; nor can this act be *life,* for this act is found in beings which do not possess a rational soul. Consequently, the act which the soul confers on the body is an intelligible actuality *(intelligere).* Now the opponent is ready for his thrust: But the intellective power confers this act; therefore the intellective power is the same as the essence of the soul.

St. Thomas' answer to this argument is important. The human soul, he says, insofar as it is essentially the form of the body, gives being *(esse)* to the body. This it does insofar as it is the substantial form of the human being. However, insofar as it is a soul, it gives being of a particular kind, namely, living being *(vivere).* Moreover, insofar as it is an intellective soul, it confers living being that is of a special type, life of an intellectual nature *(vivere in intellectuali natura).* Thus far he has said no more than he says in the *De Anima.* The next sentence makes an additional point. "To understand" *(intelligere)* can be used in two ways. Sometimes it refers to an operation, and then it arises from a power or habit. Sometimes, however, (and this is the meaning which concerns us) it means the *existential act* of an intellectual nature, and only in this second sense is its principle the very essence of the intellective soul.[13]

In another work, written after the *Questions on the Soul,* St. Thomas makes the same point. This is his work entitled *On Separate Substances.* In this work St. Thomas is primarily concerned to treat of angels, but he naturally makes a number of points which apply with equal force to the human soul since it too is an immaterial substance. The text is found in a context similar to that of the argument we have just cited, a discussion of the doctrine of the plurality of forms. St. Thomas states: "But in immaterial substances, their "to be" itself is their "to live", and their "to live" is not other than their "to be intelligent." Therefore they are living and understanding from the same principle that they are beings." [14] These two texts should control our reading of the texts in the *De Anima*. The fact that the act of existence of the composite human being is an intellective act of existence or an intellectual act of existence goes a long way toward making it clear why the human body as such can never share fully in the existence of the soul, even though the body's total existence is from the soul. It helps one see how a human being, and not simply the soul, is located on the confines of two worlds. He belongs there because he exists in his totality through an act of existence which is wholly intellectual.

What has St. Thomas accomplished in the first three questions which are the key to all the rest, and especially Question 1? He had asked whether the human soul is both a substantial form and an entity. In answering this question he seems to have effectively removed the "and," at least in the sense that "and" signifies a "plus" or an "addition." The soul is not an entity, a subsistent individual AND a form. It is rather a concrete individual, that is, a subsistent, intellectual being, which by nature is destined to achieve both the perfection of its specific nature and its perfection in the line of intellectual operation through its information of matter. In return for having conferred a wholly spiritual existence upon matter, it is enabled by the operations of its sense powers working through bodily organs to attain those intelligible objects to which such an impoverished intellectual substance is proportioned, the intelligible found in sensible, singular substances.

Even a brief glance at the subsequent questions of the *De Anima* confirms that the doctrine developed in Question 1 runs like a connecting thread through the solutions to all the succeeding questions. The two questions on the agent intellect provide a fine example. The very need for positing an agent intellect is controlled by the fact that the human soul, that is, its possible intellect, is by nature ordained to know the type of intelligibility which is found in material things. Now, since the intelligibles in sensible things are only potentially intelligible, they need to be freed from the conditions of materiality. Once again, therefore, if the fact of human understanding is to be respected, the human soul must contain a power capable of reducing these potential intelligibles to intelligibles in act. This power is the agent intellect.

The reason that the soul cannot be composed of matter and form (Question 6) is that such a composition would make it impossible for the soul as a whole to be the formal principle of existence for its body. Furthermore, the composition of matter and form in the soul would give rise to a complete species, and thus one would return to Platonic view, that the soul contains the whole specific nature of the human being. At the root of all the diverse arguments of this question is the basic conviction that the soul is *immediately* united to its body as the body's substantial form; hence nothing can be posited which would interfere with the intimacy and immediacy of this union.

Question 7 on whether an angel and the soul differ in species provides St. Thomas with the opportunity to develop at length his teaching on the order that prevails among forms, both material and immaterial. It enables him once more to reaffirm the lowly status of the human soul among intellectual substances.

Once again, there can be no doubt of the dependence of the next three questions on Question 1. All of these questions deal with the union of the soul with its body: Question 8) the fittingness of the union; Question 9) the mode of the union; Question 10) the presence of the soul within its body. The fittingness of the union is explained in terms of the soul's natural lowliness as a spiritual substance. Any medium is impossible between the soul and its body because of the intimate relation that prevails between a substantial form and its matter. Finally, since the soul confers existence on the body and on all its parts, it must be present to the parts as well as to the body as a whole.

Nor is it difficult to predict how St. Thomas will answer those persons who posit several souls in a human being, vegetative, sensitive and rational. (Question 11) For one being there can be only one substantial form. Consequently, no plurality of souls in a human being.

Few questions in the *De Anima*, however, show more closely a direct doctrinal dependence upon Question 1 than Question 14 on the immortality of the human soul. As in Question 1, St. Thomas' first effort is to prove against a materialistic view of the soul that the soul is self-subsistent. His technique is to establish that the soul is a form which possesses existence, for it is necessary that such a form be incorruptible. He establishes his point, as in Question 1, by adverting to the intellectual operations of the soul which are independent of bodily organs. His conclusion is almost identical with a similar conclusion in Question 1: "Thus it is clear that the principle by which a human being understands has an existence which transcends its body and does not depend upon the body." The intellective principle of a human being is therefore incorruptible. But, as he immediately points out, he has already established that the intellective principle of a human being is not a separate substance but something which formally inheres in the human being—that it is the soul or part of the soul. Consequently, the human soul is incorruptible.

In this question he also treats the positions of the materialist and of the separatists, all of whom in some sense denied the immortality of the human soul. Even the answers to objections in this questions repeat, in some instances almost word for word, the answers he had given to similar objections in Question 1.

There is no need to treat all the questions, but one group of questions is of singular importance. These are the questions on the soul when it is separated from its body. If I have understood St. Thomas correctly, the intellective soul is essentially dependent for its proper natural perfection on its union with its body. If this is so, then the soul should exist and operate in a less perfect way when it is separated from its body than it does when joined to its body. Do the texts confirm this?

Let us focus on just one point: how the soul knows natural things, singular things. It is his teaching that the human soul while joined to its body is able to know all natural things; it knows them even as singulars. It is appropriate, therefore, to ask: Does the separated soul know natural things and singulars. If it does, does it know them more perfectly or less perfectly than it does in this life? St. Thomas devotes Questions 18 and 20 to these problems. The answer to the first question is "Yes." The separated soul knows both natural things and it knows singulars. It is the answer to the second question, however, which is important to us. Let us turn to Question 18 in which he treats of the separated soul's knowledge of natural things.

He begins his Response by declaring that a separated soul knows all natural things; however, it does not know them without qualification but only in a certain way. He then goes on to enlarge on what these qualifications mean. The intelligible species through which things are known, he explains, are present to all intellectual substances, but not in the same way. The nobler or loftier an intellectual substance is, the more universal are the species through which it knows, and consequently the fewer of them does it require. In the highest intelligence, God, the forms of all things are contained in a unified and simple fashion. God knows all things by knowing one intelligible form, His own essence. As we go down the scale of intellectual substances, however, we see that the lower an intelligence is, the more numerous are the intelligible forms that are required for such an intelligence to know the ultimate diversity of species. He continues by saying that it would be of no use to a lower intellectual substance to receive the kind of universal species which a higher intellectual substance possesses. This is a decisive point. It is not, in other words, merely a question of possessing intelligible species, but rather of having an *intellectual power* which is proportioned to knowing certain objects. If an intellect of an inferior degree of intellectuality were to receive the universal species which properly belong to a higher intellect, it would not thereby understand better. It would be hindered in its knowing, for it would understand these forms, not clearly but indistinctly.

We are now ready for his main point. It is clear, he says, that the human soul is the lowest of intellectual substances; therefore its natural capacity is to receive the forms of things which are material. Consequently, the human soul has been united to a body so that it might receive in its possible intellect those intelligible species which are derived from material things. It is for this reason that the human soul needs an agent intellect to render these material forms intelligible in act.

Therefore, when the human soul is joined to its body in this life, from the very fact of the union, its gaze is turned to things below it, and from these material things it abstracts and receives the intelligible species which are proportioned to its intellective power. When it is separated from its body, however, there is a change. It looks above, rather than below, and receives from the intelligences above it an influx of universal intelligible species. Does it know more perfectly as a result of this? Not at all. Why not? Are not the intelligible species it receives from the superior intelligences more intelligible than the ones it received from material things. In themselves they are; but the intellectual power of the human soul, being rooted in its very essence, has not been changed by the fact of the soul's being separated from its body. It still remains a lowly type of intellect and therefore it does not attain perfect knowledge through these species. That is to say, it cannot know things determinately; it knows thing universally and indistinctly, in the way that things can be known in their universal principles.

The same point is made with equal force in Question 20 which deals with the separated soul's knowledge of singulars. Angels can know through universal species all the singulars to which these universal forms extend. Not so the human soul. The strength of the intellective power of the human soul is not proportioned to the universality of the forms which flow in upon it from above; rather it is proportioned to forms received from things; it is on this account that it is natural for the human soul to be united to a body.

The chief notion which emerges from even this brief examination of these two questions on the knowledge of the separated soul is that it is St. Thomas' evident conviction that the natural knowledge of the separated soul is less perfect than the knowledge which the soul possesses in this life. This is an inescapable consequence of the fact that the human intellect is so lowly by nature that it needs to use sense powers and consequently needs an organic body in order to complete its natural intellectual operations.

From this brief sketch of the influence of the doctrine of Question 1 on St. Thomas' development of his solutions to the questions that follow, we can draw the following conclusions. It was not by chance that St. Thomas began his disputations on the human soul with this unique and important question. It belongs by right in the place of honor because its doctrine forms the foundation upon which the whole structure of his Christian anthropology in the *De Anima* is erected. It belongs in the first place, moreover, because it contains in summary form the whole of St. Thomas' doctrine on the nature of being human, on the nature of the soul. It is not related to the other questions of the *De Anima* as to its peers; to use a mediaeval figure, it is rather related to them as a lord to his vassals; it dominates them, directs and controls the development of all the later questions; where other questions control a certain, limited doctrinal area, it wields universal dominion.

One final question: Did St. Thomas achieve his goals in these questions? Were his doctrinal and historical purposes realized? In an Aristotelian age, he had set himself the task of solving an Aristotelian problem in Aristotelian terms. The Aristotelian problem was this: To explain what it means to be a human being in its substantial unity. The Aristotelian terms were these: the form-matter relation of soul and body. Without yielding any of the cardinal points of Aristotle's metaphysics or psychology, but rather by placing the problem and its solution within the framework of his own existential metaphysics of being, St. Thomas seems to have preserved both the substantial unity of man and the subsistent actuality of the intellective soul. In doing so, he avoided that which the Platonists of his time feared most of all, the debasing of the human being to the status of a material thing. Instead, he used the psychology of the Philosopher to locate the human soul and to situate the human being at a point in reality to which even the Platonists could not object, that is, among the spiritual substances. Human beings may be the lowest of intellectual substances, but even so, they have full claim to citizenship in that kingdom.

But if St. Thomas' doctrine of the nature of the human soul seemed to him to answer a contemporary doctrinal need, it was only because it represented for him a genuine and sound explanation of the facts. Faced with the obvious fact of a human being's operation of intellectual understanding, and with the equally evident fact of a human being's dependence upon the imagination for the specification and perfection of his acts of intellection, St. Thomas made no compromise on the unity of the nature which underlay both facts. Unity of nature, unity of act of existence, unity of being—these must all be accounted for. His explanation of the nature of the human soul (and of the human person) respects all of these unities. Wholly intellectual, a human being seems almost to be a creature of another world; but since in his very intellectuality his soul is ordered to matter, a human being is never a stranger in this world. His being is an incarnate existence; he knows discursively and decides deliberately. His being is extended through time and space; his being is historical. In fact, human beings are the only beings who have a history, a culture, a civilization. All of these facts point to the very special kind of intellectual being a human being is. To attain his ultimate perfection through the operations of his senses, his intellect and his will, a human being must use the material things of the earth on which he finds himself. All things are good. That the humblest things of this world are here to serve all human beings in the attainment of their ultimate perfection as spiritual substances is a lesson as valuable today as it was in the 13th century. It is a lesson whose lines are written clearly and pointedly across the *Quaestiones De Anima* of St. Thomas Aquinas.[16]

Notes

1. The translation of Alfanus has been twice published in modern times: 1) K. Holzinger, *Nemesii Emeseni libri.* Leipzig and Prague, 1887. 2) Carolus Burkhard, *Nemesii Episcopi Premnon Physicon . . . Liber a N. Alfano Archiepiscopo Salerni in Latinum Translatum.* Leipzig, Teubner, 1917. The translation of Burgundio has also been edited by Burkhard: *Gregorii Nysseni (Nemesii Emeseni) Peri physeos anthropou Liber a Burgundione in Latinum Translatus.* Vienna, 1891-1902. The five fascicles were reissued as a unit in 1902.

2. Cf. C. Burkhard, ed. cit., p. 11

3. This work is printed under the title of *De conditione hominis* in PL 67: 345-408, and the translation is attributed to Dionysius Exiguus. The Greek text and a late Latin translation are also to be found in PG 44: 125-256; the Greek of Nemesius' work and a late Latin translation are in PG 40: 485-840.

4. Albert the Great, *Summa Theol.,* P. II, tr. 12, q. 69, m. 2, a. 2. Borgnet ed., vol. 33, p. 14.

5. *De Spir. Creat.,* q. 3. ed. Keeler, p. 40

6. *De Unitate Intellectus,* 3. #62, ed. Keeler, p. 39. Cf. also #71-79.

7. Cf. De Veritate, q. 2, a. 2. This entire text is useful on this point. Cf. also, *Summa Theol.,* I, 14, 1; *ibid.,* I, 84, 2; *In II Sent.,* dist. 35, q. 1, a. 1; *De Anima,* q. 13; *De Ver.,* q. 23, a. 1; *In II De Anima,* lectio 12, #377. One of St. Thomas' most concise formulations on this point is in *De Spir. Creat.,* q. 1, ad 12, ed. Keeler, p. 17: ". . . quia immunitas a materia est ratio intellectualitatis."

8. St. Thomas is not afraid to call the human soul a material form. Cf. *In II Sent.,* dist. 17, q. 2, a. 1, ad 1. (Vol. II, p. 428-429).

9. *De Spir. Creat.,* q. 2, ad. 8. ed. Keeler, p. 31; Cf. also, q. 1, sed contra 11. ed. Keeler, p. 8.

10. Cf. A. C. Pegis, *St. Thomas and the Problem of the Soul in the Thirteenth Century.* Toronto, 1934. Cf. esp. Chapter II, "St. Bonaventure and the problem of the soul as substance," pp. 26-76 and Chapter III, "St. Albert the Great and the problem of the soul as form and substance," pp. 77-120. Cf. also E. Gilson, "L'âme raisonnnable chez Albert le Grand," in *Archives d'hist. doct. et litt. du moyen âge.* 14 (1943-45) pp. 5-72.

11. *De Anima,* q. 1, ad 13.

12. *Ibid.,* ad 1.

13. *De Spir. Creat.,* q. 11, arg. 14 and ad 14; ed. Keeler, p. 138 and 147.

14. *De Substantiis Separatis,* XI, #61. ed Lescoe, p. 100-101; ed. Perrier, IX, 62, p. 164.

15. Compare especially Ad 2 with *De Anima,* q. #1, ad 13; Ad 11 with q. 1, ad 12, ad 18; Ad 21, with q. 1, ad 13.

16. Cf. James H. Robb, "Intelligere Intelligentibus est Esse" in *An Etienne Gilson Tribute* (Milwaukee, Marquette, 1959) pp. 209-227.

QUESTION ONE

Parallel texts: *In II Sent.*, dist. I, q. 2, a. 4; dist. XVII, q. 2, a. 1; *Contra gent.*, II, 56-59, 68-70; *De Pot.*, q. 3, a. 9, a. 11; *Summa theol.*, I, q. 75, a. 2; q. 76, a. 1; *De Spir. creat.*, q. 2; *De Anima*, q. 2, q. 14; *De Unit. intell.*, cap. 3; *In II De An.*, lect 4; *In III De An.*, lect 7; *Compend. theol.*, cap. 80, 87.

The first question that is asked about the soul is this: Whether a human soul can be both a form and an entity.[1] It seems that it cannot be both.

(1) For if a soul is an entity, it is subsistent and possesses complete *per se* existence. Now whatever accrues to something over and above its substantial existence accrues to it accidentally, as whiteness, or even clothing, are accidents of a human being.[2] Consequently the body united to a soul is united to it accidentally. Therefore, if a soul is an entity, it is not the substantial form of its body.

(2) Furthermore, if a soul is an entity, it must be something that is individuated, for nothing that is universal is an entity.[3] Therefore it is individuated either by something else or by itself. If it is individuated by something else and is also the form of its body, it must be individuated by its body, for forms are individuated by their proper matter;[4] and so it would follow that if its body were removed, a soul would lose its individuation; and thus a soul could not be *per se* subsistent nor an entity. If it is self-individuated, it is either a simple form or it is something composed of matter and form. If it is a simple form, it follows that one individual soul could not differ from another except by reason of this form. However, a difference in respect to form produces a diversity of species. Therefore, it follows that the souls of diverse human beings would be specifically different.[5] Whence it also follows that human beings would differ specifically if a soul is the form of its body, since each thing acquires its species from the form proper to it. On the other hand, if a soul is composed of matter and form, it is impossible that a soul in its entirety be the form of its body, since matter is not the form of anything. It follows then that it is impossible that a soul be at one and the same time an entity and a form.

(3) Furthermore, if a soul is an entity, it follows that it is an individual. Now every individual belongs to a species and to a genus. Therefore, it follows that a soul would possess its own species and its own genus. Now it is impossible that anything which possesses its own species should receive something superadded to constitute that same species, because, as the Philosopher [6] says in Book VIII of the *Metaphysics,* [7] the forms or species of things are like numbers, whose species are changed by the addition or the subtraction of a unit. Now matter and form are united in order to constitute a species. Therefore, if a soul is an entity, it will not be united to its body as form is united to matter.

(4) Again, since God creates things on account of His goodness, which is manifested in the diverse grades of things, He created as many grades of beings as nature could accommodate. Therefore, if a human soul can subsist of itself, a point that one must admit if a soul is an entity, it follows that substantially existing souls constitute one grade of beings. Now forms do not constitute a single grade of beings apart from their matter. Consequently also a soul, if it is an entity, will not be the form of any matter.

(5) Furthermore, if a soul is an entity and subsists *per se,* it must be incorruptible, since it does not have a contrary nor is it composed of contraries. [8] But if a soul is incorruptible, it cannot be proportioned to a corruptible body such as the human body is. Every form, however, is proportioned to its matter. Consequently, if a soul is an entity, it will not be the form of the human body.

(6) Furthermore, there is nothing subsistent which is pure act except God. If, therefore, a human soul is an entity, namely, as something subsisting *per se,* there will be in it at least some composition of act and potency. And thus it will not be able to be a form because potency is not the act of anything. Therefore, if a soul is an entity, it will not be a form.

(7) Furthermore, if a soul is an entity that can subsist *per se,* it ought not be joined to a body except for the good of the soul itself. [9] Therefore, it would be united to its body either for the sake of an essential good or for the sake of an accidental good. It does not need to be united to its body for the sake of an essential good because it can subsist apart from its body; nor need it be united for the sake of an accidental good, a preeminent example of which would seem to be the knowledge of truth, which a human soul acquires through the senses, which cannot exist apart from bodily organs, since the souls of still-born infants are said by some to possess a perfect knowledge of things which they obviously did not acquire through their senses. Consequently, if a soul is an entity, there is no reason why it should be united to its body as a form.

(8) Furthermore, form and entity are distinguished as opposites. For the Philosopher says in Book II of the *De Anima* [10] that substance has three divisions, one of which is form, another, matter, and the third, entity. Now opposites are not predicated of the same thing. Therefore a human soul cannot be both a form and an entity.

(9) Furthermore, whatever is an entity subsists *per se.* Now the proper characteristic of a form is that it be in another; and these two characteristics seem to be opposites. Consequently, if a soul is an entity, it does not seem to be a form.

But an objector was arguing that after the dissolution of its body, a soul remains an entity and subsists *per se;* but at that moment it ceases to function as a form.

(10) On the contrary, whatever can be withdrawn from something while the being's substance remains belongs to this thing accidentally. Therefore, if, while a soul continues to exist apart from its body, a soul ceases to function as a form, then being a form belongs accidentally to a soul. But a soul is united to its body in order to constitute a human being only insofar as a soul is form. Consequently it is united to its body accidentally, and as a result a human being is an accidental being; and this is not so.

(11) Furthermore, if a human soul is an entity, existing *per se,* it must have an essential operation because each being which exists *per se* possesses an essential operation. Now a human soul does not possess an essential operation because the act of understanding which especially seems to be its essential operation does not belong to the soul, but to the human being, through his soul, as is said in Book I of the *De Anima.* [11] Therefore a human soul is not an entity.

(12) Furthermore, if a human soul is the form of its body, it must possess some dependence on its body; for form and matter are mutually dependent. However, whatever depends on another is not an entity. Consequently, if a soul is a form of its body, it is not an entity.

(13) Furthermore, if a soul is the form of its body, the soul and the body must possess one act of existing; for from matter and form there arises a being with one act of existing. However, there cannot be one act of existing for a soul and its body since they belong to diverse genera. For a soul is in the genus of incorporeal substance while a body is in the genus of corporeal substance. Consequently a soul cannot be the form of its body.

(14) Furthermore, a body's act of existing is corruptible, arising from quantitative parts. On the other hand, a soul's act of existing is incorruptible and simple. Therefore there is not one act of existing for the soul and the body.

However, an objector was arguing that the human body owes its very existence as a body to its soul.

(15) On the contrary, the Philosopher says in Book II of the *De Anima* [12] that the soul is the act of a physical, organic body. Consequently that which is related to the soul as matter to its act is a body which is already physical and organic, and this the body cannot be except through a form which constitutes it in the genus of body. Consequently, the human body has its own act of existing besides the act of existing of the soul.

(16) Furthermore, the principles of essence, which are matter and form, are ordered to the act of existing. But if something in reality can be brought about by one principle, then two principles are superfluous. Therefore, if a soul, since it is an entity, possesses in itself its own act of existing, then its body will not in the natural order be united to it as matter to form.

(17) Furthermore, the act of existing is related to the substance of a soul as its act, and hence it must be that which is highest in a soul. Now the lower does not attain to that which is above it through that which is highest in the superior being but rather through that which is lowest. For Dionysius says in the seventh chapter of the *De Divinis Nominibus* [13] that the divine wisdom joins the ends of the primary beings to the beginnings of the secondary beings. As a result the body, which is lower than the soul, cannot directly attain to the act of existence which is the loftiest principle in the soul.

(18) Furthermore, whatever has one act of existing has one operation. Therefore, if the act of existing of a human soul is joined to its body, then its operation which is the act of understanding will belong both to the soul and the body; but this is impossible, as is proved in Book III of the *De Anima*. [14] Therefore there is not a single act of existing for both the human soul and its body. Consequently it follows that the soul is not both a form and an entity.

On The Contrary,

Each being achieves its species through its essential form. Now a human being is human insofar as he is rational; therefore a rational soul is the essential form of a human being. Now a soul is an entity and subsists *per se* since it operates *per se;* for the action of understanding does not take place through a bodily organ, as is established in Book III of the *De Anima*. [15] Therefore a human soul is both an entity and a form.

(2) Furthermore, the ultimate perfection of a human soul consists in the knowledge of truth which is achieved through the intellect. Now in order that a soul be perfected in knowing the truth it needs to be united to a body, since a soul understands through phantasms which

cannot exist apart from a body. Therefore a soul must be united to its body as a form even if it is an entity.

The Response:

It must be said that an entity in the proper sense of the term is an individual in the genus of substance. For the Philosopher says in the *Categories* [16] that by first substances we unqualifiedly mean entity; however, second substances, although they seem to mean entity, really mean qualified entity. Now to be an individual in the genus of substance does not simply mean to be that which can subsist *per se* but also to be complete in a given species and genus of substance. Whence the Philosopher, still speaking in the *Categories*, [17] says that a hand, a foot and things like that are parts of substances rather than first or second substances. For although they are not in another as a subject, and this is essentially what we mean by substance, still they do not share fully in the nature of a species; hence they do not belong to a species nor to a genus except by reduction.

Now some men have denied to a soul the two characteristics that belong to the definition of an entity, declaring that a soul is a harmony, as Empedocles did, [18] or that it is a mixture, as did Galen, [19] or something else of this sort. For if they are correct, then a soul cannot subsist *per se* nor will it be complete in a species or a genus of substance, but will be simply a form like other material forms. Now this position is not tenable even with respect to the vegetative soul, whose operations must possess a principle which transcends active and passive qualities, [20] which in the process of nutrition and growth are instrumental qualities only, as is proved in Book II of the *De Anima*. [21] Mixture and harmony, however, do not transcend elemental qualities.

Furthermore, that position cannot be maintained with respect to a sensitive soul, whose operations consist in receiving species free from matter, as is proved in Book II of the *De Anima*; [22] for since active and passive qualities exist as the dispositions of matter, they do not transcend matter. Much more untenable is this position with regard to a rational soul, whose operations consist in abstracting species, not only from matter but also from all individuating, material conditions, and these operations are required for knowing a universal.

However, it is essential to consider something further with repsect to a rational soul, for not only does it acquire intelligible species, free from matter and the conditions of matter, but also in its essential operation no bodily organ has any share, so that there would be a corporeal organ of understanding in the way that an eye is the organ of seeing, as is proved in Book III of the *De Anima*. [23]

Thus it is necessary that an intellective soul operate *per se,* inasmuch as it possesses an essential operation in which the body does not share. And because each being acts insofar as it is actual, it is necessary that an intellective soul possess an independent *per se* act of existing which is not dependent on its body. For forms which have an act of existing which depends on matter or on a subject do not possess *per se* operations; heat, for instance, does not act, but rather something which is hot. And for this reason later philosophers [24] decided that the intellective part of the soul is something which is *per se* subsistent. For the Philosopher says in Book I of the *De Anima* [25] that the intellect is a substance and it is not corrupted. And the position of Plato is practically the same when he teaches that the soul is immortal and *per se* subsistent from the fact that it is self-moving. For Plato took motion in a broad sense to apply to any kind of operation, and thus it is to be understood that an intellect moves itself because it operates through itself. [26]

But Plato goes further and holds that a soul not only subsists *per se* but even that it possesses in itself the fullness of a specific nature. For he held that the full nature of the species is in the soul, defining a human being not as something composed of soul and body but as a soul using a body, and thus the relation of the soul to its body is that of a sailor to his ship or of a clothed man to his garments. [27]

However this position cannot be maintained; for it is clear that that by which the body lives is its soul. Now to live is the "to be" of living things. Therefore the soul is that by which a human body actually exists; but to confer being is a characteristic of a form. Therefore, a human soul is the form of its body. Again, if a soul were in its body as a sailor is in a ship, it would not give to its body nor to its parts their specific nature; whereas the contrary seem to be true from the fact that when the soul leaves its body, the individual parts of the body do not retain their original names except in an equivocal sense. For the eye of a corpse, like the eye in a portrait or the eye of a statue, is only equivocally called an eye, and the same would be true of any other part of the body. Furthermore, if a soul were in its body as a sailor is in a ship, it would follow that the union of soul and body is accidental. Consequently death, which signifies the separation of soul and body, would not be a substantial corruption, and this is obviously false. Therefore, one must maintain that the soul is an entity, as being able to subsist *per se* but not as possessing in itself a complete specific nature, but rather as completing human nature insofar as it is the form of its body; and thus at one and the same time it is a form and an entity.

As a matter of fact this same point can be made from a consideration of the order of natural forms. For one observes that among the forms of lower bodies, the higher a form is, the more it is like and approximates higher principles. This can be observed from the essential operations of these forms. For the forms of elements, which are the lowest forms and those closest to matter, do not possess any operation which exceeds active and passive qualities, as rarified and compact and other qualities which seem to be dispositions of matter. Now above these forms are the forms of compounds, which over and above the aforementioned operations have an operation which follows upon the nature which they derive from celestial bodies, as, for example, that magnets attract iron, not because of heat or cold or any quality of this sort, but because they participate in some fashion in celestial power. Again, above these forms are the souls of plants, which possess a likeness not only to celestial bodies but also to the movers of the celestial bodies inasmuch as these souls are the principles of a certain kind of motion, namely, that belonging to beings which move themselves.

Still higher than these are the souls of animals, which moreover possess a likeness to the substance which moves the heavenly bodies, not only in the operation by which they move their bodies but also because they are in themselves capable of knowledge, although the knowledge of animals is of material things only and they know in a material way; hence they need bodily organs. Higher still than these are human souls, which bear a likeness to higher substances[28] even in the genus of knowledge, since they are able to know immaterial things through the operation of understanding. However, human souls differ from these higher substances in this, namely, that they possess the nature of acquiring the immaterial knowledge of the intellect from that knowledge which comes from sensing material things.

Thus in such a fashion from the operation of the human soul the mode of its very existence can be known. For insofar as a soul possesses an operation which transcends material things, its very existence is raised above and does not depend on its body. But insofar as a soul by nature acquires its immaterial knowledge from what is material, it is clear that the fulfillment of its nature cannot be achieved apart from union with a body. For a thing is not complete in nature unless it possesses those things which are demanded for the proper operation of that nature. In this way, therefore, a human soul insofar as it is united to its body as its form still possesses an act of existence which is elevated above the body and does not depend on it; clearly then this soul is constituted on the boundary line between corporeal and separate substances.

Replies to the Opposing Arguments:

(1) Although a soul has a complete act of existence, it does not follow that its body is accidentally united to it: both because that identical act of existence which belongs to the soul is communicated to its body in order that there might be one act of existence for the whole composite, and also because of the fact that although a soul could subsist *per se,* it does not possess a complete nature, but its body is joined to it to complete its nature.

(2) Each being possesses its act of existing and its individuation in accordance with the same factor. For universals do not exist in the universe of things insofar as they are universals, but only inasmuch as they are individuated. Consequently, therefore, a soul's act of existence comes from God as from an active principle, and is in its body as in matter. Still, a soul's act of existing does not perish when the body ceases to be, nor does a soul's individuation, although this individuation is related to its body, perish along with the body.

(3) A human soul is not an entity in the sense of being a complete substance which possesses its specific nature but rather in the sense of being part of a being which has a complete specific nature, as is clear from what has been said. Consequently the conclusion of the argument does not follow.

(4) Although a human soul is able to subsist *per se,* still it does not *per se* possess a complete specific nature. Whence it would not be possible that separated souls would constitute a distinct grade of beings.

(5) A human body is matter that is proportioned to a human soul since the body is to its soul as potency is to act. Still it does not necessarily follow that the body equals the soul in its power of existing; because a human soul is not a form totally circumscribed by matter, as is clear from the fact that one of a soul's operations transcends matter. However, according to the teaching of faith a different explanation can be given, namely, that in the beginning the human body was constituted as in some way incorruptible, and that through sin it incurred the necessity of dying from which it will once again be freed in the resurrection. Hence it is merely accidental that the body does not achieve the immortality of soul.

(6) A human soul, although it is subsistent, is composed of potency and act; for the substance of a soul is not identical with its act of existing but rather is related to it as potency is related to act. Nor does it follow from this that a soul cannot be a form of its body; because even in other forms that which is form and act in relation to one thing is potential in relation to another. For example, transparency, which acts as form with respect to the atmosphere, is potential with respect to light.

(7) A soul is united to its body both for a good that is a substantial perfection, namely, that its specific nature might be achieved, and also for a good that is an accidental perfection, namely, that a soul might be perfected in achieving intellectual knowledge, which a soul acquires through the senses. For this mode of understanding is natural to a human being; nor is it a valid objection that the separated souls of children and other human beings make use of a different mode of understanding, for that mode is appropriate to these souls by reason of their being separated rather than by reason of their being specifically human.

(8) It is not essential to an entity that it be composed of matter and form, but only that it can subsist *per se.* Hence it follows that although a composite is an entity, this does not prevent something other than a composite from being an entity.

(9) It is not of the nature of an entity to exist in another as an accident exists in a subject. But to exist in another as a part, and this is the way in which a soul exists in a human being, does not altogether prevent that which is in another from being called an entity.

(10) When the body ceases to be through corruption, the soul does not lose that essential feature by which it is appropriate to the soul to be a form, although the soul does not actually perfect matter so that it is a form.

(11) To understand is the essential operation of a soul if one takes into account the principle from which the operation proceeds. For understanding does not take place in a soul by means of a corporeal organ as sight does through the medium of the eye. The body nevertheless shares in the operation of understanding from the side of the object, for phantasms, which are the objects of the intellect, cannot exist apart from the organs of the body.

(12) Although a soul depends on its body to the extent that without its body a soul does not attain the fullness of its nature, yet a soul is not so dependent on its body that a soul cannot exist apart from its body.

(13) It is necessary, if a soul is the form of a body, that there be common to both one act of existing which is the act of existing of the composite. Nor is it an objection to this that the soul and body belong to diverse genera, for neither the soul nor the body belongs to a species or to a genus except through reduction, as parts are reduced to the species or the genus of their whole.

(14) That which undergoes corruption in the proper sense is not the form nor the matter nor the act of existing but rather the composite. The body's existence is said to be corruptible insofar as the body through the process of corruption loses that act of existing which was shared by it and the soul, and which remains in the subsistent soul. For the same reason the act of existing of the body can be said to

consist of parts because it is so constituted by its parts as to be able to receive existence from the soul.

(15) Sometimes in the definitions of forms the subject is said to be without form, as when one says that motion is the act of that which exists in potency. Sometimes the subject is said to be informed, as when it is said that motion is the act of the movable thing and light is said to be the act of what is luminous. It is in this latter way that a soul is said to be the act of a physical, organic body, because a soul makes the body to be an organic body just as light causes something to be luminous.

(16) The essential principles of a given species are not ordered toward existence only, but to the existence of that species. Therefore, although a soul is able to exist *per se,* it cannot however exist in the fullness of its nature apart from it body.

(17) Although existence is the most formal of all perfections, still it is also the most communicable, although it is not shared in the same mode by those beings which are lower and higher. Hence the body shares in the act of existence of the soul but not so excellently as the soul itself does.

(18) Although the act of existing of a soul belongs in some way to the body, still the body does not succeed in participating in the existence of the soul according to the soul's full excellence and power; and consequently there is an operation of soul in which the body does not share.

Notes to Question One

1. The Latin term *hoc aliquid,* the literal translation of the Greek τόδε τι, is translated here as "entity" and denotes a particular thing which subsists of itself *(per se).*

2. Plato, *Phaedo,* 87B

3. An abstract universal cannot be termed an entity because it exists only in the intellect. See *Summa theol.,* I, q. 85.

4. "Signate" or "designated" matter, that is, matter considered as possessing determinate dimensions, is the principle of individuation. See *De ente et essentia,* chapter 2; *Summa theol.,* I, q. 29, a. 1.

5. It is St. Thomas' doctrine that all angels (all separate substances) are composed of act and potency, that is, existence and essence; but they are purely immaterial, containing no matter. Consequently the differences between these separate substances is one of essence, and as a result each one of them consitutes a complete species of being.

6. A mediaeval term of respect for Aristotle.

7. *Metaphysics,* VIII, 3 (1043b 33-1044a 2)

8. Where there is no contrariety there can be no corruption since corruption is from contrary into contrary. See *Summa theol.,* I, q. 75, a. 6.

9. St. Thomas rejects any account of the union of body and soul as a punishment for sin; the union is the natural state of human beings and it exists for the good of the soul. See *Summa theol.,* I, q. 89.

10. Aristotle, *De Anima,* II, 1 (412a 6-9)

11. Aristotle, *De Anima,* I, 4 (408b 13-15)

12. Aristotle, *De Anima,* II, 1 (412a 27-28)

13. Pseudo-Dionysius, *De Divinis Nominibus,* VIII, 3 (PG 3: 871)

14. Aristotle, *De Anima,* III, 4 (429a 24-27)

15. *Ibid.*

16. Aristotle, *Categories,* V (3B 10-23)

17. Aristotle, *Categories,* V (3a 28-31)

18. Aristotle, *De Anima,* I, 4 (407b 27-408a 28); Nemesius, *De Natura hominis,* cap. 2 (PG 40: 537), ed. Burkhard, Part II, p. 3 (27); Cf. Gregory of Nyssa, *De Anima,* Sermo Primus (PG 45: 193D). Empedocles (5th century B.C.), post-Parmenidean poet and philosopher of nature, who originated one notion of the schema of four elements (earth, water, air, fire) to explain reality.

19. Nemesius, *De Natura hominis,* cap. 2 (PG 40: 553), ed. Burkhard, p. 9; Cf. Gregory of Nyssa, *De Anima,* Sermo Primus (PG 45: 196). Galen (A.D. 129-c199) Greek physician and philosopher.

20. Classical physics held that the four elements possessed qualities categorized as active (hot and cold) and passive (moist and dry). Cf. Aristotle, *De gen. et corr.,* II, 3 (330a 30 ff)

21. Aristotle, *De Anima,* II, 4 (416b 17-30)

22. Aristotle, *De Anima,* II, 12 (424a 17-21)

23. Aristotle, *De Anima,* III, (429a 24-27)

24. Post-Empedoclean philosophers such as Socrates, Plato and Aristotle.

25. Aristotle, *De Anima,* I, 4 (408b 18-19)

26. Plato, *Phaedrus,* (245c-246A)

27. Plato, *Alcibiades,* I (129E-130C)

28. By higher substances St. Thomas means what Christian theology referred to as angels or angelic substances. Thinkers of the middle ages identified these angels with the separate substances of Aristotelean philosophy.

QUESTION TWO

Parallel texts: Most of the texts cited for Question One deal with the issues in this question. See also: *In III Sent.,* dist. 5, q. 3, a. 2; dist. 22, q. 1, a. 1; *De Ente et ess.,* 2; *Summa theol.,* I, q. 75, a. 4; *In VII Metaph.,* lect. 9.

The second question that is asked about the soul is this: Whether a human soul is separate from its body in existence. And it seems that it is.

(1) For the Philosopher says in Book III of the *De Anima* [1] that the sensitive soul cannot exist without a body whereas the intellect is separate. Now a human soul is an intellect. Therefore a human soul is separate in existence from its body.

(2) Furthermore, a soul is the act of a physical, organic body inasmuch as the body is its organ. Consequently, if the intellect is united in existence to the body as the body's form, then the body must be the intellect's organ; and this is impossible, as the Philosopher proves in Book III of the *De Anima.* [2]

(3) Furthermore, the union of form to matter is stronger than that of a power to its organ. But because of its simplicity the intellect cannot be united to the body as a power is to its organ. Much less, therefore, can it be united to the body as form is to matter.

But an objector was arguing that the intellect, that is to say, the intellective power, does not have an organ, but that the very essence of an intellective soul is united to its body as its form.

(4) On the contrary, an effect is not more simple than its cause. But a power of the soul is an effect of its essence because all the powers of the soul flow from its essence. Therefore no power of the soul is simpler than its essence. [3] Consequently, if the intellect cannot be the act of a body, as is proved in Book III of the *De Anima,* [4] neither can the intellective soul be united to its body as its form.

(5) Furthermore, every form that is united to matter is individuated through its matter. Therefore, if an intellective soul is united to its body as its form, the soul must be individuated. Consequently, the forms received in it are individuated forms. As a result, an

intellective soul will not be able to know universals, and this is clearly false.

(6) Furthermore, a universal form does not become intelligible because of a thing which exists outside the soul since all forms existing in things outside the soul are individuated. Therefore, if the forms in the intellect are universal, they must acquire this universality from the intellective soul. Consequently the intellective soul is not an individuated form; and so it is not united to its body substantially.

But an objector was arguing that intelligible forms, inasmuch as they inhere in the soul, are individuated; but inasmuch as they are the likenesses of things, are universal, representing things according to their common nature and not according to their individuated principles.

(7) On the contrary, since form is the principle of operation, an operation issues from a form according to the mode by which a form inheres in a subject. For the hotter something is, the more it heats. Therefore, if the species of things which are in the intellective soul are individuated inasmuch as they inhere in the soul, the knowledge which issues from them will be of the individual only and not of the universal.

(8) Furthermore, the Philosopher says in Book II of the *De Anima* [5] that just as a triangle is in a quadrilateral and as a quadrilateral is in a pentagon, so the nutritive soul is included in the sensitive soul and the sensitive soul is included in the intellective soul. But a triangle is not actually present in a quadrilateral, but potentially only; so also is a quadrilateral present in a pentagon. Therefore neither the nutritive nor the sensitive parts of a soul are actually present in the intellective part of a soul. Consequently, since the intellective part is not united to the body except through the medium of the nutritive and sensitive parts, from the fact that the nutritive and sensitive parts are not actually in the intellective part, it follows that the intellective part of a soul will not be united to the body.

(9) Furthermore, the Philosopher say, in Book XVI of *De Animalibus,* [6] that animal and man do not come to be at the same time, but animal comes first and man thereafter. Hence the principle by which something is animal is not the same as that by which it is man, since it is animal by reason of the sensitive soul and man by reason of the intellective soul. Therefore, the sensitive and intellective principles are not united substantially in the soul; and thus the conclusion is the same as in the previous argument.

(10) Furthermore, a form belongs to the same genus as the matter to which it is united. But an intellect is not in the genus of bodily things. Therefore an intellect is not a form united to its body as to matter.

(11) Furthermore, from two actually existing substances no being that is one comes into existence. But the body as well as the intellect is an actually existing substance. Consequently, the intellect cannot be united to its body so that from them one being may result.

(12) Furthermore, every form that is united to matter is brought into act through motion and through alteration of the matter. Now the intellective soul is not brought into act from the potency of matter, but comes from without, as the Philosopher says in Book XVI of *De Animalibus.*[7] Therefore it is not a form which is united to matter.

(13) Furthermore, everything operates according to the way in which it exists. Now an intellective soul has an essential operation that it performs independently of its body, namely, to understand. Therefore it is not united to its body in existence.

(14) Furthermore, it is impossible that whatever is in the slightest degree unsuitable be attributed to God. But it is unsuitable for an innocent soul to be confined in a body which is like a prison. Therefore it is impossible that God should have united the intellective soul to a body.

(15) Furthermore, no craftsman who is wise puts an impediment in the way of the product which he makes. But the body is a very great impediment to the intellective soul in its achieving the knowledge of truth, in which the soul's perfection consists, according to the text in Chapter IX of the *Book of Wisdom,* "A corruptible body weighs down upon the soul."[8]

(16) Furthermore, those things which are united to each other possess a mutual affinity for each other. But the intellective soul and the body oppose each other because "the flesh lusts against the spirit and the spirit against the flesh," *Galatians, V.*[9] Therefore the intellective soul is not united to the body.

(17) Furthermore, the intellect is in potency to all intelligible forms, possessing none of them in act, just as prime matter is in potency to all sensible forms, and has none of them in act. For this reason there is one prime matter for all things and one intellect for all men, and thus the intellect is not united to a body which would individuate it.

(18) Furthermore, the Philosopher proves, in Book III of the *De Anima,*[10] that if the possible intellect had a bodily organ, it would have a determinate nature within the realm of sensible things and consequently would not be able to receive and to know all sensible forms. Now form is more closely united to matter than a power is to its organ. Therefore, if the intellect be united to its body as its form, it will have a sensible determinate nature and consequently will not be receptive of or able to know all sensible forms, and this is impossible.

(19) Furthermore, every form united to matter is received in

matter. But whatever is received in something exists in it according to the mode of the recipient. Therefore, every form united to matter is in matter according to the mode of matter. But the mode of sensible and corporeal matter does not permit it to receive anything in accordance with an intelligible mode. Therefore, since the intellect possesses intelligible being, it is not a form united to corporeal matter.

(20) Furthermore, if the soul is united to corporeal matter, the soul must be received in it. Now whatever is received by that which has been received by matter is itself received in matter. Therefore, if the soul is united to matter, whatever is received in the soul is received in matter. But the forms of the intellect cannot be received by prime matter, rather they become intelligible through abstraction from matter. Therefore a soul which is united to corporeal matter is not receptive of intelligible forms. And so the intellect which is capable of receiving intelligible forms will not be united to corporeal matter.

On The Contrary,

The Philosopher states in Book III of the *De Anima* [11] that it is as unnecessary to ask whether the soul and the body are one as to ask whether the wax and its shape are one. But the shape of the wax cannot in any way be separated in existence from the wax. Therefore, neither can the soul be separated from the body. But the intellect is a part of the soul, as the Philosopher states in Book III of the *De Anima*. [12] Therefore the intellect is not separate in existence from its body.

(2) Furthermore, no form is separate in existence from its matter. But the intellective soul is the form of its body. Therefore, it is not separate in existence from matter.

THE RESPONSE:

In order to clarify this question one must note that wherever something is sometimes in potency, sometimes in act, it is necessary that there be a principle through which that thing is in potency, as a man is sometimes sensing in act and sometimes in potency. It is because of this that we must posit in a human being a principle of sensibility that is in potency to sensible things. For if a human being were always sentient in act, the forms of sensible things would actually be present at all times in the principle of sensibility. In like fashion, since a human being is sometimes understanding in act and is sometimes only in potency to understand, we must admit that there is in a human being an intellective principle which is in potency to intelligible things. And this principle the Philosopher, in Book III of the *De Anima,* [13] calls the possible intellect. The possible intellect must therefore be in potency to and able to receive all those things which are intelligible to a human being, and must therefore be devoid of all of them. This follows from the principle that whatever is capable of receiving things and is in potency to them is of itself without any of them, just as the pupil of the eye, which is capable of receiving all colors, has itself no color. Now a human being is naturally capable of understanding the forms of all sensible things. Consequently, the possible intellect must in itself be devoid of all sensible forms and natures, and as a result it is necessary that it have no bodily organ. For if it possessed a bodily organ, the possible intellect would be determined to a particular sensible nature; just as the power of sight is restricted to the nature of the eye.

Now this demonstration of the Philosopher eliminates the position of the ancient philosophers, who held that the intellect was no different from sensitive powers, [14] as well as the position of those other thinkers who taught that the principle by which a human being understands is a form or a power which is intermingled with the body just as other material forms and powers are. [15] Now other men, seeking to avoid this mistake, fall into the opposing error. For they hold that the possible intellect is so devoid of any sensible nature and so unmixed with body that it is a substance separate in existence from the body so that it should be in potency to all intelligible forms. [16]

However, this position is untenable. For we are concerned with the possible intellect only inasmuch as it is that through whose agency a human being understands. For it was in this way that Aristotle himself came to know about it. This is clear from what he says in Book III of the *De Anima,* where he begins his treatment of the possible intellect: "Now we must treat that part of the soul by which the soul knows and cognizes." [17] In another passage he says: "Now I call the possible intellect that by which the soul understands." [18] Now if the possible intellect were a separate substance, it would be impossible that a human being should understand by means of it. For if a substance performs a given operation, it is impossible that that operation be attributed to another substance that is diverse from the first. For although one of two substances can be the cause of operation in the other as principal agent in relation to its instrument, still the action of the principal agent is not one in number with the action of the instrument, for the action of the principal agent consists in moving the instrument while the action of the instrument consists in being moved by the principal agent and in moving something else. Consequently, if the possible intellect be a substance which is separate in existence from this human being or from that human being, it is impossible that the act of understanding of the possible intellect belong to either human being. Now, since the operation of understanding is not attributed to any principle in a human being other than the possible intellect, it follows that no human being understands anything. Hence this position can be refuted by the same kind of argument as that used against those who deny the first principle; this is clear from the way Aristotle argues against them in Book IV of the *Metaphysics*. [19]

However, striving to avoid this difficulty, Averroes, [20] a follower of this position, stated that the possible intellect, although separate in existence from the body, is nevertheless conjoined to man through the mediation of phantasms. For, as the Philosopher says in Book III of the *De Anima*, [21] phantasms are related to the possible intellect as sensible objects are related to the senses and as colors are to sight. As a result, therefore, an intelligible species has two subjects, one in which it exists according to the mode of intelligible being, and this is the possible intellect; and another subject in which it exists according to the mode of real being, and this subject is the phantasms. There is, therefore, a conjoining of the possible intellect with the phantasms insofar as the intelligible species is in some fashion in both, and it is because of this conjunction that a human being understands by means of the possible intellect.

However, this conjunction is not adequate to explain human knowing, for something is not said to be capable of knowing from the fact that knowable species are present to it, but rather because of the fact that it possesses a power of knowing. Now it is clear if one accepts the above-mentioned position that there would be present to a human being nothing but the intelligible species alone; and the power of understanding, namely, the possible intellect, is utterly separate. As a consequence, then, of the conjunction-theory just described, a human being will not be the one who understands; but rather his intellect, or a species of something belonging to his intellect be understood. This can be clearly seen from the analogy used above. For if phantasms are related to the intellect as colors are related to sight, then, according to the aforementioned position, the union of the possible intellect with us through phantasms will be no different from that of sight with a wall through color. Now from the fact that colors are in it, it does not follow that a wall sees, but only that it is seen. Also it does not follow from the fact that phantasms are present in a human being that a human being understands, but only that he be understood.

Furthermore, a phantasm is not the subject of an intelligible insofar as the intelligible species is understood in act, but rather it is through abstraction from phantasms that an intelligible species becomes understood in act. Now the possible intellect is not the subject of an intelligible species except insofar as the species is already actually understood and has been abstracted from phantasms. Hence there does not exist some one entity that could exist both in the (separate) possible intellect and in the phantasms, through which the possible intellect might be joined to us. Furthermore, if someone understands through intelligible species only when the species are actually understood, it follows from the aforementioned position that we are in no way intellectual knowers; for the intelligible species would be present to us only as they are found in phantasms, that is to say, only as potentially understood.

Clearly, then, the conjunction-theory is impossible from the viewpoint of human cognition; and the same conclusion is also clear from the viewpoint of the nature of separate substances. Since separate substances are possessed of a very high degree of perfection, it is unthinkable that in their own essential operations they should depend upon material things or on the operations of material things, or that they should be in potency to other things which are of this kind; for this is true even of celestial bodies, which are inferior to the aforesaid substances. Therefore, since the possible intellect is in potency to the species of sensible things, and since its operation cannot be achieved without phantasms, which depend upon a body, it is impossible and unthinkable that the possible intellect be one of the separate substances.

Hence we must hold that the possible intellect is a potency or power of the human soul. For although the human soul is a form united to a body, still it is united in such a way that it is not entirely contained by the body as if immersed in it, as are other material forms, but rather it surpasses the capability of all corporeal matter and because of the fact that its power exceeds corporeal matter, there is grounded in it the potential for intelligible objects, and this potency belongs to the possible intellect; however, insofar as the soul is united to its body, it possesses operations and powers in which the body shares, such as the powers of the nutritive and sensitive parts of the soul.

In this way we can maintain the nature of the possible intellect as Aristotle held it to be,[22] since on the one hand the possible intellect is not a power grounded in a corporeal organ; and yet on the other hand a human being understands through the possible intellect because it is located in the essence of the human soul, which is the form of a human being.

Replies to the Opposing Arguments:

(1) The intellect is said to be separate but not the power of sense

because when the body is corrupted, the intellect continues to exist
in the separated soul but the sensitive powers do not. Or a better reply
might be to say that the intellect does not use a bodily organ in its
operation as the senses do.

(2) The human soul is the act of an organic body because the
body is its organ. But it does not follow that the body must be the
soul's organ with respect to every one of its potencies and powers,
since the human soul transcends its relation to its body, as has already
been stated.

(3) The organ of a power is that power's principle of operation.
Hence if the possible intellect were united to an organ, its operation
would also be the operation of that organ. From this it would follow
that it would be impossible for the principle by which we understand
to be free of all sensible natures. For the principle by which we understand would be at one and the same time the possible intellect and
its organ, just as the principle by which we see is the power of sight
and the pupil of the eye. But even though the human soul is the form
of its body and the possible intellect is a power of the soul, it does
not follow that the possible intellect is restricted to a particular sensible
nature, because the human soul transcends its relation to its body,
as we have already said.

(4) The possible intellect belongs to the human soul to the degree
that the soul surpasses corporeal matter. Consequently, the possibly
intellect, from the fact that it is not the act of any organ, does not
wholly transcend the essence of the soul, but rather is that which is
highest in the soul.

(5) The human soul is an individuated form and so are its power
which is called the possible intellect and the intelligible forms which
are received in this intellect. But this fact does not hinder these forms
from being actually understood. Something is actually understood from
the fact that it is immaterial, not because it is universal; rather, a
universal is intelligible because it is abstracted from individuating
material principles. For it is clear that separate substances are intelligible in act, and nevertheless they are individuals; as Aristotle says
in Book VII of the *Metaphysics,*[23] the separate forms which Plato posited
were individuals. Thus it is clear that if individuation were incompatible with intelligibility, those who claim that the possible intellect
is a separate substance would be faced with the same problem; for
it would follow that the possible intellect would be an individual and
would individuate the species received in itself. Therefore, it must
be maintained that although the species received in the possible intellect
are individuated by the fact that they inhere in the possible intellect,
still these species, because they are immaterial, are the means by which
we know the universal which is conceived through abstraction from

individuating principles. For universals, with which the sciences deal, are that which is known through intelligible species; they are not the intelligible species themselves; and it is clear that not all sciences are concerned with species that are intelligible but only physics and metaphysics. For an intelligible species is that *by which* the intellect understands, not *that which* the intellect understands, except through reflection when the intellect understands that it understands and that by which it understands.

(6) The intellect bestows universality on forms which are understood because it abstracts these forms from individuating material principles. Hence it is not necessary that an intellect be universal, but that it be immaterial.

(7) A specific kind of operation follows upon the specific form, which is the principle of operation, although the failure of the operation to achieve its end follows upon the form insofar as it inheres in a subject. For by the fact that a form is heat, it heats; but it heats to a greater or lesser degree in proportion to the way in which it perfects its subject. Now to understand universals belongs to the species of intellectual operation; hence to understand universals follows upon an intellectual species according to its proper operation. But from the fact that this intellectual species belongs more or less perfectly to the one who understands, it follows that someone understands more perfectly or less perfectly.

(8) The likeness which the Philosopher notes between geometrical figures and parts of the soul bear upon this point, that just as a quadrilateral possesses whatever a triangle has and something more, and as a pentagon has whatever a quadrilateral has, so the sensitive soul possesses whatever the nutritive soul does and the intellective soul possesses whatever belongs to the sensitive soul and more. It does not follow from this that the nutritive and sensitive differ essentially from the intellective, but rather that one of them includes the other.

(9) Just as animal and human being are not conceived at one and the same time, so neither are animal and horse, as the Philosopher says in the same text. Consequently, the necessary meaning of the statement is not that there is in a human being one substantial principle, namely, the sensitive soul, by which he is an animal, and another principle, the intellective soul, by which he is human, since one cannot say that in a horse there are diverse principles by one of which the horse is an animal and by another of which it is a horse. Rather the statement means that in the embryo there first appear less perfect operations and afterwards more perfect operations appear, just as all generation involves a change from the imperfect to the perfect.

(10) A form does not belong to a genus, as we have said. Consequently, since the intellective soul is the form of the human being,

it is not in another genus than that of the body; rather it is only by reduction that either of them is said to belong to the genus 'animal' or the species 'human being.'

(11) A substantial unit cannot be produced from two substances which are actually existing and are complete in their own species and nature. However, the soul and the body are not substances of this kind, since they are parts of human nature. Consequently nothing prevents them from becoming a substantial unit.

(12) Although it is a form united to a body, the human soul nevertheless transcends all of corporeal matter, and consequently the soul cannot be brought to actual existence from the potency of matter by motion or mutation as are other forms that are immersed in matter.

(13) The human soul does have an operation in which the body does not participate, but this operation belongs to that part of the soul which wholly transcends its body. But this does not prevent the soul from being united to its body in some fashion.

(14) This operation is based on the position of Origen,[24] who taught that souls were originally created without bodies, along with spiritual substances, and later these souls were united to bodies as if being imprisoned. But he also said that souls suffered this indignity as a just punishment for their guilt, the result of an earlier sin. Origen, following Plato's teaching, held that a human soul possessed a complete species, and that its body was united to it accidentally. Now since this position is false, as we showed earlier, it is no loss to a soul to be united to its body, but rather the union perfects the soul in its nature. And if it be true that the body imprisons the soul and corrupts it, this situation is a punishment for original sin.

(15) It is natural to the human soul to attain intelligible truth by a mode of understanding that is inferior to the way in which higher spiritual substances grasp intelligible truth: souls, that is, receive such knowledge from sensible things. But even in this mode a soul is hindered by the corruption of the body which follows upon the sin of Adam.

(16) The very fact that the flesh lusts against the spirit indicates the soul's affinity for its body. For 'spirit' means the superior part of the soul by which a human being surpasses other animals, as Augustine says in his *Super Genesim Contra Manichaeum*.[25] Now the flesh is said to 'lust' because those parts of the soul that are united to the flesh desire those things which are pleasant to the flesh, and sometimes these desires are at war with the spirit.

(17) From the fact that the possible intellect does not possess an intelligible form in act, but only in potency, just as prime matter does not possess a sensible form in act, it does not follow that the possible intellect is one for all men, but only that it is one with respect to all

intelligible forms, just as prime matter is one with respect to all sensible forms.

(18) If the possible intellect had a corporeal organ, it would necessarily follow that the principle by which we understand would be that organ along with the possible intellect, just as the pupil of the eye along with the power of sight is the principle by which we see. And consequently the principle by which we understand would possess a determinate sensible nature, and this is obviously false, as is clear from Aristotle's demonstration cited above.[26] But this consequence does not follow from the fact that the soul is the form of the human body, since the possible intellect is a power of the soul insofar as the soul transcends its relation to its body.

(19) The soul, although it is united to the body according to the body's mode, nevertheless possesses an intellectual nature by virtue of that part of the soul which transcends the body; and thus the forms received in the soul are intelligible and not material.

From this last response the solution to the twentieth argument is clear.

Notes to Question Two

1. *De Anima,* III, 4 (429b 4-5)
2. *De Anima,* III, 4 (429a 27-28)
3. In my translation, I have adopted the reading *'esssentia'* instead of *'esse,'* which is in the Latin text.
4. *De Anima,* III, 4 (429a 24-27; 429b 4-5)
5. *De Anima,* II, 3 (414b 28-32)
6. *De Generatione animalium,* II, 3 (736b 1-5)
7. *De Generatione animalium,* II, 3 (736b 27-29)
8. *Wisdom,* 9: 15.
9. *Galatians,* 5: 17.
10. *De Anima,* III, 4 (429a 24-27)
11. *De Anima,* II, 1 (412b 6-7)
12. *De Anima,* III, 4 (429a 10-13, 22-23)
13. *De Anima,* III, 4 (429b 30-31)
14. The Ionian philosophers. See *De Anima,* II, 3 (427a 21-29)
15. See Averroes, *Commentarium magnum in Aristotelis De Anima,* III, 5. ed. Crawford, p. 395.
16. *Ibid,* III, 20, lines 29-33, 294-295; Cf. III, 5.
17. *De Anima,* III, 4 (429a 10-13)
18. *De Anima,* III, 4 (429a 22)
19. *Metaphysics,* IV, 4 (1005b 35ff.)
20. Averroes, *op. cit.* III, 5, lines 500-527; ed. Crawford, pp. 404-405.
21. *De Anima,* III, 7 (431a 14-15)

22. *De Anima,* III, 4 (429a 10-29)

23. *Metaphysics,* VII, 15 (1040a 8-9); VII, 14 (1039a 25)

24. Origenes, *Peri Archon,* II, 9 (PG 11:229); III, 5 (PG 11:330)

25. *De Genesi contra Manichaeos,* II, 8 (PL 34: 202)

26. *De Anima,* III, 4 (429a 18-27)

QUESTION THREE

Parallel texts: In I Sent., dist. 8, q. 5, a. 2, ad 6; *In II Sent.*, dist. 17, q. 2, a. 1; *Contra gent.*, II, 59, 73, 75; *Summa theol.*, I, q. 75, a. 2; *De Spir. creat.*, a. 9; *In III De An.*, lect. 7, 8; *Compend. theol.*, cap. 85.

The third question that is asked about the soul is this: Whether the possible intellect or the intellective soul is one for all human beings. And it seems that it is.

(1) A perfection is proportioned to that which is capable of being perfected. But truth is the perfection of an intellect; for the true is the good of the intellect, as the Philosopher says in Book VI of the *Ethics*.[1] Therefore, since the truth which all human beings understand is one, it seems that there is one possible intellect for all human beings.

(2) Furthermore, Augustine says in his book, *On the Quantity of the Soul*,[2] "I do not know what to say to you about the number of souls. For if I say that the soul is one, you will be confused by the fact that in one person this soul is happy and in another wretched, for one thing cannot be happy and sad at the same time. If I assert that the soul is one and many simultaneously, you will laugh, and I shall not easily have at hand the means to suppress your mirth. If I say souls are many only, I shall laugh at myself, and I can endure my own discomfiture less easily than I could yours." Therefore that there are many souls for many human beings seems ridiculous.

(3) Besides, whatever is distinguished from another is distinguished by means of a determinate nature which it possesses. Now the possible intellect is in potency to every form, possessing no form in act. Therefore the possible intellect has no basis for distinction. Consequently, it cannot be multiplied in order to be many in diverse human beings.

(4) Besides, the possible intellect is empty of anything which is intelligible, because before the act of understanding it is none of the things which are, as is said in Book III of the *De Anima*.[3] Now, as is said in the same book, the possible intellect is intelligible just as other (intelligible realities) are. Therefore it is empty (barren) of itself

and thus has no basis which would enable it to be multiplied in diverse human beings.

(5) Furthermore, there must be something common to all beings that are distinct and many. For man is common to many men and animal is common to many animals. But the possible intellect has nothing in common with anything, as is stated in Book III of the *De Anima*. [4] Consequently the possible intellect cannot be made distinct and many in diverse human beings.

(6) Furthermore, as Rabbi Moses says,[5] Among those things that are separate from matter, the only basis for plurality is the relation between a cause and its effect. Now the intellect, or the soul, of one human being is not the cause of the intellect or the soul of another human being. Therefore, since the possible intellect is separate, as is said in Book III of the *De Anima*,[6] the possible intellect will not be multiplied in diverse human beings.

(7) Furthermore, the Philosopher says, in book III of the *De Anima*,[7] that the intellect and that which is understood are the same. But that which is understood is the same in all human beings. Consequently, the possible intellect is also one for all human beings.

(8) Furthermore, that which is understood is a universal, which is one in many. Now the form intellectually grasped does not derive this unity from the thing which is understood; for there is no form of a human being in reality except as individuated and multiplied in diverse human beings. Therefore the form derives this unity from the intellect. Consequently the intellect is one in all human beings.

(9) Furthermore, the Philosopher, in Book III of the *De Anima*,[8] declares that the soul is the "site of species." But a site is common to the diverse beings which are in that place. Therefore the soul is not multiplied in diverse human beings.

But an objector was arguing that the soul is called the "site of species" because the soul is able to contain species.

(10) On the contrary, just as a soul is able to contain intelligible species, so a sense is able to contain sensible species. Therefore, if the intellect is the site of species because it is able to contain them, then for a like reason a sense will be the site of species. Now this position is opposed to what the Philosopher says in Book III of the *De Anima*,[9] namely, that the soul is the site of species, but not the whole soul, only the intellective part.

(11) Furthermore, nothing operates except in the place where it is. Now the possible intellect operates everywhere; for it understands the things that are in the heavens and those things that are on earth and those things which are everywhere. Therefore the possible intellect is one in all human beings.

(12) Furthermore, whatever is restricted to one particular thing

possesses determinate matter, because matter is the principle of individuation. Now the possible intellect is not subject to the limitations imposed by matter, as is proved in Book III of the *De Anima*. [10] Therefore it is not limited to any particular individual, and consequently it is one for all human beings.

But an objector raised this argument, namely, that the possible intellect does possess matter in which it exists, to which it is restricted, namely, the human body.

(13) On the contrary, individuating principles ought to belong to the individuated essence. Now the human body does not pertain to the essence of the possible intellect. Therefore the possible intellect cannot be individuated by the body, and consequently cannot be multiplied.

(14) Furthermore, the Philosopher states, in Book I of the *De Caelo et Mundo*, [11] that if there were many worlds, there would be many first heavens. But if there were many first heavens, there would be many first movers. And thus it would follow that the first movers would be material. Therefore, for a like reason, if there were many possible intellects in many human beings, the possible intellect would be material, and this is impossible.

(15) Furthermore, if there are many possible intellects in many human beings, they would have to remain many after the dissolution of their bodies. But since then the only difference among possible intellects would be a specific difference, they would have to differ specifically. But the possible intellects could not acquire a different species after the dissolution of their bodies, because nothing changes from one species to another unless it itself undergoes corruption. Therefore, the possible intellects did not differ specifically even before the disssolution of their bodies. Now a human being possesses his specific nature through the intellective soul. Therefore diverse human beings do not belong to the same species, and this is clearly false.

(16) Furthermore, something that is separate from body cannot be multiplied through bodies. Now the possible intellect is separate from body, as the Philosopher proves in Book III of the *De Anima*. [12] Consequently it cannot be multiplied nor individualized by bodies. Consequently there are not many possible intellects in many human beings.

(17) Furthermore, if the possible intellect is multiplied in diverse human beings, then intelligible species must be multiplied in diverse human beings; and so it follows that these species would be individual forms. Now individual forms are not understood except potentially; for it is necessary that the universal be abstracted from them, and it is the universal which is properly speaking understood. Therefore, it follows that the forms which are in the possible intellect will be

intelligible only in potency. Consequently, the possible intellect will not be able to understand, and this is untenable.

(18) Furthermore, the agent and the patient, the mover and the moved, have something in common. Now a phantasm is related to the possible intellect which exists in us as agent to patient and as the mover to the moved. Therefore the intellect which exists in us has something in common with phantasms. But the possible intellect has nothing in common with anything, as is said in Book III of the *De Anima*.[13] Therefore the possible intellect is other than the intellect which is in us, and thus the possible intellect is not multiplied in diverse human beings.

(19) Furthermore, each thing, insofar as it is, is one.[14] Therefore, if a thing's existence does not depend on another, neither does its unity depend on another. Now the existence of the possible intellect does not depend on the body, otherwise it would undergo corruption when the body does. Therefore the unity of the possible intellect does not depend on the body, and consequently neither does its multiplicity. Therefore the possible intellect is not multiplied in diverse bodies.

(20) Furthermore, the Philosopher states, in Book VIII of the *Metaphysics*,[15] that in those beings which are pure forms, the thing and its essence, that is, its specific nature, are identical. Now the possible intellect or the intellective soul is form only. For if it were composed of form and matter, it could not be the form of something else. Therefore the intellective soul is its own specific nature. Therefore, if the specific nature is one in all intellective souls, it is not possible that the intellective soul be multiplied in diverse human beings.

(21) Furthermore, souls are not multiplied through bodies except inasmuch as they are united to bodies. Now the possible intellect belongs to the part of the soul which exceeds the soul's union with its body.[16] Therefore, the possible intellect is not multiplied in human beings.

(22) Furthermore, if the human soul is multiplied through a multiplicity of bodies, then possible intellect is made to be many because of the plurality of souls. Now since it is clear that intelligible species must be multiplied if the possible intellect is made to be many, it follows that the ultimate principle of multiplication will be corporeal matter. Now whatever is multiplied by matter is individual, and consequently not actually intelligible. Therefore the species which are in the possible intellect will not be actually intelligible, and this is untenable. Consequently the human soul and the possible intellect are not multiplied in diverse human beings.

On The Contrary,

A human being understands by his possible intellect: for in Book III of the *De Anima* [17] it is said that the possible intellect is that by which the soul understands. Consequently, if the possible intellect were one in all human beings, it follows that whatever one human being understands, any other human being would understand, and this is obviously untrue.

(2) Furthermore, the intellective soul is related to its body as form is to matter, and as a mover is related to its instrument. Now every form demands determinate matter and every mover requires determinate instruments. Therefore it is impossible that there be only one intellective soul in diverse human beings.

The Response:

It must be stated that the solution of this questions depends to some degree on the preceding question. For if the possible intellect is a substance that is separate in existence from a body, then there must necessarily be only one possible intellect. For those things which are separate in existence from a body can in no way be multiplied through the multiplication of bodies. However, the oneness of the intellect requires a special treatment because it poses a special difficulty.

For at first sight it seems impossible that there be one possible intellect for all human beings. For it is clear that the possible intellect is related to the perfections found in the sciences as a first perfection is related to a second perfection, and that through the possible intellect we are potential knowers. It is this consideration which compels us to posit the possible intellect. Now it is clear that the perfections of the sciences are not the same in all human beings, since some human beings are found to possess sciences which others lack. Now it would seem illogical and impossible that a second perfection not be one and the same in all human beings if the first perfection is one in them; just as it is impossible that a single subject be at first both in act and in potency with respect to the same form; as, for example, that a surface be at one and the same time both actually white and potentially white.

Now in trying to avoid this difficulty, there are those who teach that the possible intellect is one for all human beings in this sense, that the intelligible species which constitute the perfection of a science, have a two-fold subject, as we said earlier, namely, phantasms themselves and the possible intellect. And since phantasms are not the same in all human beings, neither will the intelligible species be the same for all inasmuch as their subject is the phantasms. But inasmuch as their subject is the possible intellect, the intelligible species are not multiplied. And consequently it is the diversity of phantasms which accounts for the fact that one human being possesses a science which another lacks.

But that this explanation is clearly worthless follows from what we have already said. For species are not actually intelligible unless they have been abstracted from the phantasms and exist in the possible intellect. Consequently the diversity of phantasms cannot be the cause either of the oneness or of the multiplicity of a perfection which is in the order of intelligible science. Furthermore, habitual scientific knowledge does not exist in any part of the sensitive soul as in a subject, as these men maintain.

Furthermore, there is even a greater difficulty facing those who claim that the possible intellect is one in all. For it is clear that the operation called understanding flows from the possible intellect as from the first principle through which we understand, just as the operation of sensing proceeds from a sense power. Now it is true that we proved above that if the possible intellect is separate in existence from a human being, then it is not possible that understanding, which belongs to the possible intellect, is an operation of this or of that human being. But if this point be granted for the sake of our present inquiry, then it follows that this human being or that human being understands through the act of understanding of the possible intellect. Now an operation can be multiplied in only one of two ways, either from the side of the objects toward which the operation is directed, or from the side of the principle that performs the operation; one could add a third way, from the point of view of time, as when an operation is performed intermittently.

Therefore, the act of understanding, which is the operation of the possible intellect, can be multiplied from the point of view of the objects of intellection; for example, it is one thing to understand a human being and another thing to understand a horse; and understanding can be multiplied, according to time, as for example, the act of understanding that occurred yesterday is numerically different from the one that takes place today, provided of course that the operation of understanding be not continuous. However, the act of understanding cannot be multiplied from the point of view of the principle which performs the operation if there is only one possible intellect. Therefore, if the act of understanding itself of the possible intellect is the act of understanding of this human being or of that human being, then this human being or that human being could indeed have different acts of understanding if they understood diverse objects; and the diversity of phantasms might provide some sort of explanation for this diversity of the acts of understanding, as these men claim. Likewise there could be a multiplication of the act of understanding itself, namely, if one human being understands something today and another human being understands it tomorrow, for this too could be explained by a diversity in the use of phantasms. But if there are two human beings who understand one and the same thing, at one and the same time, it is necessary that their act of understanding be one and the same in number, and this is clearly impossible. As a result, it is impossible that the possible intellect, by which we formally understand, be one for all human beings.

If, however, we were to understand through the possible intellect as through an active principle which makes us understand through some principle of understanding existing in us, then the position would be more reasonable. For one cause can move diverse agents to perform their operations; but it is utterly impossible that diverse agents should function formally in virtue of a single principle. Furthermore, the forms and species of natural things are known through their essential operations. Now the essential operation of a human being, insofar as he is human, is to understand and to reason. Hence it is necessary that the principle of this operation, namely, the intellect, be that by which a human being is specifically what he is; and this principle cannot be the sensitive soul or one of its powers. Therefore, if the possible intellect is one in all human beings, like some kind of separate substance, it would follow that all human beings would be specifically human through a single, separate substance; and this doctrine would be like the doctrine of ideas and open to the same objections.

Consequently it must be said without qualification that the possible intellect is not one for all human beings, but rather is multiplied in diverse human beings. And since it is a power or faculty of the human soul, it is multiplied just as the substance of the soul is multiplied, and this multiplication must be understood as follows. If something is multiplied by reference to and because of some common essential feature, then this common feature is multiplied numerically while the species remains the same. For instance, flesh and bones belong to the very nature of animal; hence the distinction in animals which is based on their bodily features produces diversity in number but not in species.

Now it is clear, from what we have said above, that it is of the essence of the human soul that it be capable of union with the human body, since it does not possess in itself a fullness of species, but is a part of the species in the composite itself. Hence it follows that a soul, from the fact that it is unitable to this or to that body, is multiplied numerically and not specifically, just as this whiteness differs from another whiteness numerically because it belongs to this or to that subject of whiteness. Still the soul differs from other forms in this respect: that its existence does not depend upon the body; consequently neither does its individuated existence depend upon its body. For insofar as some thing is one, it is undivided in itself and is distinct from other things.

Replies to the Opposing Arguments:

(1) Truth is the conformity of an intellect to a thing. Consequently, the truth which diverse human beings understand is one because of the fact that their conceptions conform to the same thing.

(2) Augustine admits that he would be ridiculous, not if he maintained that there were many souls, but if he maintained there were only many, that is to say, that they were many both numerically and specifically.

(3) The possible intellect is not multiplied in diverse human beings according to a formal difference, but according to the multiplication of the substance of the soul whose power the possible intellect is.

(4) It is not necessary that every intellect lack that which it understands, but only an intellect in potency; just as any recipient lacks the nature of what it receives. Hence if there is an intellect which is solely act, such as the divine intellect, it understands itself through itself. But the possible intellect, just like other intelligible realities, is said to be intelligible because it understands itself through the intelligible species of other intelligible realities. For from its object it knows its own operation, and from this it comes to a knowledge of itself.

(5) The possible intellect must be understood as not having anything in common with any of the sensible natures from which it acquires its intelligibles; however, one possible intellect is specifically like any other possible intellect.

(6) In those things which are separate in existence from matter there can be no distinction except a specific distinction. Now diverse species constitute diverse grades of being. Hence they are said to be like numbers, in which diverse species are set up by the addition or subtraction of a unit. And therefore, according to the position of those men who hold that things which are lower in being are caused by those which are higher, it follows that in those beings which are separate from matter multiplication takes place in terms of cause and the caused. But this position runs counter to what faith teaches. Furthermore, the possible intellect is not a substance that is separate in existence from matter and consequently the argument is irrelevant.

(7) Although an intelligible species by which the intellect formally understands is in the possible intellect of this human being and of that human being because the possible intellects are many, still that which is understood through such a species is one, if we consider, in reference to the thing understood, that the universal which is understood by both is the same for all. And the fact that that which is one for all can be understood through species which are multiplied in diverse individuals is due to the immateriality of the species, which represent the thing without the individuating material conditions which permit a nature that is specifically one to be multiplied numerically in diverse individuals.

(8) According to the Platonists,[18] the reason that something is understood as one with reference to many particulars is not due to the intellect but to the thing; for unless there existed some one reality participated in by many particulars, when the intellect understands the one in many, it would seem that the intellect is deluded, since there is nothing in reality that corresponds to its cognition. Hence they were driven to posit the Ideas by participation in which natural things acquire their specific natures and our intellects come to understand universals. Now according to the teaching of Aristotle,[19] the fact that the intellect understands one in the many through abstraction from individuating principles is due to the intellect itself. Nor is the intellect fickle or false even though nothing abstract exists in reality; for when two things exist together, we can truly understand or name one of them without the other, even though it is impossible that we should truly understand or assert that one of them exists without the other. Consequently, therefore, one can with truth consider or speak of that which in an individual belongs to its specific nature, in which it is like others, without considering the individuating principles by which it is distinguished from all others. In this way, therefore, through its act of abstraction, the intellect produces the unity of a universal, not because the intellect is one in all men but because it is immaterial.

(9) The intellect is the site of species because it contains species. Hence it does not follow that the possible intellect is one for all human beings but that it is one for and common to all species.

(10) A sense of power does not receive a species without an organ and consequently it is not called the site of species as the intellect is.

(11) The possible intellect can be said to operate everywhere, not because its operation is everywhere, but because its operation has to do with things which are everywhere.

(12) The possible intellect, although it does not have determinate matter, nevertheless is a power of the substance of the soul, which does have determinate matter, not as a constitutive principle from which the soul arises, but as that in which the soul is received and exists.

(13) Not all forms have their individuating principles as part of their essence; this is true only of forms that are composites.

(14) The First Mover of the heavens is wholly separate from matter, even in existence; hence it can in no way be multiplied numerically. But the same is not true of the human soul.

(15) Separated souls do not differ in species; but they differ numerically because they are unitable to one body or to another.

(16) Although the possible intellect is separate from the body with respect to the intellect's operation, the intellect is still a power of the soul which is the act of the body.

(17) Something is said to be understood potentially not because it is individual but because it is material. Hence it follows that intelligible species which are received immaterially in the intellect, even if they are individuated, are actually understood. And furthermore, the same difficulty posited in the objection would follow from the position of those who hold that the possible intellect is one, because if the possible intellect is one as a separate substance is, it is necessary that it be an individual, as Aristotle argued against the ideas of Plato.[20] And for the same reason the intelligible species in the intellect would be individuated, and they would also be diverse in diverse separate intellects, since every intelligence is full of intelligible forms.

(18) A phantasm moves the possible intellect inasmuch as the phantasm is made to be intelligible in act by the power of the agent intellect, to which the possible intellect is related as potency to an agent; and in this way the phantasm is related to the possible intellect.

(19) Although the existence of the intellective soul does not depend on its body, still it has a natural relation to its body in order to achieve its specific perfection.

(20) Although the human soul does not have matter as a part of itself, it is still the form of a body. And therefore its quiddity or essence involves a relation to its body.

(21) Although the possible intellect exceeds the body, it does not transcend the whole substance of the soul, which is multiplied according to its relation to diverse bodies.

(22) The argument would be valid if the body were so united to the soul as to envelope the whole essence and power of the soul. For then whatever would be in the soul would have to be material; but this is not so, as I clearly showed above, and hence the argument is not valid.

Notes to Question Three

1. *Nicomachean Ethics*, VI, 2 (1139a 27-30).

2. St. Augustine, *On the Quanity of the Soul*, 32, 69 (PL 32:1073).

3. *De Anima*, III, 4 (429a 21-22).

4. *De Anima*, III, 4 (429b 22-25).

5. Moses Maimonides, *Dux seu director dubitantium aut perplexorum*, II, fol. 39r, Propositio XVI; Cf. *The Guide of the Perplexed*, p. 337, Premise 16, ed. S. Pines, Chicago, 1963.

6. *De Anima*, III, 4 (429b 5).

7. *De Anima*, III, 4 (430a 3-4).

8. *De Anima*, III, 4 (429b 5).

9. *De Anima*, III, 4 (429a 27-29).

10. *De Anima*, III, 4 (429a 18-30).

11. *De Caelo*, I, 9 (279a 8). Cf. Aristotle, *Metaphysics*, XII, 8 (1074a 31-38).

12. *De Anima*, III, 4 (429a 24-27).

13. *De Anima*, III, 4 (429b 23-24).

14. In the metaphysics of St. Thomas being and unity are identical and the terms are, therefore, convertible. See *De Veritate*, q. 1. a. 1.

15. *Metaphysics*, VIII, 6 (1045a 36).

16. Although the rational soul is the single substantial form of a human being, its intellectual powers are not exhausted in informing the body.

17. *De Anima*, III, 4 (429a 23).

18. Cf. Plato, *Republic*, 475E-476A; 478E-480A.

19. Aristotle, *De Anima*, III, 4 (429b 20-22).

20. Aristotle, *Metaphysics*, VII, 14 (1039a 24-26); 15 (1040a 8-9).

QUESTION FOUR

Parallel texts: *Contra gent.*, II, 77; *Summa theol.*, I, q. 54, a. 4; q. 79, a. 3; *De Spir. creat.*, a. 9; *In III De An.*, lect. 10; *Compend. theol.*, cap. 83.

The fourth question that is asked about the soul is this: Whether it is necessary to posit an agent intellect. And it seems that it is not necessary.

(1) For whatever in nature can be brought about by one agent is not done by many. Now a human being can adequately understand through a single intellect, namely, the possible intellect; therefore it is not necessary to posit an agent intellect. Proof of the minor premise: Powers which are grounded in the single essence of a soul mutually affect one another. As a result, a change brought about in a sense power leaves an impression on the imagination; for imagination is a movement brought about by one of the senses insofar as the sense is in act, as is stated in Book III of the *De Anima*.[1] Consequently, if the possible intellect exists in our soul and is not a separate substance, as has already been shown,[2] it must be in the same essence of the soul as the imagination is. As a result, a movement in the imagination affects the possible intellect; and consequently it is not necessary to posit an agent intellect which would produce intelligible objects from the phantasms by abstraction from them.

(2) Furthermore, touch and sight are diverse powers. Now because of a change brought about in the imagination by the sense of touch, it happens that the imagination of a blind man is stimulated to imagine something that is appropriate to the sense of sight; and this happens because sight and touch are grounded in one and the same essence of the soul. Therefore, if the possible intellect is a power of the soul, for a like reason, from a movement in the imagination there will come about a modification of the possible intellect; and consequently it is not necessary to posit an agent intellect.

(3) Furthermore, the reason for postulating an agent intellect is that it might make actually intelligible those objects which are only potentially intelligible. Some things become actually intelligible because

they are abstracted from matter and from the conditions of matter. Consequently, an agent intellect is posited in order that intelligible species might be abstracted from matter. Now this can be brought about without an agent intellect,; for since the possible intellect is immaterial, it must receive whatever it receives in an immaterial way, for whatever is received is in the receiver according to the mode of being of the recipient. Therefore, it is unnecessary to posit an agent intellect.

(4) Furthermore, Aristotle, in Book III of his *De Anima,*[3] compares the agent intellect to light. Now light is not necessary for seeing except insofar as it makes the medium of sight to be actually luminous. For color is essentially visible and has the power to move what is actually luminous, as is stated in Book II of the *De Anima.*[4] Now it is not necessary that there be an agent intellect to render the possible intellect capable of being receptive because the possible intellect is by nature in potency to intelligible objects. Therefore it is not necessary to posit an agent intellect.

(5) Furthermore, the intellect is related to intelligible objects just as the senses are related to sensible objects. Now sensible objects do not need an agent sense in order to move a sense power, although it is by a spiritual mode of existence that sensible objects are present in one of the senses which is capable of receiving sensible things without their matter, as is said in Book III of the *De Anima.*[5] They exist in the same way in the medium as well, for it receives the species of sensible things in a spiritual manner. This is evident from the fact that a sense in the same part of itself is receptive of contraries, for example, black and white. Therefore neither do intelligible objects require an agent intellect.

(6) Furthermore, in order for something in potency in the realm of natural things to become actualized, all that is needed is something actual in the same genus. For example, matter which is potentially afire becomes actually afire through actual fire. Therefore, in order that the intellect which is potential in us becomes actualized, nothing more is required than an intellect in act; either the intellect of the one who understands, as when from a knowledge of principles we arrive at a knowledge of conclusions; or the intellect of another, as when a person learns from a teacher. Therefore it does not seem necessary to posit an agent intellect.

(7) Furthermore, the agent intellect is posited that it might illumine our phantasms as the light of the sun illumines colors. But for our illumination nothing more is needed than the divine light which enlightens every man who comes into this world, as is said in the *Gospel of John,* Chapter I.[6] Therefore it is not necessary to posit an agent intellect.

(8) Furthermore, the act of an intellect is to understand. Therefore, if there are two intellects, namely, an agent and a possible intellect, the act of understanding of one man will be two-fold, and this seems inappropriate.

(9) Furthermore, an intelligible species seems to be the perfection of an intellect. Consequently, if there are two intellects, namely, a possible and an agent intellect, there are two acts of understanding as well. But this number seems to be excessive.

On The Contrary,

We can cite the position of Aristotle, as given in Book III of the *De Anima*,[7] that as in the whole of nature there is that which is agent and that which is potential, it is necessary that both of these elements be in the soul: one of them is the agent intellect, the other is the possible intellect.

The Response:

It must be said that it is necessary to posit an agent intellect. To make this clear we must note that since the possible intellect is in potency to intelligible objects, it is necessary that intelligible objects move the possible intellect. But that which does not exist cannot move anything. Now the intelligible object understood by the possible intellect does not exist in reality as intelligible. For our possible intellect understands something as one in many and as common to many. But an entity of this kind is not to be found subsisting in reality, as Aristotle proves in Book VII of the *Metaphysics*.[8] Therefore, if the possible intellect is to be moved by an intelligible object, it is necessary that such an intelligible object be produced by an intellect. And since it is impossible for something that is in potency to another to produce this latter, it is necessary, over and above the possible intellect, to posit an agent intellect which makes to be actually intelligible those objects which move the possible intellect.

Now the agent intellect does this by abstracting from matter and from those material conditions which are the principles of individuation. Now none of those elements which belong to the nature of a species inasmuch as it is species enables it to be multiplied in diverse individuals: the principles that individuate a species are something outside the specific nature. Hence the intellect can apprehend the species apart from all the conditions that make it individual; and thus the intellect apprehends it as one. And for this same reason the intellect, by abstracting from specific differences, grasps the nature of a genus as one in many species and common to them all.

Now if universals subsisted in reality of themselves, as the Platonists taught,[9] there would be no necessity to posit an agent intellect, because these intelligible realities would of themselves actuate the possible intellect. It was for this reason that Aristotle seems to have felt compelled to posit an agent intellect, namely, because he did not agree with the teaching of Plato that one must posit ideas. Now there are in fact intelligible beings which of themselves actually subsist in reality, for example, immaterial substances. However, the possible intellect is not able to know these substances directly, but arrives at some knowledge of them by means of what it abstracts from material and sensible things.

Replies to the Opposing Arguments:

(1) Our operation of understanding cannot be completed through the possible intellect alone. For the possible intellect cannot understand unless it is moved by an intelligible object; and since this intelligible object does not pre-exist in reality, it must be produced by the agent intellect. Now it is true that two powers which are grounded in the single essence of a soul mutually affect one another; but this influence can be understood to operate in two ways. In the first way, one power is hindered in its action or is prevented from acting at all when the other power operates vigorously; but this situation has no bearing on the present discussion. In the second way, one power is moved by another, as when the imagination is stimulated by a sense power; and such an occurrence is in fact possible because a form in the imagination and a form in a sense power belong to the same genus, for both forms are individual. And consequently forms which are in a sense power are able to leave their own impressions on the forms which are in the imagination by actuating the imagination, since these forms are similar to each other. However, the forms in the imagination, inasmuch as they are individual, cannot cause intelligible forms since such forms are universal.

(2) Using species received in the imagination from the sense of touch, the imagination would not be able to form shapes or figures pertaining to the sense of sight unless there pre-existed forms which through the power of sight have already been received and stored up in the treasure house of memory or imagination. For a man who is blind from birth cannot imagine color by means of other sensible species.

(3) The nature of a recipient cannot change a species that it

receives from one genus to another; however, the recipient can change the mode of existence of the species it has received while the species remains in the same genus. And hence it is that since a universal and a particular species differ generically, the condition of the possible intellect alone is insufficient to cause the particular species which are in the imagination to become universal; but rather there must be an agent intellect which would bring this about.

(4) As the Commentator says in Book II of the *De Anima,*[10] there are two theories about light. For there are those who say that light is necessary for seeing because light gives to colors the power to be able to move the sense of sight, as if color were not visisble of itself but only because of light. Aristotle seems to reject this position when he states, in Book III of the *De Anima,*[11] that color is essentially visible, and this would not be so if color possessed visibility solely because of light. Consequently, others offer what seems to be a better interpretation, namely, that light is necessary for seeing insofar as light actuates what is transparent, causing it to be actually luminous. Hence the Philosopher says, in Book II of the *De Anima,*[12] that color has the power of setting in motion what is actually transparent. Nor can it be objected that those who are in the dark can see things which are in the light and not vice versa. This happens because it is necessary that the transparent which surrounds the things to be seen be illuminated in order that it might receive the species of the visible thing. Now a species remains visible just as far as action of light which illuminates the transparent extends its influence, even though the closer the light is, the more perfectly it illuminates, and the farther away it is, the more weakly it illuminates the transparent. Therefore the comparison between light and the agent intellect is not valid from every point of view, since the agent intellect is necessary to make potential intelligible objects to become actually intelligible. And this is what Aristotle means in Book III of the *De Anima* when he said that the agent intellect is somehow like light.[13]

(5) A sensible, because it is something particular, cannot impress, either in a sense power or in the medium, a species of a different genus, since species, both in the medium and in the sense power, can be nothing other than particular. Now the possible intellect does receive species which belong to another genus than those which are in the imagination, since the possible intellect receives universal species and the imagination contains only particular species. And therefore, for intelligible objects, we have need of an agent intellect, but in the realm of sensible objects we do not need an additional active power, but rather all the sense powers are passive powers.

(6) The possible intellect, brought to actualization, is inadequate to cause knowledge in us unless we presuppose that there is an agent

intellect. For if we are speaking of the actualized intellect of a person who is learning, it is a fact that his possible intellect is in potency with respect to something and is in act with respect to something else; and that through this actual knowledge his possible intellect can also be brought to actual knowledge of that to which it had been in potency: for example, one who actually knows principles can come actually to know conclusions, which he previously knew potentially. However, the possible intellect cannot have actual knowledge of principles except through the agent intellect; for a knowledge of principles is derived from sensible things, as it is stated near the end of the *Posterior Analytics,* [14] but intelligible objects cannot be derived from sensible realities except by the agent intellect's abstraction. And so it is obvious that an actual understanding of principles is not adequate to change the possible intellect from potency to act without an agent intellect. Now in the process of this actualization the agent intellect is like an artisan and the principles of demonstration are like tools. However, if we speak of the actualized intellect of one who is teaching, it is clear that the teacher does not cause knowledge in the learner as if he were an interior agent, but only as assisting the pupil from without; just as a physician heals by assisting from without, while nature heals by acting from within.

(7) Just as in natural things there are in each genus essential active principles, although God is the first efficient cause of them all, so although God is the First Light which illumines all human beings in general, there also must be in a human being an intellectual light which is essentially his.

(8) Each of the two intellects, possible and agent, has its own action. The action of the possible intellect is to receive intelligible objects, while the action of the agent intellect is to abstract intelligible objects. However, it does not follow from this that there are two acts of understanding in a human being, because it is necessary that both of these actions unite to produce one act of understanding.

(9) One and the same intelligible species is related to both the agent intellect and the possible intellect; but it is related to the possible intellect as to that which receives the species, while it is related to the agent intellect as to that which produces species of this sort through abstraction.

Notes to Question Four

1. Aristotle, *De Anima,* III, 3 (428b 30 - 429a 2).

2. See above, Question II.

3. Aristotle, *De Anima,* III, 5 (430a 15-16).

4. Aristotle, *De Anima,* II, 7 (418a 31 - 418b 2).

5. Aristotle, *De Anima,* III, 2 (425b 24).

6. *John* 1: 9.

7. Aristotle, *De Anima,* III, 5 (430a 10-14).

8. Aristotle, *Metaphysics,* VII, 13 (1038b 35-36).

9. Plato, *Timaeus,* 52A; *Phaedo,* 73-79; Cf. Aristotle, *Metaphysics,* I, 6 (987b 7-10); I, 9 (991b 2-3); III, 2 (997b 11).

10. Averroes, *Commentarium magnum in Aristotelis De Anima,* II, 67, 13-21, ed. Crawford, p. 231.

11. Aristotle, *De Anima,* II, 7 (418a 29-30).

12. Aristotle, *De Anima,* II, 7 (418a 31 - b 2).

13. Aristotle, De Anima, III, 5 (430a 15-16).

14. Aristotle, *Posterior Analytics,* II, 19 (100a 9-11).

QUESTION FIVE

Parallel texts: *In II Sent.*, dist. 17, q. 2, a. 1; *De Ver.*, q. 10, a. 6; *Contra gent.*, II, 76, 78; *Summa theol.*, I, q. 79, a. 4, 5; *De Spir. creat.*, a. 10; *In III De An.*, lect. 10; *Compend theol.*, cap. 86.

The fifth question that is asked about the soul is this: Whether the agent intellect is one and separate. And it seems that it is.

(1) Because the Philosopher says, in Book III of the *De Anima*,[1] that the agent intellect does not sometimes understand and sometimes not understand. Now we have no experience of an uninterrupted act of cognition of this sort. Therefore, the agent intellect is separate in existence and consequently is one for all men.

(2) Furthermore, it is impossible that something be at one and the same time in potency and in act with respect to the same thing. Now the possible intellect is in potency to all intelligible objects; however the agent intellect is in act with respect to them since it is the act of intelligible species. Consequently, it seems impossible that the possible and agent intellects be grounded in one and the same substance of the soul. And thus, since the possible intellect is located in the essence of the soul, as is clear from what has already been said, the agent intellect is separate.

But an objector was arguing that the possible intellect is in potency to intelligibles and the agent intellect is in act with respect to intelligible objects according to diverse modes of existence.

(3) On the contrary, the possible intellect is not in potency to intelligible objects insofar as it possesses them, for in this respect the possible intellect is already actualized by them. Therefore the possible intellect is in potency to intelligible species insofar as they exist in phantasms. Now in reference to species as they exist in phantasms, the agent intellect is in act, since it causes these species to become intelligible in act by the process of abstraction. Therefore the agent intellect is in potency to intelligible objects with respect to the mode of existence according to which the agent intellect is related to these intelligible objects as producing them.

(4) Furthermore, in Book III of the *De Anima*,[2] the Philosopher

attributes to the agent intellect features which seem proper only to separate substances, for he says that "This alone is perpetual, and incorruptible and separate." Therefore it seems that the intellect is a separate substance.

(5) Furthermore, the intellect is not dependent on the dispositions that affect the body since it is independent of any bodily organ. Now the faculty of understanding which belongs to us varies according to the diverse dispositions within its body.[3] Consequently this faculty of understanding does not belong to us because of the intellect which is in us, but it seems that the agent intellect is separate.

(6) Furthermore, in order that there be an action, nothing more is required than an agent and a patient. Therefore, if the possible intellect whose function is that of the patient in the action of understanding is something that belongs to our soul, as has already been shown; and if the agent intellect is also something belonging to our soul, it seems that in ourselves we possess whatever is required for us to be able to understand. Therefore nothing further is necessary for us in order to understand. However, this is clearly false; for we also require the senses, from which we derive experiences needed for knowing. Hence he who lacks a particular sense, such as sight, lacks a particular type of knowledge, in this case that of colors. Also, in order to understand, we need instruction, which is done by a teacher; and in addition to this we require illumination, which comes from God, according to Chapter I of John's *Gospel,* "He was the true light, and so on."[4]

(7) Furthermore, the agent intellect is related to intelligible objects as light is related to visible things, as is clear in Book III of the *De Anima.*[5] Now a single separate light, namely, that of the sun, is adequate to make all things actually visible. Therefore, in order to make all things actually intelligible, a single separate light is enough. And hence there is no necessity for positing an agent intellect in us.

(8) Furthermore, the agent intellect is likened to art, as is clear from Book III of the *De Anima.*[6] Now art is a principle that is separate from the things produced by the art. Therefore the agent intellect is also a separate principle.

(9) Furthermore, the perfection of any nature consists in its becoming like the agent that produces it; for example, something that is generated reaches its perfection when it achieves a likeness to that which generates it; and a work of art, when it achieves a likeness to the form which is in the artist. Therefore, if the agent intellect is something that belongs to our soul, the ultimate perfection and happiness of our soul will be located in something which belongs to the soul itself, and this is clearly false; for if that were true, then the soul would be forced to find its satisfaction in itself. Therefore the agent intellect is not something existing in us.

(10) Furthermore, the agent is nobler than the patient, as is said in Book III of the *De Anima.*[7] Therefore, if the possible intellect is in some way separate from the body, the agent intellect will be still more separate. Now this cannot be so, it seems, unless the agent intellect is held to be entirely extrinsic to the substance of the soul.

On The Contrary,

in Book III of the *De Anima,*[8] it is said that just as in the whole of nature there is something that is comparable to matter and something that is productive, these two different features must exist in the soul as well; the possible intellect belongs to one of these classes, the agent intellect belongs to the other. Therefore both the possible intellect and the agent intellect are something in the soul.

(2) Furthermore, the operation of the agent intellect is to abstract intelligible species from phantasms and this is something we constantly experience. Now it seems that if the agent intellect were a separate substance, there would be no reason why abstraction of this kind would sometimes take place and at other times not occur. Therefore the agent intellect is not a separate substance.

The Response:

It must be stated that to hold that the agent intellect is one (unique) and separate seems to be more reasonable than to assert this about the possible intellect. For it is the possible intellect through which we understand, sometimes indeed only potentially, but at other times actually. Now it is the agent intellect which causes us to be actually understanding. Now an agent exists as separate from the things which it actualizes, but it seems clear that that through which something is in potency is wholly within the thing.

Consequently there are many who asserted that the agent intellect is a separate substance while the possible intellect is something in our soul. Furthermore, they maintained that this agent intellect is a separate substance, which they call the intelligence.[9] This "intelligence," they said, is related to our souls and to the whole sphere of active and passive powers in the same way as higher separate substances, which they call "intelligences," are related to the souls of the celestial bodies which they say are animated, and are related to the heavenly bodies themselves; just as these higher bodies receive their motion from the separate substances of which we just spoke, and as the souls of the celestial bodies receive intelligible perfection, so also lower bodies here on earth receive their forms and essential movements from the separate agent intellect, while our souls receive intelligible perfections from it.

Now because the Catholic faith asserts that God, and not any other separate substance, operates in nature and in our souls, some Catholic teachers therefore maintained that the agent intellect is God Himself, who is the "light which enlightens every man who comes into this world." [10] However, this position, if a person examines it carefully, does not seem to accord with the facts. For higher substances are related to our souls in the same way as celestial bodies are related to lower bodies. Now just as the powers of higher bodies are active, universal principles with respect to lower bodies, so the divine power and the power of other, secondary substances, if there are effects that flow from them into us, are related to our souls as active universal principles. However, we see that in addition to active universal principles, which are the powers of the celestial bodies, there must be active particular principles, which are powers that belong to lower bodies and which are structured toward the essential operations of one thing or another.

That there be active particular principles is especially demanded in higher animals. For there are imperfect animals for whose production nothing more is needed than the power of a celestial body, as is clear in those animals which are generated from the decomposition of matter. But for the generation of fully developed animals, in addition to celestial power, there is also required a particular power which is found in the semen. Consequently, since what is most perfect in all lower bodies is intellectual operation, in addition to active universal principles, which are the power of God who enlightens us or the power of some other separate substance, there must be in us an essential active principle of our own, through which we are made to be actually understanding, and this principle is the agent intellect.

One must also take into account the fact that if the intellect is asserted to be a separate substance other than God, then there follows a consequence which is opposed to our faith, namely, that our final perfection and happiness consists in the union of our soul, not with God, as the teaching of the *Gospel* holds, saying "This is eternal life, to know the true God," [11] but rather in union with another separate substance. For it is clear that the final beatitude or happiness of a human being is located in his highest operation, which is to understand, and the ultimate perfection of understanding must consist in this, that our (possible) intellect is joined to its active principle. For anything that is passive attains its fullest perfection when it reaches that essential, active principle which is the cause of its perfection. Consequently, those who assert that the agent intellect is a separate substance teach that final happiness for a human being consists in his being able to understand the agent intellect.

Furthermore, if we examine the question carefully, we shall discover that the reason it is impossible for the agent intellect to be a separate substance is the same reason that it is impossible for the possible intellect to be separate, and this we have shown above. For just as the operation of the possible intellect is to receive intelligible objects, so the essential operation of the agent intellect is to abstract them; for in this way it makes them to be actually intelligible. Now we experience both of these operations taking place within ourselves, for we both receive intelligible objects and we abstract them. Now in anything which operates there must be a formal principle by which this being formally operates; for nothing can operate formally through that which is separate in existence from itself. Even if that which is separate be a principle of motion, directed toward operation, nevertheless there must be an intrinsic principle by which a thing operates formally, whether this principle be a form or some kind of influence. Therefore there must be in us a formal principle by which we receive intelligible objects and another formal principle by which we abstract them, and we call these principles the possible intellect and the agent intellect. Consequently both of these intellects are something existing within us. Now it is not enough to say that the action of the agent intellect, which consists in abstracting intelligible objects, is communicated to us by means of those phantasms which are illuminated in us by the agent intellect itself. For the agent intellect is related to the phantasms which it illuminates as an artisan is to the object he produces; and no artifact can ever perform the action by which the artisan produced it.

Now it is not difficult to consider how both of these intellects can be found in the very substance of the soul, namely, the possible intellect, which is in potency to all intelligible objects, and the agent intellect, which produces them. For it is not impossible that something be in potency with respect to a thing and also in act with respect to it, although under different aspects. Therefore, if we carefully examine the phantasms themselves in relation to the human soul, they are found to be in potency, namely, insofar as they can be abstracted, but are not yet abstracted, from individual conditions; however, from another perspective, they are in act in relation to the soul, namely, insofar as they are the likenesses of determinate things. Therefore it is possible to discover potentiality in the soul with respect to the phantasms insofar as they are representative of determinate things, and this potentiality belongs to the possible intellect, which is essentially in potency to all intelligible objects, but is determined to the knowledge of a specific object through a species abstracted from phantasms. It is also possible to discover in the soul a power that can produce immateriality and which abstracts the phantasms from their material conditions. And the special characteristic of the agent intellect is that it should be an active intellect, as if it were a power that participates in some higher substance, namely, God. Hence the Philosopher teaches that the agent intellect is a kind of constant state, like light;[12] and *Psalm* 4 says: "The light of Thy countenance, O Lord, is signed upon us."[13] And something somewhat similar to this is true of animals who see by night, for the pupils of their eyes are in potency to all colors in that they possess no determinate color in act; but by means of an innate light they somehow cause colors to be actually visible.

Furthermore, there are some men who hold that the agent intellect is nothing more than our habit of indemonstrable principles. But this cannot be true because we know even these indemonstrable principles by abstracting from singulars, as the Philosopher teaches near the end of the *Posterior Analytics*.[14] Hence it is necessary that the agent intellect exist prior to the habit of indemonstrable principles as its cause. For these principles are themselves related to the agent intellect as its instruments, because by means of these principles the agent intellect makes other things to be actually intelligible.

Replies to the Opposing Arguments:

(1) The Philosopher's statement that "the intellect at one time understands and at another time does not understand"[15] is not to be taken with reference to the agent intellect, but rather to the intellect in act. For after Aristotle established his position on the possible and agent intellects, it was necessary that he state his position on the intellect in act; and first he showed how it differs from the possible intellect; for the possible intellect and the things which are understood are not the same. However, understanding or actual knowledge is the same as the thing actually known; he made the same statement about sensation, declaring that the sense and the sensible in potency differ, but that the sense and the thing actually sensed are one and the same. Next he treats the relation of the possible intellect to the intellect in act, because at one and the same time the intellect in potency is prior to the intellect in act, though not without qualification; as he said on many occasions about things which go from potency to act. After this he adds the statement cited above in which he points out the difference between the possible intellect and the intellect in act: to the effect that the possible intellect sometimes understands and sometimes does not; this cannot be said about the intellect in act. In Book III of the *Physics*[16] he points out a similar difference between causes in potency and causes in act.

(2) The substance of a soul is in potency and in act with respect to the very same phantasms, but not from the same point of view, as was explained above.

(3) The possible intellect is in potency to intelligible objects with respect to the mode of existence that they have in phantasms; and with respect to the same mode of existence, the agent intellect is in act with reference to them, but for different reasons, as has been shown.

(4) The statement of the Philosopher that this alone is separate and immortal and perpetual cannot be understood as applying to the agent intellect; for he also said earlier that the possible intellect is separate. However, they must be understood as applying to the intellect in act, in view of the context of the earlier citations, as has already been said. For the intellect in act comprises both the possible intellect and the agent intellect. And only that part of the soul which contains the agent and possible intellects is separate and perpetual and immortal, for the other parts of the soul do not exist apart from its body.

(5) Diversity of composition causes the power of understanding to be better or less good because of the powers from which the intellect does its abstracting, and these are all powers that make use of bodily organs, such as imagination, memory and the like.

(6) Although there is in our soul both an agent and a possible intellect, still something extrinsic to them is demanded in order that we be able to understand. First of all, for instance, phantasms derived from sensible things are required, by means of which the likenesses of determinate things are made present to the intellect. For the agent intellect is not the kind of act in which the determinate species of all things can be received in order to be known, just as light cannot actuate sight according to determinate species of color unless these colors are present to actuate sight. Furthermore, since we asserted that the agent intellect is a power of our souls by participation, as a sort of light, it is necessary to posit a cause, independent of the agent intellect, in which that light participates. And this cause we call God, who teaches from within, in that He pours forth this kind of light into our souls; and over and above this kind of natural light, out of His goodness, He generously grants other lights, such as the light of faith and the light of prophecy, in order that we may know those things which natural reason cannot reach.

(7) Colors which move the sense of sight are exterior to the soul, but the phantasms which move the possible intellect are within us. And consequently, although the exterior light of the sun is adequate to make colors actually visible, an interior light is required in order to make phantasms to be actually intelligible, and this is the light of the agent intellect. Furthermore, the intellective part of the soul is more perfect than the sensitive part. Hence it is necessary that the

principles required for its essential operation be present to it more perfectly; this is why in the intellective part of the soul there takes place both a receiving of intelligible objects and an abstraction of them, as if there existed in us, insofar as we are intellectual beings, both active and passive powers; this is not true with respect to sensation.

(8) Although there is a likeness between one who knows intellectually and art, it is not necessary that the likeness be valid in all respects.

(9) The agent intellect of itself is inadequate to actuate the possible intellect since the determinate principles of all things do not exist in it, as we have said. And consequently, for its highest perfection, the possible intellect must be united in some way to that agent in Whom exist the principles of all things, namely, God.

(10) The agent intellect is nobler than the possible intellect, as an active power is nobler than a passive one; and it is more separate than the possible intellect because it is less like matter than the possible intellect. But it is not so far removed from matter that it is a separate substance.

Notes to Question Five

1. Aristotle, *De Anima,* III, 5 (430a 22)
2. Aristotle, *De Anima,* III, 5 (430a 17-19)
3. See *Summa theol.,* I, q. 85, a. 7.
4. *John,* 1: 9.
5. Aristotle, *De Anima,* III, 5 (430a 14-17)
6. *Ibid.*
7. Aristotle, *De Anima,* III, 5 (430a 18-19)
8. Aristotle, *De Anima,* III, 5 (430a 10-13)
9. Avicenna, *De Anima,* V, 5 (fol. 25rb)
10. William of Auvergne, (Gulielmus Alvernus — Parisiensis), *De Anima,* VII, 6.
11. *John,* 17: 3.
12. Aristotle, *De Anima,* III, 5 (430a 15-16)
13. *Psalms* 4: 7.
14. Aristotle, *Posterior Analytics,* II, 19 (100a 15 - 100b 5)
15. Aristotle, *De Anima,* III, 5 (430a 22)
16. Aristotle, *Physics,* III, 1 (201a 19-25) Cf. also *Metaphysics,* V, 2 (1014a 15-25).

QUESTION SIX

Parallel texts: *In I Sent.*, dist. 8, q. 5, a. 2; *In II Sent.*, dist. 3, q. 1, a. 1; dist. 17, q. 1, a. 2; *De Ente et ess.*, 5; *Quodl.*, IX, q. 4, a. 6; q. 4, a. 1; *Super Boet. De Hebdom.*, lect. 2; *In lib. Boet. De Trin.*, q. 5, a. 4, ad 4; *Contra gent.*, II, 50, 51; *De Pot.*, q. 6, a. 6, ad 4; *Summa theol.*, I, q. 50, a. 2; q. 75, a. 5; *De Spir. creat.*, a. 1; a. 9, ad 9; *Quodl.*, III, q. 8, a unica; *De Subst. sep.*, cap. 5, 7, 19.

The sixth question that is asked about the soul is this: Whether a soul is composed of matter and form. And it seems that it is.

(1) For Boethius says in his book *De Trinitate:*[1] A simple form cannot be a subject. But a soul is a subject, namely, of sciences and of virtues. Therefore it is not a simple form. Therefore it is composed of matter and form.

(2) Furthermore, Boethius states in his book *De Hebdomadibus:*[2] That which is can participate in something but *esse* itself participates in nothing. And for a like reason, subjects participate but not forms, as something white can participate in something besides whiteness, but whiteness cannot. Now a soul participates in something, namely, in those things from which it acquires form. Therefore, a soul is not form only. Consequently it is composed of matter and form.

(3) Furthermore, if a soul is form alone and if it is in potency to something, it seems very likely that its very to-be would be its act; for a soul is not its own to-be. Now for a potency which is simple there can be only one act. Consequently a soul cannot be the subject of anything except its to-be. However, it is clear that a soul is the subject of other things. Consequently it is not a simple substance, but is composed of matter and form.

(4) Furthermore, accidents which belong to the form can be attributed to the whole species; but accidents following upon matter belong to this or to that individual. For form is a principle of the species, whereas matter is the principle of individuation. Therefore, if a soul is form only, all of its accidents will pertain to the whole species. Now this is clearly false, for to be a musician or a grammarian

and things of this sort do not pertain to the whole species. Consequently a soul is not a form only, but is composed of matter and form.

(5) Furthermore, form is the principle of action; but matter is the principle by reason of which a thing is the recipient of an action. Therefore, wherever there is action and passion, there is composition of form and matter. But in a soul there is action and passion. For the operation of the possible intellect consists in being acted upon, and this is why the Philosopher says that to understand is to undergo something.[3] However, the operation of the agent intellect consists in acting, for it causes those things which are potentially intelligible to become actually intelligible, as is said in Book III of the *De Anima*.[4] Therefore in a soul there is composition of form and matter.

(6) Furthermore, whatever contains the properties of matter must be composed of matter. But in a soul we find the properties of matter, namely, to be in potency, to receive, to be subject to, and other things of this kind. Therefore a soul is composed of matter.

(7) Furthermore, things that act and things that are the recipient of that action must have a matter common to both, as is explained in Book I of the *De Generatione*.[5] Therefore whatever can be affected by something which is material itself possesses matter. Now a soul can be affected by something material, namely, the fire of hell, which is a corporeal fire, as Augustine proves in Book XXI of the *De Civitate Dei*.[6] Therefore a soul itself possesses matter.

(8) Furthermore, the action of an agent does not terminate in the form alone, but rather in the composite of form and matter, as is proved in Book VII of the *Metaphysics*.[7] Now the action of that agent who is God terminates in the soul. Therefore a soul is composed of matter and form.

(9) Furthermore, that which is solely form is at the same time a being and one and does not need anything to make it a being and one, as the Philosopher states in Book VIII of the *Metaphysics*.[8] Now a soul needs something which causes it to exist and to be one, namely, God as creating. Therefore a soul is composed of matter and form.

(10) Furthermore, an agent is necessary if something is to be reduced from potency to act. Now to be reduced from potency to act belongs only to those beings in which there is matter and form. Consequently, if a soul is not composed of matter and form, it does not need an efficient cause, and this is clearly false.

(11) Furthermore, in his book *De Intellectu*,[9] Alexander states that a soul has a material intellect. By material is meant prime matter. Therefore there is prime matter in a soul.

(12) Furthermore, everything that exists is either pure act, or pure potency, or is composed of potency and act. Now a soul is not pure act since this is true of God alone. Nor is a soul pure potency because,

if it were, it would not differ from prime matter. Therefore it is composed of potency and act. Consequently, since form is act, a soul is not form alone.

(13) Furthermore, whatever is individuated is individuated by matter. Now a soul is not individuated by the matter in which it is, namely, its body; for if this were so, its individuation would be lost when it loses its body. Therefore it is individuated by the matter of which it is constituted. Consequently part of a soul is matter.

(14) Furthermore, there must be something common to an agent and a patient, as is clear from Book I of the *De Generatione*.[10] Now a soul is affected by sensible things, which are material. Nor can one say that in a human being the substance of the sensible soul is other than the substance of the intellective soul. Therefore a soul possesses something in common with material things, and consequently it seems that a soul possesses matter.

(15) Furthermore, since a soul is not simpler than an angel, it must belong to a genus as a species of the genus, for this is true of an angel. Now whatever is in a genus as a species of that genus would seem to be composed of matter and form. For genus corresponds to matter, while specific difference corresponds to form. Therefore a soul is composed of matter and form.

(16) Furthermore, a form that is common to many is diversified in the many by a division of matter. Now intellectuality is a form that is common, not only to souls, but also to angels. Therefore it is necessary that both in angels and in souls there be matter through whose division the form is multiplied in many individuals.

(17) Furthermore, whatever is moved has matter. But a soul is moved. For this is the way that Augustine uses to show that the soul is not divine in nature, namely, that it is subject to change.[11] Therefore a soul is composed of matter and form.

On The Contrary,

Everything that is composed of matter and form has a form. Consequently, if a soul is composed of matter and form, a soul has a form. But a soul is a form. Therefore a form has a form, and this seems impossible because it would lead to an infinite regress.

The Response:

It must be said that on this question people hold diverse positions. Some say that the soul, and in fact every substance except God, is composed of matter and form. The first authority to hold this position seems to be Avicebron, the author of the book *Fons Vitae*.[12] The basis of this position, which has been mentioned in the objections, is that it is necessary that there be matter in any being in which the properties of matter are found. Accordingly, since in a soul are found the properties of matter, for example, to receive, to be a subject, to be in potency, and other similar properties, he thought that there is necessarily matter in a soul.

Now this argument is worthless and his position is impossible. The weakness of the argument becomes clear from the fact that to receive, to be subject and other features of this kind do not belong to a soul and to prime matter in the same way; for prime matter receives actuation through transmutation and motion. Now since all transmutation and motion may be reduced to local motion as to that which is the first and most universal kind of motion, as is proved in Book VIII of the *Physics*,[13] it follows that matter is found only in those beings which have potency to place. Now the only beings of this kind are bodies, which are located in a place. Hence matter is found only in corporeal beings, according to what the philosophers have said about matter, unless one wishes to use the term "matter" equivocally. Now a soul is not actuated through motion and transmutation; but rather through being separated from motion and things subject to motion, according to what is said in Book VII of the *Physics*,[14] namely, that a soul becomes knowing and prudent while at rest. Hence the Philosopher also says, in Book III of the *De Anima*,[15] that to understand is to undergo something, but to undergo something in this context has a meaning different from that which it has in corporeal things. Therefore, if anyone wishes to draw the conclusion that a soul is composed of matter because it receives something or undergoes something, he is clearly led into error because of an equivocation. Therefore it is obvious that the argument cited above is worthless.

Furthermore, that this position is impossible can be made obvious is many ways: in the first place because a form accruing to matter constitutes a species. Therefore, if a soul is composed of form and matter, then from this union of the form to the matter of the soul a species would be constituted in reality. Now whatever possesses its species through itself does not enter into union with another in order to constitute a species unless the other one of the two is corrupted in some way, in the way that elements are united to produce the species of a mixture. Therefore, a soul is not united to its body in order to constitute the human species, but rather the whole human species would be located in the soul alone; now this is obviously false, because if the body did not belong to the human species, then the body would be united to the soul accidentally. Nor does this permit one to say that neither is the hand composed of matter and form because the hand does not possess a complete specific nature, but is a part of a species. For it is clear that the matter of the hand is not separately perfected by its own form, but rather there is one form which simultaneously perfects the matter of the entire body and of all its parts; and this could not be asserted of a soul if the soul were composed of matter and form. For then the order of nature would require that the matter of the soul should first be completed by its own form, and that thereafter the body should be brought to completion by the soul; unless perchance one were to say that the matter of the soul is a part of corporeal matter, and this would be totally absurd.

. Secondly, the aforesaid position is shown to be impossible from the fact that in everything that is composed of matter and form, matter is that which receives existence but it is not that by which something exists; for this latter characteristic belongs essentially to form. Therefore, if a soul is composed of matter and form, it is impossible that the entire soul be the formal principle of existence for its body. Consequently not the soul, but only a part of the soul, will be the form of its body. But the soul is that element, whatever it is, that is the form of the body. Hence the soul is not that composite of matter and form which they posit, but only the form of this composite.

This position seems to be impossible for a third reason. For if a soul is composed of matter and form, and body likewise, each of them will have its unity through itself. And consequently it will be necessary to posit a third reality by which the soul will be united to its body, and in fact some of those who subscribe to the aforesaid position admit this. For they say that a soul is united to its body by means of light: the vegetative soul by means of the light of the sidereal heaven; the sensitive soul by means of the light of the crystalline heaven; and the rational soul by means of the light of the empyrean heaven. All these explanations are fanciful. For it is necessary that a soul be directly united to its body as act is united to potency, as is clearly stated in Book VIII of the *Metaphysics.* [16] From this it is clear that a soul cannot be composed of matter and form. This does not preclude that there be act and potency in a soul, for potency and act exist not only in movable things but are found also in immutable things; for act and potency have a more universal meaning, as the Philosopher says in Book VIII of the *Metaphysics,* [17] while matter exists only in movable things.

Now the way in which act and potency exist in a soul is to be considered by advancing from material things to those that are immaterial. For in substances composed of matter and form we note three factors, namely, matter, form, and thirdly existence, of which form is in fact the principle; for matter participates in existence because it receives a form. Therefore existence follows upon the form, yet form is not identical with its own existence since form is the principle of existence. And although matter does not achieve existence except through its form, still the form, insofar as it is form, does not need matter for its own existence since existence follows upon the form itself; but it needs matter since it is the kind of form which is not essentially subsistent. Consequently there is no reason why a form that is separate from matter should not have its own existence; and in a form of this kind the very essence of the form is related to existence as to its proper act. And in this way potency and act are to be found in forms which subsist through themselves, inasmuch as the existence itself is the act of the subsisting form, which is not identical to its existence. Now if there be something which is its own existence (and this is proper to God), there will not be potency and act it in, but pure act. And it is becaue of this that Boethius says in his *De Hebdomadibus* that in all things other than God the to-be *(esse)* and that which is differ. Or as some put it, that by which something is and what it is differ; for existence itself is that by which something is, as running is that by which someone runs. Consequently, since a soul is a form that is capable of subsisting of itself, there is in it the composition of act and potency, that is, of existence and essence, but there is not the composition of matter and form.

Replies to the Opposing Objections:

(1) In the text cited, Boethius is speaking of the form which is unqualifiedly simple, namely, the divine essence, which is simply incapable of being a subject because it contains no potency, but is pure act. However, other simple forms, even though they be subsistent, as angels and souls are, can be subjects inasmuch as they possess potency as a result of which they are able to receive something.

(2) The act of existing itself is the highest act, which can be participated in by everything, but does not itself participate in anything. Hence, if there be something which is a subsistent act of existing, as we say God is, we assert that it participates in nothing. But the same argument is not valid with respect to other subsistent forms, which of necessity participate in existence and are related to it as potency is related to act. And since these forms are somehow in potency, they are able to participate in something else.

(3) Not only is a form related to its existence as potency to act, but there is also no reason why one form cannot be related to another form as potency to act, just as the transparent is related to light and the moist is related to heat. Thus, if transparency were separate and

self-subsistent, not only would it be receptive of its own existence but also of light. In like fashion there is nothing to prevent subsistent forms, such as angels and souls, from being receptive, not only of their own existence, but also of other perfections. However, the higher in perfection these subsistent form are, the fewer are the forms in which they need to participate in order to achieve their own perfection, because they possess essentially and by nature a higher degree of perfection.

(4) Although human souls are forms without matter, nevertheless they are forms that are individuated in bodies and are multiplied numerically along with the multiplication of bodies. Hence nothing prevents souls from having certain accidents which accrue to them because they are individuated, and which do not belong to the entire species.

(5) Passion, as found in a soul and attributed to the possible intellect, does not belong to that genus of passions which is attributed to matter, but 'passion' is predicated of these two equivocally. This is clear from what the Philosopher says in Book III of the *De Anima*, [19] since the passion of the possible intellect consists in its reception of something in an immaterial way. Similarly, the action of the agent intellect is not of the same kind as the action of material forms; for the action of the agent intellect consists in abstracting forms from matter, while the action of material agents consists in impressing forms upon matter. Consequently, from the kind of action and passion which are found in a soul it does not follow that a soul is composed of matter and form.

(6) To receive, to be a subject of, and other characteristics of this kind belong to a soul in a way that is different from the way in which they belong to prime matter. Hence it does not follow that the properties of matter are found in the soul.

(7) Although the fire of hell which afflicts the soul is material and corporeal, the soul is not affected by this fire in a material way, as bodies are. The soul experiences instead a spiritual suffering inasmuch as the fire is an instrument of the sentence imposed by divine justice.

(8) The action of one who generates terminates in a composite of matter and form because a natural generator is a cause which produces its offspring out of matter. But the action of one who creates does not produce its effect out of matter. As a result it is not necessary that the action of creating terminate in a composite of matter and form.

(9) Those beings which are subsistent forms do not require a formal cause to be one and to be a being since they are forms. They do, however, have an extrinsic cause which gives them existence.

(10) An agent which acts through motion reduces something from potency to act. However, an agent which acts without motion does not reduce something from potency to act, but it causes something

which of its nature is able to exist to exist actually, and this kind of agent is a creator.

(11) The possible intellect is called the 'ylealis' or material intellect by some authorities, not because it is a material form, but because it possesses a likeness to matter, insofar as it is in potency to intelligible forms just as matter is to sensible forms.

(12) Although a soul is neither pure act nor pure potency, still it does not follow that it is composed of matter and form, as is clear from what has already been said.

(13) A soul is not individuated by matter *out of* which it is composed, but rather because of its relation to the matter *in* which it exists. How this is possible has been shown in earlier questions.

(14) It is the composite being, not the sensitive soul, which is affected by sensible things; for to sense, which is a form of affectivity, does not belong to the soul alone but to the animated organ.

(15) The soul is not in a genus in the proper sense, as if it were a species, but only as part of the species "man." Hence it does not follow that it is composed of matter and form.

(16) Intellectuality does not belong to many individuals as if it were a single specific form given to many individuals because of the division of matter, since intellectuality is an immaterial form; but rather intellectuality is diversified because of a diversity of forms, whether these forms differ specifically, as human being and angel, or whether they differ only numerically, as the souls of diverse human beings.

(17) A soul and angels are said to be changeable by nature because they can undergo change through choice, which is truly a change from one operation to another. Matter is not necessary for this kind of change but only for natural changes, as from one form to another form, or from one location to another.

Notes to Question Six

1. Boethius, *De Trinitate,* II (PL 64:1250) Boethius (c. 480-524). Roman statesman and philosopher, executed by Theodoric the Ostrogoth. His most noted work, *On the Consolation of Philosophy,* written while he was in prison, is a Stoic-neoplatonic argument. Boethius also translated a number of Aristotle's works, and was the author of several theological treatises, including the *De Trinitate.*

2. Boethius, *De Hebdomadibus* (PL 64:1311)

3. Aristotle, *De Anima,* III, 4 (429a 13-15)

4. Aristotle, *De Anima,* III, 5 (430a 14-16)

5. Aristotle, *De Generatione et corruptione,* I, 7 (324a 34-35)

6. St. Augustine, *The City of God,* XXI, 10 (PL 41; 724-725)

7. Aristotle, *Metaphysics,* VII, 8 (1033b 16-19)

8. Aristotle, *Metaphysics,* VIII, 6 (1045a 36- b 7)

9. Alexander of Aphrodisias, *De Intellectu et intellecto;* ed. G. Théry in *Autour du décret de 1210;* II; Alexandre d'Aphrodise, Le Saulchoir, 1926 (Bibliothèque Thomiste, VII) p. 74 ff.

10. Aristotle, *De Generatione et corruptione,* I, 7 (323b 33)

11. Alcher of Clairvaus (Pseudo-Augustine), *Liber de spiritu et anima,* XL (PL 40: 809)

12. Avicebron, *Fons Vitae,* I, 17; III, 18. Avicebron (1020-1070) held that all created things, including the angels, are composed of matter and form.

13. Aristotle, *Physics,* VIII, 7 (260a 27 - 261a 27: VIII, 9 (265b 16 - 266a 5)

14. Aristotle, *Physics,* VII, 3 (247b 9-13)

15. Aristotle, *De Anima,* III, 4 (429a 29- b4)

16. Aristotle, *Metaphysics,* VIII, 6 (1045b 17-22)

17. Aristotle, *Metaphysics,* VIII, 5 (1044b 27-29)

18. Boethius, *De Hebdomadibus* (PL 64: 1311)

19. Aristotle, *De Anima,* III, 4 (430a 6-9)

QUESTION SEVEN

Parallel texts: *In II Sent.,* dist. 3, q. 1, a. 6; *Contra gent.,* II, 94; *Summa theol.,* I, q. 75, a. 7.

The seventh question that is asked about the soul is this: Whether an angel and a soul differ specifically. And it seems that they do not.

(1) Those beings which have the same essential and natural operation belong to the same species, for the nature of a thing is known through its operation. Now the essential and natural operation of a soul and of an angel, namely, to understand, is the same. Therefore soul and angel belong to the same species.

But an objector was arguing that a soul's act of understanding is discursive while an angel's is not; and hence a soul and an angel do not have the same specific operation.[1]

(2) On the contrary, one and the same power is not the source of operations which are diverse specifically. Through one and the same power, the possible intellect, we understand certain truths, the first principles, without a reasoning process; while other truths, conclusions from the first principles, we understand by a process of reasoning. Therefore to understand through a reasoning process and to understand without reasoning do not diversify species.

(3) Furthermore, to understand with or without a reasoning process seems to differ as to be in motion differs from to be at rest; for reasoning is a movement of the intellect from one thing to another. Now to be in motion and to be at rest do not diversify species; for motion ultimately belongs to the genus in which is found the terminus of the motion, as the Commentator says in Book III of the *Physics.*[2] And the Philosopher says in the same text[3] that there are as many species of motion as there are species of being, that is, of things in which motion terminates. Therefore, to understand through a reasoning process and to understand without reasoning do not differ specifically.

(4) Furthermore, just as angels understand things in the Word, so also do the souls of the blessed. Now the knowledge which is in

the Word is not discursive; hence Augustine says in Book XIV of his *De Trinitate* ⁴ that in heaven thoughts will not be subject to change. Therefore a soul does not differ from an angel on the basis of understanding through a reasoning process or without reasoning.

(5) Furthermore, not all angels are specifically alike, as many authorities assert, and yet all angels understand without reasoning. Consequently to understand through a reasoning process and to understand without a reasoning process do not cause a diversity of species in intellectual substances.

However an objector was arguing that some angels understand more perfectly than other angels.

(6) On the contrary, more and less do not bring about diversity of species. Now to understand more perfectly and to understand less perfectly do not differ except in terms of more and less. Therefore angels do not differ specifically because they understand more or less perfectly.

(7) Furthermore, all human souls belong to the same species, and nevertheless they do not all understand in equal degree. Therefore a specific difference in intellectual substances does not come about because they understand more or less perfectly.

(8) Furthermore, a human soul is said to understand discursively because it understands a cause through its effect and vice versa. But this also occurs in angels. For it is said in the *Liber de Causis* ⁵ that an intelligence understands the intelligence that is above itself because it is caused by it, and it understands the intelligence which is below itself because the intelligence is the cause of it. Consequently an angel does not differ from a soul on the basis of understand discursively or non-discursively.

(9) Furthermore, things which are perfected by the same perfection seem to be specifically the same; for an act that belongs to them as a property proceeds from one of their essential powers. Now an angel and a soul are perfected by the same perfections, namely, grace, glory or charity. Therefore they belong to the same species.

(10) Furthermore, things which have the same end seem to belong to the same species; for a thing is related to its end through that form which is the principle of its species. Now angels and souls have the same end, namely, eternal happiness, as is clear from what is said in the *Gospel* of Matthew, chapter 22,⁶ namely, that the children of the resurrection will be like angels in heaven. And Gregory states that souls will be elevated to the ranks of the angels.⁷ Therefore an angel and a soul belong to the same species.

(11) Furthermore, if an angel and a soul differ specifically, it necessarily follows that in the order of nature an angel is higher than

a soul, and as a result will occupy a rank midway between the soul and God. But, as Augustine holds,[8] there is no middle state between our mind and God. Consequently an angel and a soul do not differ in species.

(12) Furthermore, the impression of the same image in diverse recipients does not make them diverse in species; for the image of Hercules in gold and in silver is specifically the same. Now the image of God is in a soul just as it is in an angel. Therefore an angel and a soul do not differ specifically.

(13) Furthermore, things which have the same definition are specifically the same. Now the definition of an angel is applicable to a soul. For Damascene teaches that an angel is an incorporeal substance, constantly moving, possessing free choice, ministering to God, and able to achieve immortality through grace, not by nature.[9] Now all these characteristics are applicable to a soul. Therefore a soul and an angel are specifically the same.

(14) Furthermore, things which are alike with respect to their ultimate difference belong to the same species, because the ultimate difference constitutes the species. Now an angel and a soul are alike with respect to their ultimate difference, namely, with respect to intellectual being; this must be the ultimate difference since there is nothing higher in the nature of a soul or of an angel, and the ultimate difference is always that which is most perfect. Consequently an angel and a soul do not differ specifically.

(15) Furthermore, things which do not exist in a species cannot differ specifically. Now a soul is not in a species but rather is part of a species. Therefore it cannot differ specifically from an angel.

(16) Furthermore, a definition, in the proper sense, applies to a species. Consequently things that are not definable do not seem to belong to a species. Now an angel and a soul are not definable since they are not composed of matter, as was proved earlier. For in every definition there is something like matter and something like form, as is clear from Book VIII of the *Metaphysics,*[10] where the Philosopher states that if the species of things were free of matter, as Plato taught, they would not be definable. Therefore an angel and a soul cannot in the proper sense of the term be said to differ specifically.

(17) Furthermore, every species is constituted from a genus and specific differences. Now the genus and the difference are grounded in diverse realities, as the genus of man, which is 'animal,' is grounded in his sensitive nature; and as man's specific difference, which is 'rational,' is grounded in his intellective nature. Now in an angel and in a soul there are not diverse realities upon which genus and specific difference can be grounded. For their essence is a simple form, and their existence cannot be either a genus or a difference. For the

Philosopher proves in Book III of the *Metaphysics* [11] that being is not a genus nor a specific difference. Consequently an angel and a soul do not possess genus and specific difference and hence they cannot differ specifically.

(18) Furthermore, beings which differ specifically differ because of contrary differences. Now there is no contrariety in immaterial substances because contrariety is the principle of corruption. Therefore an angel and a soul do not differ specifically.

(19) Furthermore, an angel and a soul would seem to differ especially in this, that an angel is not united to a body while a soul is. Now this difference cannot cause a soul to differ specifically from an angel; for the body is related to the soul as the soul's matter; now matter does not confer species upon the form, but rather the reverse is true. Hence there is no way at all in which an angel and a soul differ specifically.

On The Contrary,

Things which do not differ specifically but only numerically do not differ except because of matter. Now an angel and a soul do not possess matter, as we clearly showed in an earlier question. Consequently, if an angel and a soul do not differ specifically, then they are not numerically different; and this is obviously false. It follows, therefore, that they differ specifically.

The Response:

Some authorities hold that the human soul and angels belong to the same species; and Origen [12] seems to have been the first to take this position. For he wished to avoid the errors of certain heretics of old who attributed the diversity of things to diverse principles, thus introducing the idea of different principles of good and evil. He therefore held that all diversity in things resulted from free choice. For he said that in the beginning God made all rational creatures equal; and some of them, adhering to God, became better in proportion to their adherence to God; but some of them, turning away from God through their free choice, became worse in proportion to the degree of their abandonment of God. And so some of them were embodied in celestial bodies; others, in human bodies; and some became perverted to the level of demonic malice, even though they were all alike at the moment when they proceeded from the principle that created them.

Now so far as one can follow his argument, Origen seems to have focused on the good of individual creatures while neglecting to consider the good of the whole. But a wise workman, in organizing the parts of his work, does not consider only the good of this or that part but also, and even more so, the good of the whole. Hence a builder does not make all the parts of a house equally valuable, but makes them more or less so, as he judges each of them appropriate to the suitable arrangement of the house. So too not all the parts of an animal's body possess the clarity of the eye, for then the animal would be imperfect; but there is diversity in the parts of an animal in order that the animal may be perfect. So also God in His widsom did not make all things equal, for, if He had, the universe would be imperfect, since it would lack many grades of being. Consequently, to ask why God in His activity made one creature better than another is the same as asking why an artisan provides a diversity of parts in his work.

Without reference then to this argument of Origen, there are men who follow his position and assert that all intellectual substances belong to a single species for reasons that have been touched upon in the objections of this question. But their position seems to be untenable. For if an angel and a soul are not composed of form and matter, but are only forms, as we have asserted in the preceding question, it is necessary that the specific difference by which one angel is distinguished from another angel, as well as from a soul, be a formal difference. This is true unless, of course, one were to hold that angels are also united to bodies, as souls are, so that from their relationship to bodies there could be a material difference in them, as we stated earlier about souls. Now this view is not widely taught, and even if it were, it would not support this position. For it is clear that bodies such as these would be specifically different from human bodies to which souls are united, and it is necessary that for bodies which are specifically diverse there be perfections which are specifically diverse. Therefore, if one rejects the position that angels are the forms of bodies on the ground that they are not composed of matter and form, there can be no difference between one angel and another angel or between an angel and a soul except a formal difference. Now a formal difference produces a difference in species, for it is the form what makes a thing to be what it is specifically; and so it follows that not only do angels differ specifically from souls, but they differ also from one another.

Now even if someone holds that angels and souls are composed of matter and form, still that they belong to the same species cannot be defended. For if there were, in both angels and souls, a matter that by itself is one (as there is one matter in all earthly bodies), and this one matter is diversified only by forms, then the division of that one common matter would necessarily be also the principle which distinguishes angels from one another and from souls. Now since it is of the very definition of matter that of itself it lacks any form, that (supposed) division of matter before it receives a form (which itself is multiplied according to the disposition of matter) can be understood only as a division through quantitative dimensions. Thus the Philosopher, in Book I of the *Physics,* [13] teaches that a substance remains indivisible if quantity is not present. But things that are composed of quantified matter are not merely united to a body, they are bodies. Therefore, according to this position, an angel and a soul are bodies, something that no sane person has maintained, especially since it has been proved that the operation of understanding could not be the act of any body. However, if the matter of angels and souls is not a single, common matter but belongs to diverse orders, this can only be because this matter is proportioned to diverse forms, for the same reason that they hold that there is not a single common matter for celestial and earthly bodies. And hence such a difference in matter will produce a diverse species. Hence it seems impossible that angels and souls belong to the same species; but we have still to consider how it is that they differ in species.

Now in order for us to arrive at a knowledge of intellectual substances, we must begin by reflecting on material substances. Now in material substances a diverse grade of natural perfection constitutes a diversity of species. And this is in fact very obvious if one examines the genera of material substances. For it is clear that mixed bodies are superior to the elements in the hierarchy of perfection; plants are superior to minerals and animals are superior to plants; and in any given genus we discover that species are diversified in relation to the level of natural perfection. For among the elements, earth is the lowest but fire is the highest. And in the same way among minerals, nature is discovered to progress step by step through diverse species until the species of gold is reached; among plants, until one reaches the species of fully developed trees; and among animals, until one reaches the species of human being. Yet for all that, some animals are almost like plants, for example, animals which do not have the ability to move and possess only the sense of touch; and in the same way some plants are very like inorganic bodies, as is clear from what the Philosopher says in his book *De Vegetabilibus.* [14] It is because of this that the Philosopher, in Book VIII of the *Metaphysics,* [15] states that the species of natural things are like the species of numbers, in which the addition or the subtraction of a unit brings about a change in species. In a similar fashion, therefore, a diverse grade of natural perfection brings about a difference of species in immaterial substances.

Nevertheless, the way in which species are diversified among immaterial substances is different in some respects from their

diversification in material substances. For wherever there is diversity
in levels of perfection, the levels of perfection must be treated according to their relation to a single principle. Consequently, among
material substances the diverse levels of perfection which diversify
species are recognized by their respective proximity to their first principle, which is matter. Hence it is that the first species, the ones closest
to matter, are the least perfect, but later species are more perfect,
since they contain perfections that are added to those of a more
primitive species; for example, compounds have a species that is more
perfect than the species of the elements, because in themselves they
possess whatever belongs to the elements and something more as well.
Further, the relation of plants to inorganic bodies and of animals to
plants is similar.

But among immaterial substances the basis for a hierarchy of
diverse species is found not in their relation to matter, which they
do not have, but rather in their relation to the First Efficient Cause,
which must be the most perfect of all. Consequently in immaterial
substances the first species is more perfect than the second because
the first species is more like the First Efficient Cause; and the second
species is lower in perfection than the first; and so this lessening of
perfection continues until the last of them is reached. Now the supreme
perfection of the First Efficient Cause consists in His possessing in
simple unity the totality of goodness and perfection. Hence the closer
an immaterial substance is to the First Efficient Cause, the more perfectly it possesses its goodness in its own simple nature, and the less
it needs inhering forms for its own fulfilment. And indeed this process
continues step by step down to the human soul, which holds the lowest
rank among immaterial substances, just as prime matter does in the
genus of sensible things. Hence a soul does not possess intelligible
perfection in its own nature but is in potency to intelligible objects,
just as prime matter is in potency to sensible forms. Hence in order
to perform its essential operations, a soul needs to be actualized by
intelligible forms, acquiring them from external things through its
sense powers. And since the operation of a sense takes place through
a bodily organ, it is appropriate for the soul, because of the very way
its nature is constituted, that it be united to a body and that it be
part of the human species, since of itself a soul is not complete in
species.

Replies to the Opposing Arguments:

(1) The act of understanding of an angel and that of a soul are
not specifically the same. For it is clear that if the forms which are

the principles of operations are specifically different, then the operations themselves must be specifically different; for example, the acts
of heating and of cooling differ just as heat and cold differ. Now the
intelligible species by which souls understand are abstracted from
phantasms. And consequently they are not of the same kind as the
intelligible species by means of which angels understand, namely,
species which are innate to them, according to the statement in the
Liber de Causis [16] that every intelligence is full of forms. Hence the
act of understanding of a human being and of an angel do not belong
to the same species. It is because of this difference that an angel understands without a reasoning process, whereas a soul understands discursively; and this it must do in order to achieve a knowledge of the power
of causes from their sensible effects, and to arrive from sensible accidents at a knowledge of the essences of things which are accessible
to the senses.

(2) An intellectual soul understands principles and conclusions
through species which have been abstracted from phantasms; therefore
the acts of understanding are not specifically diverse.

(3) Motion is reduced to the genus and to the species of that in
which the motion terminates; inasmuch as it is the self-same form
which prior to motion is in potency only, which while motion is in
progress is midway between act and potency, and which at the termi-
nation of the motion is fully in act. Now the act of understanding
of an angel, which takes place without a reasoning process, and the
act of understanding of a soul, which is discursive, do not occur
through the same specific form. Hence it is not necessary that angels
and souls belong to one species.

(4) The species of a thing is revealed through that operation that
belongs to it according to its essential nature, and not through an
operation that belongs to it because of its participation in the nature
of something else. For example, the specific nature of iron is not
revealed because it is burning since this feature belongs to it because
it has been set on fire; for then the species of wood and iron would
be judged to be the same, since wood can also burn when set afire.
I say, then, that "to see in the Word" is an operation which transcends
the nature of a soul and of an angel, and which belongs to both of
them because they participate in a nature superior to them, namely,
the divine nature, through the light of glory. Consequently one cannot
conclude that an angel and a soul belong to the same species.

(5) Even in diverse angels the intelligible species are not all of
the same nature. For the higher an intellectual substance is and the
closer it is to God, Who understands all things through a single principle which is His essence, the more lofty are the intelligible forms
which exist in it, and the more efficacious are they as the source of

more extensive knowledge. Hence it is said in the *Liber de Causis* [17] that the nobler intelligences understand by means of forms which are more universal. And Dionysius says, in Chapter XII of his *De Coelesti Hierarchia,* [18] that the higher angels have knowledge that is more universal. Consequently the acts of understanding of diverse angels are not specifically the same, although both acts take place without reasoning because angels understand through species which are innate and not received from outside.

(6) More and less have two meanings: in one sense, as matter shares in the same form according to diverse modes, as wood participates in whiteness; and in this sense more or less do not diversify species. In a second sense, more and less can refer to diverse grades of the perfection of forms, and in this sense a diversity of species results. For colors are diverse in species insofar as they are more or less closely related to light; and in this sense more or less is found in diverse angels.

(7) Although all souls do not understand equally well, still they all understand by means of species which are specifically the same, namely, species derived from phantasms. Hence the fact that souls understand in different degrees is due to the diversity of their sensitive powers from which species are abstracted, and this diversity can be traced also to diverse dispositions of their bodies. [19] And thus it is clear that more and less, in the sense of understanding better or less well, do not diversify the species, since they are the result of material diversity.

(8) To know something through something else can happen in two ways: in one way, to know one thing that is known through another also known, so that there is a distict knowledge of both, as a human being knows a conclusion through a principle by considering both of them separately; in another way, as to know something that is known through a species by means of which it is known, as when we see a stone through the species of the stone which is in the eye. Therefore to know one thing through another in the first way mentioned results in discursiveness, but not in the second way. But it is in this second way that angels know a cause through its effect and an effect through its cause, inasmuch as the very essence of the angel is a likeness of its cause and makes its effect to be like itself.

(9) The perfections of grace belong to a soul and to an angel through participation in the divine nature. Hence it is said in the *Second Epistle of Peter,* "through whom He has given us these great and precious gifts so that we might be partakers of the divine nature, etc." [20] Hence merely because angels and souls share in these perfections, one cannot conclude that they are one in species.

(10) Those beings whose proximate and natural end is one and the same are one in species. However, eternal beatitude is a final and

supernatural end. Hence the argument does not follow.

(11) Augustine does not mean that there is nothing intermediate between our mind and God according to the levels of dignity and grace, because even one soul is nobler than another; but he means that our mind is directly justified by God and finds its beatitude in Him. In the same way one might say that an ordinary soldier is immediately subject to his king, not that he has no superiors between him and the king, but in the sense that no one except the king has dominion over him.

(12) Neither a soul nor an angel is a perfect image of God, but only the Son of God is. Consequently it is not necessary that they belong to the same species.

(13) The aforesaid definition does not apply to a soul in the same way as it does to an angel. For an angel is an incorporeal substance, both because it is not a body and because it is not united to a body. This latter cannot be said of a soul.

(14) Those who assert that a soul and an angel are specifically the same consider that this argument provides the strongest support for their position, but the conclusion does not necessarily follow; for the ultimate difference ought to be higher, not only with respect to the nobility of nature but also with respect to the very constituting of nature, because the ultimate difference is, as it were, act with respect to all the perfections which precede it. Therefore, to be intellectual is not what is noblest in an angel or in a soul, but to be intellectual in a particular mode; the same is true in the realm of sensible things; for if it were not so, all brute animals would belong to the same species.

(15) A soul is part of a species and nevertheless is the principle which confers specific nature, and it is from this latter perspective that we are now inquiring whether the species of the soul is different from that of angels.

(16) Although in the proper sense of the term, only a species can be defined, nevertheless it is not necessary that every species be definable. For the species of immaterial things are not known through definition nor through demonstration as something is known in the speculative sciences, but they are known through a simple intuition. Consequently, an angel, in the proper sense of the term, cannot be defined. For we do not know what an angel is, but we can gain some knowledge about angels through certain negative judgments we make about them, or through positive indications that are given us.

(17) The terms 'genus' and 'specific difference' can be understood in two ways: first, with reference to the real order, as the metaphysician and philosopher of nature deal with them; and taken in this way genus and specific difference must be grounded in diverse natures. And from this point of view there is no objection to saying that in

spiritual substances there is neither genus nor specific difference, but that such substances are forms only and simple species. Secondly, genus and specific difference can be understood with reference to the logical order; and from this point of view genus and specific difference need not be grounded in diverse natures, but upon a single nature in which the logician distinguishes a proper and a common element. And there is no reason why one should not say that genus and specific differences, taken in this sense, are found in spiritual substances.

(18) If one speaks of genus and of specific difference as they are in order of nature, it is necessary that specific differences be contraries. For matter, upon which the nature of genus is grounded, is capable of receiving contrary forms. However, if one examines the issue from the point of view of logic, any kind of opposition between specific differences will do, as is clear in the differences between numbers, between which there exists no contrariety. The same is true with respect to spiritual substances.

(19) Although matter does not confer species, nevertheless the nature of a form depends upon the relationship of matter to that form.

Notes to Question Seven

1. For St. Thomas, human understanding involves intellectual movement, for example, from first principles, from premises to conclusions. It involves composition and division in that by simple apprehension the human intellect apprehends some quidditative notion, and then moves to understand the various dispositions affecting the essence by proceeding from one composition and division to another; the divine and angelic intellects know with immediacy what the human intellect knows by discursive reasoning. See *Summa theol.*, I, q. 75, a. 7.
2. Averroes, *III Physics*, T.C. 4, ed. Venetiis, 1574, fol. 87.
3. Aristotle, *Physics*, III, 1 (201a 8-9)
4. St. Augustine, *De Trinitate*, XV, 16 (PL 42: 1079)
5. *Liber de Causis*, VII; ed. Bardenhewer, p. 170, 25-27.
6. *Matthew*, 22: 30.
7. Pope Gregory I (540-604) *In Evang.*, II, 34 (PL 76:1252).
8. St. Augustine, *De Trinitate*, XV, 1 (PL 42: 1057).
9. St. John Damascene, *De Fide orthodoxa*, II, 3 (PG 94: 865).
10. Aristotle, *Metaphysics*, VII, 6 (1031b 4-6) VIII, 6 (1045a 33-35)
11. Aristotle, *Metaphysics*, III, 3 (998b 22-27).
12. Origen, *Peri Archon*, II, 8 (PG 11: 220).
13. Aristotle, *Physics*, I, 2 (185b 3-4).
14. Aristotle, *De Plantis*, I, 2 (816a 39-40; 817b 24).
15. Aristotle, *Metaphysics*, VIII, 3 (1043b 33 - 1044a 2).
16. *Liber de Causis*, IX, ed. Bardenhewer, p. 173, 18.
17. *Ibid.*, p. 173, 2-24.
18. Pseudo-Dionysius, *De Coelesti hierarchia*, XII, 2 (PG 3: 292).
19. Cf. *Summa theol.*, I, q. 85, a. 7.
20. *II Peter*, 1: 4.

QUESTION EIGHT

Parallel texts; *In II Sent.*, dist. 1, q. 2, a. 5; *Contra gent.*, II, 90; *Summa theol.*, I, q. 76, a. 5; *De Malo*, q. 5, a. 5.

The eighth question that is asked about the soul is this: Whether a rational soul ought to be united to a body such as the human body. And is seems that it ought not to be.

(1) For a rational soul is the loftiest of those forms which are united to a body. Now earth is the lowest of bodies. Therefore it is not fitting that a soul be united to an earthy body.

But an objector was arguing that an earthy body, because it is formed by a balanced combination of elements, is like the body of the outermost heaven, which has no contraries at all, and is thus so ennobled that a rational soul might fittingly be united to it.

(2) On the contrary, if the nobility of the human body is due to its likeness to a celestial body, it follows that a celestial body is nobler than it. Now a rational soul is nobler than any body whatsoever because through the capability of its intellect it transcends all bodies. Consequently a rational soul ought rather to be united to a celestial body.

But an objector was arguing that a celestial body is perfected by a perfection which is loftier than a rational soul.

(3) On the contrary, if that which perfects a celestial body is nobler than a rational soul, it must be an intellect; for any intelligent being whatsoever is more noble than any which is not intelligent. Consequently, if a celestial body is perfected by a spiritual substance, this substance will either be its mover only, or its form as well. If it is its mover only, it will still be true that a human body is perfected in a higher way than is a celestial body. For a form confers species on that of which it is the form, but a mover does not. Hence there is nothing to prevent those things which of their own nature are very lowly from being the instruments of a very lofty agent.

However, if an intellectual substance is the form of a celestial body, then a substance of this kind possesses only an intellect, or, along with its intellect, it possesses sense powers and other powers.

If it possesses sense powers and other powers, then, since sense powers of this kind must be the acts of those organs which they require for operating, it follows that a celestial body is an organic body; and this is opposed to a celestial body's simplicity, uniformity and unity. But if the intellectual substance possesses only an intellect which acquires nothing from the senses, then such a substance has no need to be united to a body, since the operation of the intellect does not take place through a bodily organ. Therefore, since the union of body and soul is not for the sake of the body but for the sake of the soul (because matter exists for the sake of form and not vice versa), it follows that an intellectual substance is not united to a celestial body as its form.

(4) Furthermore, every created intellectual substance is by nature capable of sinning because it can turn away from the Supreme Good, God. Consequently, if certain intellectual substances were united as forms to celestial bodies, it would follow that they will be able to sin. Now the penalty for sin is death, that is to say, the separation of a soul from its body, and the torment of sinners in hell. Therefore it could happen that the celestial bodies would die by being separated from their souls and that their souls would be thrust down into hell.

(5) Furthermore, every intellectual substance is capable of achieving beatitude. Therefore, if celestial bodies are animated by intellectual souls, then such souls are able to achieve beatitude. And consequently in the state of eternal beatitude there will not be only angels and human beings but also beings of an intermediate nature, although the Christian doctors teach that the society of the saints is composed of angels and human beings.

(6) Furthermore, the body of Adam was proportioned to receive a rational soul. Now our body is not like his body; for his body, before he sinned, was immortal and incapable of suffering, and our bodies are not. Therefore the kind of bodies that we possess are not proportioned to receive a rational soul.

(7) Furthermore, a very lofty mover deserves instruments which are best ordered and obedient to its operation. Now a rational soul is more noble than any of the lower movers. Consequently it ought to have a body which is responsive in the highest degree to its operations. Now this is not the kind of body which we possess; for the flesh wars against the spirit, and the soul is pulled in all directions because of its struggle against the desires of the flesh. Therefore a rational soul ought not to have been united to such a body.

(8) Furthermore, it is fitting that a rational soul should have a profusion of spirits in the body which it perfects. For the human heart is the most fiery among all animal hearts in its power of generating spirits. Evidence of this is the human body's erect position, which results from the power of heat and of spirits. Consequently it would

have been far more fitting that a rational soul should have been united to a body that is completely spiritual.

(9) Furthermore, a soul is an incorruptible substance. However, our bodies are corruptible. Therefore it is not fitting that a rational soul be united to bodies such as ours.

(10) Furthermore, a rational soul is united to a body to constitute the human species, but the human species would be more adequately preserved if the body to which a soul is united were incorruptible. For then it would not be necessary that the species be kept in existence through generation, but it could be preserved in individuals whose number remains the same. Consequently, a human soul ought to have been united to incorruptible bodies.

(11) Furthermore, in order that the human body might be the loftiest among lower bodies, it ought to be very similar to a celestial body, which is the loftiest of bodies. Now there is no contrariety in a celestial body; therefore the human body ought to have the smallest degree of contrariety. However, our bodies do not have the smallest degree of contrariety, since contrariety is the principle of dissolution and other bodies, such as stones and trees, are more enduring. Consequently a rational soul ought not to have been united to the kind of bodies which we possess.

(12) Furthermore, a soul is a simple form. Now simple matter is appropriate to a simple form. Therefore, a rational soul ought to have been united to a simple body, for example, fire, or air, or something of this kind.

(13) Furthermore, a human soul would seem to have something in common with the principles of nature. Hence the earliest philosophers asserted that the soul was in fact of the same nature as these principles, as is clear in Book I of the *De Anima*.[1] Now the principles of bodies are the elements. Therefore, although the soul is not an element nor composed of elements, it ought at least to be united to an elemental body, such as fire, or air, or one of the others.

(14) Furthermore, bodies composed of similar parts are less distant from simplicity than bodies composed of dissimilar parts. Consequently, since a soul is a simple form, it ought rather to have been united to a body made up of similar parts than to a body made up of dissimilar parts.

(15) Furthermore, a soul is united to a body both as its form and as its mover. Therefore a rational soul, which is the loftiest of substantial forms, ought to have been united to a body that is quick in motion; but the opposite is true, for the bodies of birds and also of many other animals are far more rapid in motion than human bodies are.

(16) Furthermore, Plato[2] holds that forms are bestowed by a mover in proportion to what the matter deserves, that is, in proportion

to what are called the dispositions of matter. Now it seems that the human body does not have a proper disposition to so lofty a form since the human body is coarse and corruptible. Therefore a soul ought not to have been united to a body of that kind.

(17) Furthermore, the intelligible forms which exist in a human soul are far more particularized than those found in loftier intellectual substances. Now such forms would be more proper to the operation of a celestial body, which is the cause of the generation and corruption of particular phenomena. Therefore a human soul ought to have been united to celestial bodies.

(18) Furthermore, nothing is moved naturally when it occupies its own natural place, but only when it is outside its natural place. Now the heaven is moved while existing in its natural place. Therefore it is not moved naturally. Consequently it is moved spatially by a soul, and thus has a soul united to it.

(19) Furthermore, 'to proclaim' is an act of an intelligent substance. Now the heavens proclaim the glory of God, as Psalm 18 says.[3] Consequently the heavens are intelligent, and therefore possess an intellective soul.

(20) Furthermore, a soul is the most perfect of substantial forms. Therefore it ought to have been united to a perfect body. However, a human body is apparently extremely imperfect, for it does not have weapons to use for defense or attack, nor does it have protection from the weather, nor any of those things with which nature endows the bodies of other animals. Consequently such a soul ought not to have been united to a body of this kind.

On The Contrary,

One can cite *Ecclesiasticus,* chapter XVII: "God created man from earth and made him after his image."[4] Now the works which God has made are suitable, for it is said in Chapter I of *Genesis*: "God looked at all the things which He had made and they were exceedingly good."[5] Therefore it was appropriate that a rational soul in which the image of God exists be united to an earthly body.

The Response:

In settling this question one must assert that since matter exists for the sake of form and not vice versa, we must discover by reflecting on the soul what kind of body ought to be united to it. Hence it is stated in Book II of the *De Anima*[6] that a soul is not only the form and mover of its body, but also its end. Now it is clear from what we have said in previous questions that it is wholly reasonable for a human soul to be united to a body because it is the lowest in the order of intelligible substances, just as prime matter holds the lowest rank in the order of sensible things. A human soul does not possess innate intelligible species by means of which it can accomplish its essential operation, which is to understand, as higher intellectual substances do; but rather a human soul is in potency to intelligible species since it is like a wax tablet on which nothing has been written, as is said in Book II of the *De Anima*.[7] Consequently it must acquire intelligible species from things outside itself through the mediation of sense powers, which cannot accomplish their appropriate operations without bodily organs. Hence it is necessary that a human soul be united to a body.

Consequently, if the reason a human soul is unitable to a body is that it needs to acquire intelligible species from things by means of sensation, it is necessary that the body to which a rational soul is united be of such a kind that it is particularly suitable for acquiring sensible species from which intelligible species can be derived for the intellect. Consequently, the body to which a rational soul is united must be arranged in the best possible way for the operation of sensing. Now although there are a number of senses, still one of them is the foundation of all the others, namely, the sense of touch, in which is found in a special way the totality of sensitive nature. This is the reason we also find it said in Book II of the *De Anima*[8] that it is on account of this sense that living things are first called 'animal.' And hence it is that when this sense is inoperative, as happens during sleep, all other senses are inoperative. And furthermore all the other senses are not only rendered inoperative by an excess of their own proper sensible objects, as sight is by things that are excessively luminous and hearing is by sounds which are too loud, but also by an excess in the sensibles which are proper to touch, as by intense heat or cold.

Therefore, since the body to which a rational soul is united ought to be arranged in a way that best suits a sentient nature, it is necessary that this body be an extremely suitable organ for the sense of touch. For this reason it is stated in Book II of the *De Anima*[9] that our sense of touch has greater exactitude than that of all other animals, and also it is on account of the excellence of this sense that one human being is more fit than another to perform intellectual operations. For we observe that those whose flesh is pliant, who are delicate in the sense of touch, are mentally well-endowed.[10] Now no organ of any sense power ought to possess actually those contraries which that sense is capable of perceiving, but rather must be in potency to them so that it might acquire them; for a recipient must lack the thing received.

But this principle necessarily applies in a different way to the organ of the sense of touch than to the organs of the other senses. For the organ of sight, the pupil of the eye, totally lacks white and black and any kind of color whatsoever, and something like this is true of the sense of hearing and the sense of smell. But the sense of touch is capable of knowing those elements of which an animal body must be composed, namely, the hot and the cold, the moist and the dry. Hence it is impossible that the organ of the sense of touch should be totally deprived of any one of these four elements that are its sensible object; but it must rather be constituted as a kind of mean among them all, for thus it is in potency to contraries. Consequently the body to which the rational soul is united, since it must be extremely suitable for the sense of touch, must be brought to the highest possible degree of this median state through an equal blending of the four simple elements. And from this constitution of the human body we see that the entire operation of inferior powers terminates in a human being as in the perfection of nature. For we observe that the operation of nature advances gradually from simple elements, by combining them, until it achieves the most perfect mode in which things may be combined, the mode found in the human body. Therefore, in general, the ordering of the body to which a rational soul is united ought to be of a very balanced disposition.

However, if anyone wants to examine also the particular organs of the human body, he will discover that they are organized so that a human being might sense most effectively. Consequently, because a well ordered brain is necessary for the effective condition of the internal sense powers, for example, the imagination, the memory and the cogitative power, a human being was made in such a way that in proportion to his size he has a brain that is larger than that of any other animal. Also, in order that a human being's operation be more free, a human being has his head placed at the top of his body; for a human being is the only animal that stands erect, whereas other animals move along in a bent-over postion. In order to possess and to maintain this erect position, the heart must possess a great deal of heat by which many spirits may be generated, so that through the greater abundance of these spirits produced by the heat, the body might be maintained in an upright position; evidence of this is found in the fact that in old age a human being bends over, since his heat is naturally diminished. In this way one can determine the meaning of the human body with respect to the particular features which belong to a human being by nature.

However, one must also note that in those beings which are constituted out of matter, there are dispositions belonging to the matter itself on account of which matter of a particular kind is chosen for a particular form; there are also other dispositions which are the consequences of what necessarily belongs to matter and are not the result of the agent's choice. For example, in order to make a saw, an artisan selects the hardness in iron in order that the saw be suitable for cutting; but that the sharpness of the iron can be blunted and that it can become rusty are the necessary consequences of the kind of matter iron is. For the artisan would prefer to choose a kind of matter which did not have such disadvantages if he could find it; but since he cannot find it, the artisan does not refuse to use the matter which he has at his disposal to produce the saw because this matter has defects inherent to it. The same thing is true of the human body; the fact that it is compounded from the elements and its organs so arranged that it is a very suitable instrument for the operations of the sense powers results from the decision of the Maker to fashion a human being from this kind of matter. But that the body is corruptible, that it grows weary, and that it has other defects of this kind are the necessary consequences of the kind of matter the body is. For it is necessary that any body which is composed of these sorts of contraries be subject to these sorts of defects. Nor is it valid to object that God could have made things differently; because the question we should ask about the creation of nature is not what God could do, but rather how things might be constituted so that nature as a whole might exist, according to what Augustine says in his book, *Super Genesim ad Litteram*.[11]

However, it must be noted that in order to provide a remedy for these defects, God, in creating a human being, bestowed on him the assistance of original justice, whereby the body would be wholly under the control of the soul so long as the soul remained subject to God; so that neither death nor suffering nor any other defect would affect a human being unless the soul were first separated from God. But when the soul turned away from God through sin, a human being was deprived of this privilege and is now subject to those defects which are due to the nature of matter.

Replies to the Opposing Arguments:

(1) Although a soul is the loftiest of substantial forms in that it is intelligent, still because it is lowest in the genus of intelligible forms, it must be united to a body which is a balanced combination of elements, so that the soul might acquire intelligible species through the senses. For this reason it was necessary that the body to which a soul is united contain a greater measure of the heavier elements, namely, earth and water. For since fire is more powerful in its action

than are the heavier elements, if there were not a greater measure of the lower elements, the four elements could not be combined and especially not brought to a medium state, since fire would burn up the other elements. Hence, in Book II of his *De Generatione*,[12] the Philosopher states that in compound bodies there is a greater measure of earth and water.

(2) A rational soul is united to the kind of body it has, not because this body is like the body of the outermost heaven, but because it is a balanced mixture; still on this basis there follows some likeness to the body of the outermost heaven in that this body is somewhat free of contraries. However, according to the opinion of Avicenna,[13] a soul is united to this kind of body because of its resemblance to the body of the outermost heaven; for he supposed that lower realities were caused by higher ones with the result that the bodies of this world were caused by celestial bodies. And when these inferior bodies arrived at a likeness to celestial bodies through a balanced mixture of elements, they reached a form which is like the form of a celestial body, which Avicenna asserted was animated.

(3) There are diverse opinions as to whether celestial bodies are animated, both among philosophers and among Christian teachers. One of the philosophers, Anaxagoras,[14] asserted that the intellect which governs all things is entirely unmixed and separate and that celestial bodies are inanimate. He was said even to have been condemned to death because he maintained that the sun is a fiery stone, according to Augustine's account in his book, *The City of God*.[15] However, other philosophers asserted that celestial bodies are animated. Some of them declared that God is the soul of the heavens, and this belief was the basis of idolatry with the result that the heavens and the celestial bodies were accorded divine worship. Still others, like Plato and Aristotle,[16] although they held that celestial bodies are animated, nevertheless maintained that God is superior to the soul of the heavens and totally separate.

Even among Christian teachers Origen[17] and his disciples maintained that celestial bodies are animated. Some others, however, asserted that they are inanimate, as Damascene holds;[18] this latter position is generally held by present day theologians; that Augustine did not take a position is seen in Book II of his *Super Genesim ad Litteram*, and in his book *Enchiridion*.[19]

For our part, we hold it as certain that the celestial bodies are moved by some intellect, at least by one that is separate; and we support both sides of the question because of the arguments proposed. Let us therefore say that some intellectual substance is the perfection of a celestial body as its form, and that this substance possesses only intellectual, not sensible powers. This one may conclude from the

words of Aristotle in Book II of his *De Anima* and in Book XI of the
Metaphysics,[20] even though Avicenna asserts that the soul of the outermost heaven, along with its intellect, has also an imagination.[21]
However if it has intellect only, it is still united to its body as a form,
not through an intellectual operation but because of the exercise of
its active power in virtue of which it can achieve a likeness to God
by the causality it exerts in moving the heavens.

(4) Although because of their own nature all created intellectual
substances are capable of sinning, nevertheless many are kept from
sinning because of divine choice and predestination through the help
of grace, and among these one could locate the souls of the celestial
bodies, especially if the demons who sinned belonged to a lower order,
as Damascene[22] maintained.

(5) If celestial bodies are animated, their souls belong to the
company of angels. For Augustine says in his *Enchiridion:*[23] I am not
certain whether the sun and the moon and all the stars belong to the
same society, namely, that of the angels, although to some they seem
to be luminous bodies, having neither sense powers nor intellect.

(6) The body of Adam was proportioned to receive a human soul,
as was said, not only with respect to what nature demands but also
with reference to what grace bestowed, and although we have been
deprived of this grace, our nature remains the same.

(7) The struggle which goes on in a human being among contrary
desires results too from the exigencies of nature. Thus, if a human
being was to have senses, it was necessary that he then sense objects
which cause delight and that a desire for these delightful objects arise
in him, and such a desire if very often opposed to reason. But in the
state of innocence, a human being was granted a remedy against concupiscence through grace, namely, that his lower powers would not
be moved in any way that was opposed to reason. However, human
beings lost this remedy because of sin.

(8) Although spirits are transmitters of powers, they cannot be
organs of the sense powers. And consequently the body of a human
being cannot consist of spirits alone.

(9) Corruptibility arises from those defects which belong to a
human body as a result of the exigencies of matter, and particularly
as a consequence of original sin, which removed the help which grace
affords.

(10) What is better for any species is to be sought in those qualities
which are for the sake of its end as a species, not in those which result
from the exigencies of matter. Thus it would be better that an animal
body should be incorruptible only if it were according to nature that
the kind of matter which the form of an animal demands should be
incorruptible.

(11) Those things which in the scale of being are nearest to the elements and which have a great deal of contrariety, such as stones and metals, are more permanent because in them the harmony of the elements is of a simple kind and hence it is not easily broken down; for the harmony of the elements in those beings where this harmony is very complex is easily destroyed. Nevertheless, the cause of the longevity of animals is the fact that the moist element should not easily dry up nor become hardened, and that the hot element should not easily become extinguished, because the basis of life is the hot and the moist elements. Now in a human being, the elements have these qualities in proportion to the limit imposed by the fact that the human body is a blending of elements brought to a median state. As a consequence of this fact, some of the combinations of elements found in human beings are more enduring and others are less enduring, and for this reason some human beings live longer than others.

(12) The body of a human being could not be a simple body nor a celestial body because if it were, the organs of the senses and especially the organ of the sense of touch would be incapable of being affected by their sensible objects; nor can the human body be a simple elementary body because contraries exist in act in an element. On the other hand the human body must be brought to a median state.

(13) The earliest philosophers held that a soul which knows all things must actually be like all things. As a consequence they asserted that the soul was of the same nature as that element which they made the principle out of which (they said) all things are constituted; so that thus the soul would be like all things in order that it might know all things. At a later date, however, Aristotle [24] declares that a soul knows all things insofar as it resembles all things in potency, not in act. Hence the body to which the soul is united must not consist entirely of either the highest or the lowest elements, but must constitute a mean among all the elements, so that it might be in potency to contraries.

(14) Although a soul is simple in essence, yet its powers are manifold; and the more a soul will have been manifold in powers, the more perfect it will have been. For this reason a soul needs an organic body which is made up of dissimilar parts.

(15) A soul is not united to a body in order that it might move from place to place, but rather the local motion of a human being, like that of other animals, has as its end the preservation of the body which is united to the soul. But a soul is united to its body in order that it might understand, which is a soul's essential and principal operation. And consequently it is necessary that the body which is united to a rational soul be the kind of body that is best fitted for being of service to the soul in whatever understanding demands. But as for quickness of movement and other qualities of this sort, the human

body should possess them to the extent that its role as servant of a rational soul permits.

(16) Plato [25] asserted that the forms of things were self-subsistent and that participation in these forms by portions of matter is for the benefit of these portions of matter, in order that they might achieve the fullness of their being; but that this participation is not for the benefit of the forms which subsist of themselves. And consequently it followed that forms were granted to portions of matter in proportion as these portions of matter deserve them. Now according to Aristotle's teaching, [26] natural forms are not self-subsisting. Hence the union of form to matter is not for the sake of matter but for the sake of the form. Consequently, it is not because matter is ordered in a certain fashion that a particular kind of form is united to it; but rather, because the form is of a certain kind, it is necessary that its matter be ordered in such a way. And so we said earlier that the body of a human being is ordered in such a way that it is suitable to the kind of form that a human soul is.

(17) A celestial body, although it is a cause of particular things which are generated and corrupted, is nevertheless only a cause of them as being a general agent; that is why, below a celestial body, there must be determinate agents to produce determinate species. From this it follows that the mover of a celestial body need not have particular forms but only universal ones, whether this mover be a soul or a separate mover. However, Avicenna [27] asserted that the soul of the outermost heaven had to have an imagination through which it might apprehend particulars. For since this soul is the cause of the movement of the outermost heaven by which the outermost heaven rotates in this place or in that, the soul of the outermost heaven, which is the cause of this movement, must know the here and now; and consequently it must have a sensory power. But this is not necessary: first of all because the movement of the outermost heaven is always uniform and suffers no impediment, and a universal conception is sufficient to cause such a motion. But a particular concept is needed for the movements of animals because of the irregularity of these movements and the hindrances which may arise to impede them. Secondly, because the higher intellectual substances can know particular things without possessing a sensory power, as we have shown elsewhere.

(18) The motion of the outermost heaven is a natural motion because of a principle which is passive or receptive of this motion, since such a motion naturally belongs to a body of this kind; however, the active principle of this motion is an intellectual substance. Now the statement that no body which exists in its proper place moves naturally is to be understood as applying to a body which moves in a straight line, and which changes place in relation to the whole of

itself, not only abstractly but also as a subject of motion. However, a body which moves with a circular motion does not change its place as a subject, but only abstractly considered. As a consequence it is never outside its natural place.

(19) This argument has no value even though Rabbi Moses [28] proposes it. For if 'to proclaim' is taken in a strict sense when it is said that the heavens proclaim the glory of God, the heavens would have to possess not only an intellect but also a tongue. For if the text is taken literally "the heavens" are said to "proclaim the glory of God" in the sense that through them the glory of God is made known to human beings, in the same way that even creatures which do not possess sense powers are said to praise God.

(20) Other animals have a natural estimative power which is directed toward certain fixed objects, and consequently nature can adequately provide these animals with fixed aids; not, however, a human being, who because he possesses reason is open to an infinity of conceptions. And therefore, in place of all the aids which other animals possess by nature, a human being has an intellect, which is the likeness of all species, and hands, which are the organ of organs, and by means of these attributes a human being can provide himself with all that is necessary.

Notes to Question Eight

1. Aristotle, *De Anima*, I, 2 (403b 28 - 405b 30).
2. Plato, *Laws*, X, 903D.
3. *Psalms*, 18: 1.
4. *Ecclesiasticus*, 17: 1.
5. *Genesis*, 1: 31.
6. Aristotle, *De Anima*, II, 4 (415b 8-12).
7. Aristotle, *De Anima*, III, 4 (429b 30 - 430a 1).
8. Aristotle, *De Anima*, II, 2 (413b 2-5).
9. Aristotle, *De Anima*, II, 9 (421a 20-26).
10. Cf. *Summa theol.*, I, q. 85, a. 7.
11. St. Augustine, *De Genesi ad litteram*, I, 2 (PL 34: 263).
12. Aristotle, *De Generatione et corruptione*, II, 9 (334b 31 - 335a 35)
13. Avicenna, *Metaph.*, Tr. IX, cap. 4; ed. Franciscan Institute, St. Bonaventure, N.Y., 1948, pp. 297-305.
14. Anaxagoras (c. 500 B.C. - c. 428 B.C.) A pre-Socratic philosopher who posited a spiritual or intellectual principle, mind, to account for motion in the universe. Cf. Aristotle, *De Anima*, I, 2 (405a 14-17); also Aristotle, *Metaphysics*, I, 4 (985a 18).
15. St. Augustine, *The City of God*, XVIII, 41 (PL 41: 601)
16. Aristotle, *Physics*, VIII, 6 (259b 31 - 260a 10); *Metaphysics*, XII, 8 (1073a 11-37) Cf. St. Thomas Aquinas, *De Substantiis separatis*, II, 9; ed. Lescoe, 1962, p. 25.

17. Origen, *Peri Archon,* I, 7 (PG 11: 172).

18. St. John Damascene, *De Fide orthodoxa,* II, 6 (PG 94: 885).

19. St. Augustine, *De Genesi ad litteram,* II, 18 (PL 34: 279-280): *Enchiridion,* LVIII (PL 40: 260).

20. Aristotle, *De Anima,* II, 1 (413a 4-6); *Metaphysics,* XI, 2 (1060a 10 ff.); *Metaphysics,* XII, 8 (1073 a 11-37).

21. Avicenna, *Metaph.,* Tr. X, cap. 1, ed. St. Bonaventure, p. 327 ff.

22. St. John Damascene, *De Fide orthodoxa,* II, 4 (PG 94: 873).

23. St. Augustine, *Enchiridion,* XVIII (PL 40: 260).

24. Aristotle, *De Anima,* III, 4 (429a 15-16).

25. Plato, *Timaeus,* (52A - 53C)

26. Aristotle, *Metaphysics,* I, 9 (990b ff.); III, 2 (997b 5 - 12).

27. Avicenna, *Metaph.,* Tr. X, cap. 1, ed. St. Bonaventure, p. 327 ff.)

28. Moses Maimonides, *Dux seu director dubitantium aut per plexorum,* II, 5.

QUESTION NINE

Parallel texts: *In II Sent.,* dist. 1, q. 2, a. 4, ad 3; *Contra gent.,* II, 71; *Summa theol.,* I, q. 76, a. 6, 7; *De Spir. creat.,* a. 3; *In II De An.,* lect. 1; *In VIII Metaph.,* lect. 5; *Quodl.,* XII, q. 6, a. 9.

The ninth question that is asked about the soul is this: Whether a soul is united to corporeal matter through an intermediary?

And it seems that a soul is united to corporeal matter in this way.

(1) In the book *De Spiritu et Anima* [1] it is asserted that a soul has powers through which it is intermingled with its body. Now the powers of a soul are other than its existence. Therefore a soul is united to its body through an intermediary.

But an objector was arguing that a soul is united to a body by means of powers insofar as a soul is a mover, but not insofar as it is a form.

(2) On the contrary, a soul is the form of a body insofar as it is an act; but it is a mover insofar as it is a principle of operation. But a principle of operation is only such insofar as it is an act, because everything acts insofar as it is in act. Therefore a soul is both mover and form of its body under the same formality. Consequently one cannot draw a distinction between a soul as a mover of a body and a soul as its form.

(3) Furthermore, a soul, as its body's mover, is not united to the body accidentally; because, if it were, a substantial unit would not arise from the union of soul and body. Therefore a soul is united to its body substantially. But whatever is united to another substantially is united to it without an intermediary. Therefore a soul, insofar as it is a mover, is not united to its body through an intermediary.

(4) Furthermore, a soul is united to its body as a mover inasmuch as a soul is a principle of operation. Now the operations of a soul do not belong to the soul alone, but to the composite, as is said in Book I of the *De Anima.* [2] Consequently there is no intermediary between a soul and its body with respect to its operations. Therefore

a soul, insofar as it is a mover, is not united to its body through an intermediary.

(5) Furthermore, it seems that a soul is also united to its body through an intermediary inasmuch as it is form. For a form is not united to any matter whatsoever but to its proper matter. Now matter becomes proper to this or that particular form through those proper dispositions which are the proper accidents of a thing, as hot and dry are the proper accidents of fire. Consequently a form is united to matter through the intervention of its proper accidents. Now the proper accidents of beings which are alive are the powers of the soul. Therefore a soul as form is united to its body by means of its powers.

(6) Furthermore, an animal is that which moves itself. Now something which moves itself is divided into two parts, one which does the moving, the other of which is moved, as is demonstrated in Book IV of the *Physics*. [3] Now the part which does the moving is the soul. However the part which is moved cannot be unqualified matter, because whatever is purely in potency is not moved, as is said in Book V of the *Physics*. [4] Consequently heavy and light bodies, although they have movements within themselves, still do not move themselves because the only division within them is between matter and form, which cannot be moved. Therefore one must admit that an animal is divided into its soul and another part of which is composed of matter and form; and so it follows that a soul is united to corporeal matter through the mediation of some form.

(7) Furthermore, the proper matter of any form is included in its definition. Now the definition of a soul, inasmuch as it is a form, includes a physical, organic body, potentially possessing life, as is clearly stated in Book II of the *De Anima*. [5] Therefore a soul is united to a body of this sort as to its proper matter. But a physical, organic body, possessing life potentially cannot exist except through a form. Therefore a soul is united to matter through the mediation of a form which first perfects this matter.

(8) Furthermore, Chapter I of *Genesis* [6] says "God formed man from the slime of the earth and breathed into his face the breath of life." Now the breath of life is the soul. Therefore a formation took place in matter before matter's union with the soul, and consequently a soul is united to corporeal matter through the mediation of another form.

(9) Furthermore, forms are united to matter because of the fact that matter is in potency to them. Now matter is in potency to the forms of the elements before it is in potency to other forms. Consequently a soul and other forms are not united to matter except through the mediation of the forms of the elements.

(10) Furthermore, a human body, like the body of any animal,

is a compound body. But in a compound, the forms of the elements must retain their essential nature; otherwise there would be a corruption of the elements and not a compound. Consequently a soul is united to matter through the mediation of other forms.

(11) Furthermore, an intellectual soul is a form inasmuch as it is intellectual. Now to understand takes place through the mediation of other powers. Therefore a soul is united to its body as its form through the mediation of other powers.

(12) Furthermore, a soul is not united to just any kind of body, but to a body that is proportioned to the soul. Therefore there must be a proportion between a soul and its body, and by means of this proportion a soul is united to its body.

(13) Furthermore, every agent acts on a distant object through that which is closest to itself. Now the powers of a soul are extended to all parts of its body through the heart. Consequently, the heart is closer to the soul than the other parts of its body, and as a result a soul is united to its body through the mediation of the heart.

(14) Furthermore, the parts of a body are diverse and interrelated. Now a soul has simple essence. Therefore, since a form is proportioned to the matter that can be perfected by it, a soul apparently is united first to one part of its body, and, through the mediation of that part, to the other parts of its body.

(15) Furthermore, a soul is loftier than its body. Now the lower powers of a soul are connected with the higher powers of the body, for its intellect requires a body only because of the imagination and the sense powers, from which the intellect acquires species, Conversely, therefore, a body is united to its soul by means of those things which are highest and more simple within it, for instance, a spirit or a humor.

(16) Furthermore, that which when withdrawn results in the dissolution of the union between things that have been united is apparently a medium connecting them. Now when the spirit is withdrawn, when the natural heat is extinguished and the basic moisture is dried up, the union of a soul and its body is destroyed. Consequently spirit, heat and moisture are intermediaries between a soul and its body.

(17) Furthermore, just as a soul is united to a body, so this particular soul is united to this particular body. Now this body is this particular body because it possesses determinate dimensions. Consequently a soul is united to its body through the mediation of these determinate dimensions.

(18) Furthermore, things that are distinct cannot be joined except through a medium. Now a soul and a human body are apparently distinct in the highest degree, since one of them is incorporeal and simple and the other is corporeal and composed of many parts. Therefore a soul is not united to its body except through an intermediary.

(19) Furthermore, a human soul, in its intellectual nature, is like the separate substances which move the celestial bodies. But the same relation that exists between these two substances that impart movement would seem to obtain between the bodies which they move. Consequently it seems that a human body, which is moved by its soul, possesses within itself something that belongs to the nature of celestial bodies, and through the mediation of this, the soul is united to it.

On The Contrary,

The Philosopher states in Book VIII of the *Physics* [7] that form is united to matter without an intermediary. Now a soul is united to its body as its form. Therefore a soul is united to its body without an intermediary.

The Response:

Among all the elements that constitute a thing, the act of existence belongs to it most immediately and most intimately, as is said in the *Liber de Causis*. [8] Hence it is necessary, since matter possesses its act of existence through its form, that the form which gives existence to matter be understood to accrue to matter before the advent of any of the properties of matter, and that it belongs to matter more immediately than anything else. Now it is the nature of a substantial form to give to matter its existence without qualification. For the form is that through which a thing is the very thing that it is; through accidental forms a thing does not possess unqualified existence, but only qualified existence, for example, to exist as large, or colored, or something of this kind. Therefore, if there is a form which does not give unqualified existence to matter but which accrues to matter that is already actually existing through another form, then such a form will not be a substantial form.

From this it clearly follows that no intermediate substantial form can come between a substantial form and its matter, although some philosophers have postulated such an intermediate form. They assert that there is a hierarchy of diverse forms in matter which follows the hierarchy of genera, in which one genus ranks below another. Thus one might say that matter is an actual substance through one form, a body through another form, a living body through yet another form, and so on. But if one grant such a position, only the original form, which causes a substance actually to exist, would be a substantial form; whereas all the others would be accidental forms, because the substantial form is that which produces an entity, as I have already said. Consequently it is necessary to say that it is one and the same substantial form through which a thing is a substance and through which it is placed in its ultimate and most restricted species and in all the intermediate genera.

We are left then with the conclusion that the forms of natural things are like numbers, in which diversity of species arises with the addition or subtraction of a unit, as is said in Book VIII of the *Metaphysics*.[9] Hence the diversity of natural forms, through which matter in constituted in diverse species, must be understood to mean that one form bestows another perfection in addition to that conferred by another form; for instance, one form constitutes matter in corporeal existence only. Now this must be the lowest level of material forms, because of the fact that matter is in potency only to corporeal forms; for things which are incorporeal are immaterial, as I have shown in earlier questions. But another and more perfect form constitutes matter in corporeal existence and confers vital existence in addition; and yet another form confers both corporeal and vital existence on matter while giving it sensory existence as well; and so it is with other forms.

It must therefore be understood that even a more perfect form, to the extent that it constitutes matter in the perfection of a lower level of being, has to be considered, in composition with its matter, as material with respect to a higher perfection. And to carry the analysis further, this first composition, which is one of matter and form inasmuch as it is already constituted in corporeal existence, is matter with respect to the higher perfection, life. And it is for this reason that 'body' is the genus of a living body, and 'animated' or 'living' is its specific difference; for genus is derived from matter and specific difference from form. And so one and the same form, insofar as it constitutes matter in the actuality of a lower level of perfection, is in a sense intermediate between matter and itself, insofar as it constitutes matter in the actuality of a higher level of perfection. Now matter, understood as constituted in substantial existence according to the perfection of a lower level of being, can consequently be regarded as subject to accidents. For a substance, as constituted in that lower level of perfection, must have proper accidents which necessarily inhere in it. For example, because matter is constituted in corporeal existence through forms, the immediate consequence is that it has dimensions; by reason of these dimensions it is understood to be matter divisible into diverse parts, that so, through its diverse parts, it might be capable of acquiring diverse forms. Furthermore, from the fact that matter is now understood as constituted in some kind of substantial existence, one can consider matter as capable of acquiring accidents which in turn makes it a matter proper for the reception of a yet higher perfection. Now dispositions of this kind are understood as prior to the form, inasmuch as the form is induced into matter by an agent; although there are some accidents so proper to the form that they cannot be produced in matter except by the form itself. Hence such accidents are not understood as if they were dispositions existing in matter prior to the form, but rather the form is to be undestood as existing prior to them, as a cause is prior to its effect.

Therefore, since a soul is a substantial form because it constitutes a human being in a determinate species of substance, there is no other substantial form intermediate between a soul and prime matter; but it is the soul itself which perfects a human being according to diverse levels of perfection, so that he is a body, and a living body, and a rational animal.[10] But this point is to be noted with reference to matter inasmuch as it is regraded as receiving from the rational soul itself perfections of a lower level of being: for example, that it be a body, a living body, and an animal. Thus taken, matter must be understood in conjunction with its appropriate dispositions, so that it might be matter proper for the rational soul inasmuch as this soul confers on matter its ultimate perfection. Consequently the soul, inasmuch as it is a form which bestows existence, has no intermediary between itself and prime matter.

However, because the same form which gives existence to matter is also a principle of operation, for anything acts insofar as it is in act, it is necessary that a soul, just like any other form, be a principle of operation. Now one must note that corresponding to levels of forms in the order of existence, there are levels of forms with respect to their power of operating, since operations belong to something which actually exists. Consequently the higher a form is in its perfection of bestowing existence, the greater will be its power in operating. Hence more perfect forms have operations which are more numerous and more diverse than those of less perfect forms. Hence it is that in less perfect things a diversity of accidents is all that is needed for a diversity of operations; however, in things that are more perfect a diversity of parts is also needed, and the more perfect a form is, the more diversity is required. For we observe that fire has diverse operations because of its diverse accidents, for example, to move upward because of its lightness, to heat in virtue of its hotness, and so on; still each of these operations belongs to fire in virtue of any one of its parts. However, in living bodies, which possess higher forms, diverse operations are assigned to diverse parts; for example, in plants there are diverse operations for a root, a branch and a trunk. And the more perfect living bodies are, the greater must be the diversity of parts found in them because of their greater perfection. Thus, since a rational soul is the highest of material forms, we find in a human being the greatest

distinction of parts because of the diverse operations they must perform; and the soul gives to each of these parts that level of substantial
existence that corresponds to its operation. Evidence of this fact is
that when the soul departs, there remains neither flesh nor an eye
except in an equivocal sense.

But since the order of instruments must correspond to the order
of operations, one of the diverse operations which proceed from a soul
precedes another operation; thus one part of a body must be moved
to carry out its operation by means of another part. Hence it is that
a medium does intervene between a soul, inasmuch as it is a mover
and a principle of operation, and the whole extent of its body; because
the soul moves other parts of the body to perform their operations
through the medium of some part that it first moves; for example,
the heart is the intermediary through which a soul causes the body's
other members to perform their vital operations. On the other hand,
inasmuch as a soul gives existence directly to its body, it gives substantial and specific existence to every part of the body; and hence it is
that many authorities declare that a soul as form is united to its body
without an intermediary, but that soul as mover is united through
an intermediary. And this view is in line with the doctrine of Aristotle,
who teaches that a soul is the substantial form of its body.

However, some authorities, since they hold, following Plato's
view, that a soul is united to its body as one substance to another, find
it necessary to posit various media by which a soul might be united to
its body; because substances which are diverse and distinct cannot
coalesce unless there is something that brings them together. Consequently some of them asserted that a spirit and a humor were intermediaries between soul and body; other proposed light; still others, the
powers of the soul or something else of this sort.[11] However none of
these intermediaries is necessary if a soul is the form of its body, for
everything is one in the same way in which it is a being. Since then
a form gives existence to matter by its very nature, it is also united to its
proper matter by its very nature, and not by means of a bond of any sort.

Replies to the Opposing Arguments:

(1) The powers of a soul are the qualities by which it operates,
and consequently they are intermediaries that come between a soul
and its body inasmuch as a soul moves its body, but not inasmuch
as a soul gives the body its existence. It must, however, be understood
that the book entitled *De Spiritu et Anima* is not written by Augustine
and that its author holds the view that a soul is its own powers; as
a result, the objection has no point at all.

(2) Although a soul is a form inasmuch as it is act and also inasmuch as it is a mover, and consequently is a form and a mover under the same aspect, nevertheless its effect as a form is distinct from its effect as a mover. Because of this the distinction has no value.

(3) A substantial unit does not arise from the union of a mover and something moved merely from the fact that they are mover and moved; but from this mover that is a soul and this moved reality that is a body, there does arise a substantial unit because a soul is the form of its body.

(4) With reference to any operation of a soul which is attributed to the composite, there is no intermediary between a soul and any part of its body; rather there is one part through which a soul primarily performs that operation, and this part is an intermediary between a soul, taken as the principle of that operation, and all the other parts of the body which share in that operation.

(5) Accidental dispositions which make matter to be proper to a certain form are not direct intermediaries between form and matter, but rather between a form inasmuch as it confers the ultimate perfection and matter inasmuch as it is already informed by the perfection of a lower order. Now matter of itself is proper to the lowest grade of perfection, since matter of itself is in potency to substantial corporeal existence. And it needs no disposition to receive this perfection, but once it is assumed that matter has this initial perfection, dispositions are required for further perfections. Furthermore, it must be noted that the powers of a soul are its proper accidents and do not exist apart from it. Hence, considered as powers of the soul, they do not have the character of dispositions toward the soul, but only inasmuch as the powers of a lower part of a soul are said to be dispositions to a higher part, as, for example, a power of the nutritive soul is a disposition toward the sensitive soul, as can be understood from what has already been said.

(6) This argument comes to the conclusion that a soul, or better an animal, is divided into two parts, one of which is a movable body and the other a mover; and this is true. However, one must understand that a soul moves its body by means of knowledge and appetite. Now there are two kinds of knowledge and appetite in human beings. One of these belongs to the soul alone and does not take place through a bodily organ; this kind of knowledge belongs the soul's intellective part. The other kind of knowledge and appetite belongs to the composite and to the sensitive part of the soul. Now that knowledge and appetite which belong to the intellective part of the soul do not move the body except through the mediation of the knowledge and appetite belonging to its sensitive part. The reason for this is that since movement is directed towards what is singular, universal knowledge, which

belongs to the intellect, does not impart movement unless there occurs a particular motion, that which is grasped by the sense. Therefore, when a human being or an animal is divided into a part which causes motion and a part which is moved, the division is not strictly between a soul on one side and a body on the other, but rather between one part of an animated body and its soul. For that part of an animated body to which the operation of knowing and desiring belongs moves the whole body.

However, even if one supposes that the intellective part directly causes motion, so that in a human being the part which causes movement would be the soul alone, an answer based on the assertions just made will still be valid. For a human soul will be a mover through that which is loftiest within it, namely, through its intellective part. And what is moved will not be prime matter, pure and simple, but prime matter inasmuch as it has been constituted in corporeal existence of this specific kind through no other form than this same soul. Consequently there will be no necessity for positing an intermediate substantial form between a soul and prime mattter.

But there are in an animal movements that do not result from knowledge and appetite: that is, the movement of the heart and also those of growth and nutrition, which take place throughout the body. (These latter movements are found in plants as well as in animals.) With respect to movements of this kind we must say that the soul gives an animal not only those operations that properly belong to it as animal soul, but also the perfections of lower forms—this point is clear from what we have said above. For this reason, the soul is the principle of natural movements in the animal body just as lower forms are the principles of such movements in natural bodies. Hence the Philosopher says, in Book II of the *De Anima,*[12] that a soul belongs by nature to a body of such and such a kind, and because of this the operations of a soul are divided into animal operations and natural operations. Those operations are called animal operations which proceed from a soul with respect to what is proper to itself, but those operations are called natural which proceed from the soul insofar as it produces an effect proper to lower natural forms.

In consequence of this, therefore, one must say that just as fire, through its natural form, has a natural movement by which it tends upward, so also that part of an animated body in which is found the first movement which does not result from knowledge possesses this movement naturally through its soul. For just as fire naturally moves upwards, so also blood naturally moves toward its proper and determinate places. And in similar fashion a heart moves by its own proper motion, although the dissolution of spirits brought about by the blood cooperates in this movement, for by means of this dissolution the heart expands and contracts, as Aristotle states in the text where he treats of inhalation and exhalation.[13] Consequently, therefore, the first part of an animated body in which this kind of movement is verified is not a self-mover but it rather moved naturally in the way that fire is. However, this part moves the animal; and consequently the animal as a whole is a self-mover since one part of it is a mover and another part is moved.

(7) A physical, organic body is related to a soul just as matter is related to form; this is not to say that it is this kind of body because of another form, but rather that the body is the kind it is because of its soul, as we pointed out earlier.

(8) A similar answer must be given to the eighth argument; for the action spoken of in the text of *Genesis,* that "God formed man from the slime of the earth" is not prior in time to the subsequent action, "and He breathed into his face the breath of life," but has a priority of nature only.

(9) Matter is in potency to forms following a certain order, not in the sense that matter receives diverse substantial forms one after another, but rather in the sense that what is specifically proper to a higher form is not received by matter except through the mediation of that which is specifically proper to a lower form, as we have explained. It is in this way that one must understand that matter receives other forms through the mediation of the forms of the elements.

(10) The forms of the elements do not actually exist in a compound according to their essence, although Avicenna [14] holds this; for they could not exist in the same particle of matter. If, however, they did exist in diverse parts, there would not be a true compound: one, that is, which extends throughout the entire compounded body. There would be instead a mixture, which only appears to the senses to be a compound. And it is absurd to say, as Averroes does,[15] that the forms of the elements are capable of being to a greater or lesser degree the forms that they are; for they are substantial forms, and these cannot exist at a greater or lesser degree of perfection. Nor is there anything which is intermediate between a substance and an accident, as Averroes also supposed. Furthermore, one must not say that the forms of the elements are wholly corrupted, but rather that they continue to exist virtually in the compound, as Aristotle [6] teaches. They remain in the compound, that is, to the extent that their proper accidents somehow continue to exist therein, and the power of the elements is retained in these proper accidents.

(11) Although a soul is the form of its body in accordance with its essence as an intellective soul, it is not the form of its body with respect to its intellectual operation.

(12) The proportion which exists between a soul and its body

resides in the very realities that are related; consequently it is not necessary that there be a thing which is an intermediary between a soul and its body.

(13) The heart is the primary instrument through which a soul moves the other parts of its body, and consequently a soul as mover is united to other parts of its body through the mediation of the heart; although a soul as form is united essentially and directly to each part of its body.

(14) Although a soul is in essence a simple form, still it has a multiplicity of powers insofar as it is the principle of diverse operations. Now a form actuates matter not only to make it exist, but also to enable it to operate. Hence a soul, although it is a single form, must actuate the parts of its body in a diversity of ways, and actuate each part of it in a way appropriate to its operation. Because of this there must also be an order among the parts of the body that parallels the order of operations, as we have said. However, this order is grounded in the relation of a body to its soul insofar as the soul is a mover.

(15) The lower powers of a soul can be understood as connected with the higher powers of its body in relation to operation, to the extent, that is, that the higher powers depend on the operation of the lower powers which are exercised through the body. And in the same way, a body, through its higher parts, is connected to its soul with respect to operation and movement.

(16) Just as a form does not accrue to matter unless the matter is made to be proper to this form through the requisite dispositions, so also, if the proper dispositions cease to exist, a form cannot remain in the matter. And this is the way in which the union of a soul to is body is dissolved; that is, when the natural heat and moisture and other factors of this kind, through which a body is made ready to acquire a soul, are destroyed. Consequently things of this sort mediate between a soul and its body as dispositions; how this takes place has already been explained.

(17) Dimensions cannot be understood to belong to matter unless matter be understood as constituted in its substantial existence as a body by a substantial form; and in a human being this does not come about through any other form than the soul, as we have said. Hence dimensions of this kind are not understood as existing in matter prior to any union with the soul but only as being prior to the higher grades of perfection, as we explained above.

(18) A soul and its body are not different as things of diverse genera or species are, since neither of them belongs to a genus or a species, but only that which is composed of them does, as we explained in earlier questions. But a soul is essentially the form of its body and gives existence to it; hence a soul is united to its body substantially and directly.

(19) A human body shares something that belongs also to a celestial body, not in the sense that something which belongs to a celestial body, such as light, serves as an intermediary between a soul and its body, but in the sense that a human body is constituted in a balanced proportion of parts, far removed from contrariety, as we explained in earlier questions.

Notes to Question Nine

1. Alcherius Claravallensis (Pseudo-Augustine), *Liber de spiritu et anima,* XX (PL 40: 794).
2. Aristotle, *De Anima,* I, 4 (408b 13-15).
3. Aristotle, *Physics,* VIII, 4 (255a 10-15); VIII, 5 (257b 13-14).
4. Aristotle, *Physics,* V, 1 (225a 20-23).
5. Aristotle, *De Anima,* II, 1 (412a 27-28).
6. *Genesis,* 2: 7.
7. Aristotle, *Metaphysics,* VIII, 6 (1045b 17-22).
8. *Liber de Causis,* IV; ed. Bardenhewer, p. 166, 19-20.
9. Aristotle, *Metaphysics,* VIII, 3 (1043b 33 - 1044a 2).
10. Thomas Aquinas rejects the doctrine of the plurality of forms, commonly held in his day. He insists that there is only one substantial form for a material, composite being. In holding this position, he denies that there is a *forma corporeitatis,* by which the body is made to be a body, a body which is then made to be a living body through another substantial form, the soul.
11. Among the various thinkers that St. Thomas has in mind at this time are Avicebron, Alfredus Anglicus, Hugo of St. Victor, St. Bonaventure and others whose names are not known to us.
12. Aristotle, *De Anima,* II, 2 (414a 25-28).
13. Aristotle, *De Partibus animalium,* I, 1 (642a 31 - b 8).
14. Avicenna, *In De Generatione,* Lib. I, T.C. 90 (V.370K), Venetiis, 1562-1576.
15. Averroes, *De Coelo,* III, T.C. 67. ed Venetiis, 1560, fol. 231-232.
16. Aristotle, *De Generatione et corruptione* (334b 8-30).

QUESTION TEN

Parallel texts: *In I Sent.*, dist. 8, q. 5, a. 3; *Contra gent.*, II, 72; *Summa theol.*, I, q. 76, a. 8; *De Spir. creat.*, a. 4; *In I De An.*, lect. 14.

The tenth question that is asked about the soul is this: Whether a soul exists in the whole body and in each of its parts? And it seems that it does not.

(1) A soul is in its body as a perfection in that which is perfectible. Now that which is capable of being perfected by a soul is an organic body; for a soul is the act of a physical, organic body, potentially possessing life, as is stated in Book II of the *De Anima*.[1] Consequently a soul exists only in an organic body. Now not every part of an organic body is an organic body. Therefore a soul is not in each part of its body.

(2) Furthermore, a form is proportioned to its matter. Now a soul, inasmuch as it is the form of its body, is a simple essence. Consequently matter that is made up of different parts is not proportioned to a soul. But the diverse parts of a body, either that of a human being or of an animal, are similar to matter that is made up of different parts, in that they exhibit very great diversity when compared to one another. Therefore a soul is not the form of each part of its body, and consequently a soul is not in each part of its body.

(3) Furthermore, no part of a whole exists outside of the whole. Consequently, if a soul as a whole is in each part of its body, no part of a soul exists outside that part of the body. Therefore it is impossible that a soul be wholly in each part of its body.

(4) Furthermore, the Philosopher says in his book *De Causa Motus Animalium*,[2] "One must consider an animal to correspond to a state that is well governed by laws. For when order has once been established in a state, there is no need for an independent monarch who would have to control all the individual things that are done; but each does whatever is assigned to his authority and one thing is done after another in its customary order. Now in animals the same order occurs because of nature; and because each part is by nature so constituted as to perform its own proper task, there is no need for a soul to be in each part, but the soul exists in a fundamental part of the body; the other

parts live because they are so structured by nature; moreover they perform their proper tasks because of nature." Therefore the soul is not in each part of its body but only in one part.

(5) Furthermore, the Philosopher says, in Book VIII of the *Physics,*[3] that the mover of the heaven must be either in the center or in a section of the circumference, since these two are the principles of circular motion. And he proves that the mover cannot be at the center but is rather at the circumference, because the closer things are to the circumference, and the farther they are from the center, the swifter is their motion. Therefore, for a similar reason, it is necessary that the movement of a soul be in that part of an animal in which motion is most perceptible. Now this is the heart. Consequently a soul is only in the heart.

(6) Furthermore, the Philosopher says, in his book *De Juventute et Senectute,*[4] that plants possess a nutritive principle located midway between their upper and lower parts. Now just as plants have higher and lower parts, so animals have parts that are higher and lower, on the right side and on the left, to the front and to the rear. Consequently the principle of life, which is the soul, must be located at a place midway among these various parts. This place is the heart. Therefore a soul is only in the heart.

(7) Furthermore, any form which is in a whole and in every part of the whole is predicated of the whole and of every one of its parts, as is clearly true of the form of fire, for each part of fire is fire. However, each part of an animal is not an animal. Therefore a soul is not in each part of its body.

(8) Furthermore, the operation of understanding belongs to some part of the soul. But the operation of understanding is not in any part of the body. Therefore the soul is not wholly in each part of its body.

(9) Furthermore, the Philosopher says, in Book II of the *De Anima,*[5] that a part of the soul is related to a part of the body just as the soul is related to the body. Consequently, if a soul is in the whole body, it will not be present as a whole in each part of its body but only a part of it will be.

But an objector was arguing that the Philosopher was speaking about the soul and its parts insofar as the soul is a mover and not insofar as it is a form.

(10) On the contrary, the Philosopher says in the same work[6] that if an eye were an animal, sight would be its soul. But a soul is the form of an animal. Therefore a part of the soul is in the body as its form, and not merely as its mover.

(11) Furthermore, a soul is the principle of life in an animal. Therefore, if a soul were in each part of its body, then each part of the body would acquire life directly from the soul; and consequently

one part would not depend upon another part for its life. Now this is obviously false, since the other parts of the body depend upon the heart in order to live.

(12) Furthermore, a soul is accidentally moved when the body in which that soul exists moves; and in like fashion a soul is accidentally at rest when the body in which it exists is at rest. Now it can happen that while one part of the body is at rest, another part moves. Consequently, if a soul is in each part of its body, it will necessarily follow that a soul is at one and the same time moving and at rest, and this is apparently impossible.

(13) Furthermore, all the powers of a soul are grounded in the essence of the soul. Therefore, if the essence of a soul were in each part of its body, it would be necessary that each power of a soul be in each part of its body. Now this is obviously false, for the power of hearing is not in the eye, but only in the ear, and the same is true of the other powers.

(14) Furthermore, every thing which exists in another is in the other in accordance with the mode of that in which it is. Therefore, if a soul is in a body, it must be in it in accordance with the mode of a body. But the mode of a body is such that where one part is, another part cannot be. Consequently where one part of a soul is present, another part does not exist; and consequently a soul is not wholly in each part of its body.

(15) Furthermore, some imperfect animals, which are called ringed, continue to live after they have been cut in pieces; because in these animals the soul remains in each part after the cutting has taken place. But a human being and other perfect animals do not continue to live after having been cut into pieces. Consequently in them the soul does not exist in each part of the body.

(16) Furthermore, just as a human being or an animal is a whole made up of diverse parts, so is a house. Now the form of a house is not in each part of a house but in the whole house. Consequently a soul also, which is the animal's form, is not wholly in each part of its body but only in the whole body.

(17) Furthermore, a soul gives existence to its body inasmuch as it is the body's form. Now a soul is form by its very essence, which is simple. Therefore it gives existence to its body in accordance with its simple essence. But from one principle there proceeds only something that is one by nature. Therefore, if a soul is in each part of its body as a form, it follow that it gives the exact same existence to each part of its body.

(18) Furthermore, a form is more closely united to its matter than a thing located in a place is united to its place. But a thing located in one place cannot at the same time be located in diverse places,

not even a spiritual substance can do this. For the masters of theology do not admit that an angel exists in diverse places at one and the same time. Consequently neither can a soul exists in the diverse parts of its body.

On The Contrary,

Augustine says in Book VI of his *De Trinitate* [7] that a soul is wholly in the whole body and wholly in each part of it.

(2) Furthermore, a soul does not give existence to its body except insofar as it is united to it. Now a soul gives existence to the whole body and to every part of it. Therefore a soul is in the whole body and in each of its parts.

(3) Furthermore, a soul operates only where it is. Now the operations of a soul can be observed in every part of its body. Therefore a soul exists in each part of its body.

The Response:

The true answer to this question depends on our response to the preceding question. For there it was proved that a soul, inasmuch as it is the form of its body, is not united to the whole body through the mediation of one of the body's parts, but is directly united to the whole body. For the soul is the form of the entire body and of each of its parts: this must be asserted. For since the body of a human being or of any other animal is a natural whole, it will be called one because it has one form; and by this one form it is completed in a way far different from the mere aggregation or assembling of parts that is found in a house and in other artifacts of this kinds. Hence it is necessary that each part of a human being and of an animal receive its existence and specific nature from its soul as from its essential form.

Hence the Philosopher [8] states that when a soul departs, neither eye, nor flesh, nor any other part of the body remains except in an equivocal sense. Now it is impossible that something acquire its existence and specific nature from something separate from it as if this latter were its form. (This position would be similar to that of Plato, who asserted that sensible things acquire their existence and specific nature through their participation in separate forms.) But the form must be something that belongs to the thing to which it gives existence, for form and matter are the intrinsic principles which constitute the essence of a thing. If, then, a soul as form gives existence and specific nature to each part of its body, as Aristotle maintains, it must exist in each part of its body; for the same reason a soul is said to exist in the whole body because it is the form of the whole. Hence, if it is the form of any part, it must be in every part and not only in the whole nor in one part only. The very definition of 'soul' proves this point; for soul is "the act of an organic body." Now an organic body is made up of diverse organs. Therefore, if a soul were in only one part as a form, it would not be the act of an organic body, but the act of only one organ, for example, of the heart or of some other organ; and the other parts of the body would be actuated by other forms. And thus the whole body would not be a natural unit, but merely something made up of parts. Therefore it follows that a soul is in the whole body and in each of its parts.

But since there is the further question as to whether a soul is totally in the whole body or totally in each of its parts, we must consider the precise meaning of this question. Now totality can be attributed to a form in three ways, corresponding to the three ways in which a things can be said to have parts. For a things has parts in one way as a result of the division of quantity: that is, as a number or a magnitude is divided. Now the totality of a number or of a magnitude is not attributed to a single form except perhaps by accident; for example, in forms which are accidentally divided through the division of a continuum, as when whiteness is divided when a surface is divided. Secondly, something can be called a whole in relation to the essential parts of its specific nature, as matter and form are called parts of a composite, and genus and difference are in a sense called the parts of a species. This mode of totality is attributed even to essences which are simple by reason of their perfection, because just as composites possess a complete species through the conjunction of their essential principles, so also simple substances and simple forms possess a complete species in virtue of themselves. Thirdly, something is called a whole in relation to the divisions of its capability or power, and these parts are named in accordance with a division of operations.

We may therefore consider a form which is divided by the division of a continuum, and ask whether such a form is wholly in each part of its body: whether, for example, whiteness is wholly in each part of the surface. If 'whole' is thus understood in relation to quantitative parts — and this is a totality that in fact belongs to whiteness accidentally — then the form is not wholly in each part, but is wholly in the whole and partially in each part. However, if we inquire about the kind of totality which belongs to a species, then the form is wholly in each part, for one part is just as white as the whole is. However, it is true that considered in terms of its power, a form in not wholly in each part. For the whiteness which exists in one part of a surface cannot reflect as much light as the whiteness which exists in the entire surface, just as the heat of a small fire cannot produce so much warmth as the heat of a large fire.

Let us assume for the moment that there is only one soul in a human body (for this question will be taken up later on): then this soul is not divided by the division of quantity that belongs to number. It is also clear that this soul is not divided as a continuum is divided; this is especially true of the souls of complete animals, which do not continue to live after being cut into pieces. The same would not perhaps be true of worm-like animals, which possess one soul in act and several in potency, as the Philosopher teaches.[9] Hence it follows that in speaking of the soul of a human being and of any complete animal, the term 'totality' can be used only in reference to the perfection of the species and in reference to power or capability. Therefore we declare that since the fullness of specific nature belongs to a soul by its own essence, and since a soul by its own essence is the form of its body, and since as form of its body it is in every part of its body, as we have shown, it follows that the whole soul is in every part of its body according to the fullness of its specific perfection.

However, if 'totality' is used in reference to capability and power, then in this sense a soul is not wholly in every part of its body, nor even totally in the whole body if we are discussing the soul of a human being. For it has been established in earlier questions that a human soul, because it transcends the capacity of its body, possesses the power of exercising some operations without the cooperation of the body, for example, to understand and to will. Hence the intellect and the will are not the acts of any bodily organ. However, in reference to those other operations which a soul carries out through bodily organs, its whole capability, its power, is in the whole body but not in each part of the body, because diverse parts of the body are fitted to diverse operations of the soul. Hence a soul is in a particular part of its body according to that power only which is directed towards the operations which the soul carries on through that part of its body.

Replies to the Opposing Arguments:

(1) Since matter exists for the sake of form, whereas a form is ordered to its proper operation, the matter of any form must be such as is appropriate to the operation of that form; for example, the matter of a saw must be iron-like because such matter, on account of its hardness, it suitable for sawing. Therefore, since a soul, because of the fullness of its powers, is able to perform diverse operations, it is necessary that a soul's matter be a body made up of parts that are fitted to the diverse operations of the soul, and these parts are called organs.

Because of this the entire body to which a soul is primarily related as form is an organ; but its parts exist for the sake of the whole. Consequently a part of a body is not related to its soul as that which the soul essentially and primarily perfects, but inasmuch as it is something which is ordered to the whole. Hence it is not necessary that each part of a body be an organic body, even though the soul is its form.

(2) Since matter exists for the sake of form, a form gives being and specific nature to matter in a way that is appropriate to the form's operation. And a body that can be perfected by its soul requires a diversity of parts so that it might be fit for the diverse operations of that soul. Consequently, although the soul is one and simple in essence, it perfects the parts of its body in diverse ways.

(3) Since a soul is in one part of its body in the way just explained, nothing belonging to a soul is outside the soul which is in this part of its body. But it does not follow that nothing belonging to the soul is outside this part of the body, but that nothing belonging to the soul is outside of the entire body; and it is the entire body that the soul primarily perfects.

(4) In the text cited the Philosopher is speaking of a soul's motive power. For the principle of a body's movement is in one part of the body, namely, in the heart; and by means of this part it moves the entire body. This is clear from the example he cites about a ruler.

(5) So far as its substance is concerned, the mover of the heaven is not confined to a particular place. But what the Philosopher wishes to point out is where the mover is, insofar as it is a principle of motion. From this point of view, as principle of motion, the soul is in the heart.

(6) Even in plants a soul is said to occupy a position that is midway between what is above and what is below, insofar as a soul is the principle of various operations; the same thing is true of animals.

(7) It does not follow that each part of an animal is an animal as each part of a fire is fire; because all the operations of fire are verified in each part of the fire, but not all the operations of an animal are verified in each of its parts; this is especially true of complete animals.

(8) This argument concludes that a soul, according to its powers of operating, is not wholly in each of the parts of its body; and we have said that this is true.

(9) The Philosopher here understands 'parts of the soul' not in reference to the soul's essence, but in reference to its power; and hence he says that just as a soul is in the whole body, so also a part of a soul is in a part of its body. For just as the whole organic body is constituted in order to assist those operations of the soul which are carried out through it, so also a single organ is so constituted that it may assist in a particular operation.

(10) A power of a soul is grounded in its essence, and consequently

the essence of a soul is present wherever a power of a soul is. Therefore the Philosopher's statement that if the eye of an animal were an animal, sight would be its soul is not to be understood as referring to a power of a soul apart from the soul's essence. In the same way the sensible soul is said to be the form of the entire body through its essence, but not through its sensitive power.

(11) A soul operates on the other parts of its body through one part that it activates first of all. Now the body is disposed in such a way that it is made fit for existence through the action of its soul, which is the efficient cause of the body, as Aristotle teaches in Book II of the *De Anima.*[10] It is necessary that the disposition of the other parts, according to which they can be perfected by the soul, should depend upon a single primary part, namely, the heart; and to this extent the life of the other parts of the body does depend on the heart, because once any part loses its requisite disposition, the soul is no longer united to it as form.

(12) It is only by accident that a soul moves or is at rest when its body moves or is at rest. Now no difficulty arises if by accident the same thing moves and is at rest at the same time; just as no difficulty arises because something is moved accidentally by contrary motions, for example, if someone on a ship is carried in a direction that is contrary to the direction of the ship.

(13) Although all the powers of a soul are grounded in the essence of a soul, nevertheless each part of its body receives the soul in a way that is appropriate to that part. Consequently the soul is in diverse parts through diverse powers, and it is not necessary that the soul be in each part through all of its powers.

(14) When something is said to be in another according to the mode of that in which it is, this is to be understood as referring to the mode of the recipient's capacity, not to its nature. For it is not necessary that something which is in another possess the nature and the properties of that in which it is, but rather that it be received in the other according to the other's capacity. For it is obvious that water does not have the nature of a water jug. Neither then is it necessary that a soul possess the nature of a body so that where one of its parts is another part cannot be.

(15) Worms continue to live after being cut into pieces not merely because their soul is in each part of the body, but because the soul of such animals, since it is imperfect and capable of a limited number of actions, requires a limited diversity of parts; and this diversity is found in the living, severed part. Hence, since this part retains the disposition by means of which the entire body can be perfected by its soul, the soul remains in it; however, this is not so in higher animals.

(16) The form of a house, like other artificial forms, is an accidental

form. Hence it does not give existence and specific nature to the whole house and to each of its parts; nor is the whole a unit without qualification, but rather is one as an aggregate is one. However, a soul is the substantial form of its body and it gives existence and specific nature to the whole body and to its parts; and the whole constituted from these parts is one without qualification. Hence the two instances are not the same.

(17) Although a soul is one and simple in essence, it still possesses powers that are ordered to diverse operations; and inasmuch as a soul is the form of its body through its essence, it naturally confers a specific kind of existence on that which can be perfected by it. Now because attributes which occur naturally are for an end, the soul must establish in its body a diversity of parts that are appropriate to diverse operations. And it is true that because the reason for diversity of this kind is derived from the end and not only from the form, it is easier to see in the constitution of living beings that nature operates for the sake of an end than it is to see this in other natural things, in which a single form perfects in a uniform way that which is capable of being perfected by it.

(18) The simplicity of a soul and an angel is not to be conceived in the same way as that of a point, which has a determinate location in a continuum, and thus, because it is simple in this way, cannot at one and the same time be in diverse parts of a continuum. But an angel and a soul are said to be simple because they are entirely without quantity; and consequently they cannot come into contact with a continuum except by applying their power to it. Hence the whole with which an angel is in contact through its power, but of which it is not the form, is but a single place in relation to an angel; but such a whole is related to a soul, which is united to it as form, as one body that can be perfected. And just as an angel is wholly in each part of its place, so also a soul is wholly in each part of that body which can be perfected by it.

Notes to Question Ten

1. Aristotle, *De Anima*, II, 1 (412a 27-28).
2. Aristotle, *De Motu animalium*, X (703a 30 - b 2).
3. Aristotle, *Physics*, VIII, 10 (267b 6-9).
4. Aristotle, *De Juventute et senectute*, II (468a 20-28).
5. Aristotle, *De Anima*, II, 1 (412b 17-25).
6. Aristotle, *De Anima*, II, 1 (412b 18-19).
7. St. Augustine, *De Trinitate*, VI, 6 (PL 42: 929).
8. Aristotle, *De Anima*, II, 1 (412b 17-25).
9. Aristotle, *De Anima*, II, 2 (413b 16-21).
10. Aristotle, *De Anima*, II, 4 (415b 8-12).

QUESTION ELEVEN

Parallel texts: *Quodl.* XI, q. 5, a. 1; *Contra gent.,* II, 58; *De Pot.,* q. 3, a. 9, ad 9; *Summa theol.,* I, q. 76, a. 3; *De Spir. creat.,* a. 3; *De Anima,* q. 9; *Compend. theol.,* 90-92.

The eleventh question that is asked about the soul is this: Whether the rational, sensitive and nutritive soul in a human being is one substance. And it seems that it is not.

(1) For wherever a soul's act is, there also is the soul. Now in an embryo the act of the nutritive soul precedes the act of the sensitive soul; and the act of the sensitive soul precedes the act of the rational soul. Therefore, in the fetus the nutritive soul is prior to the sensitive soul, and the sensitive soul is prior to the rational soul; and thus they are not the same substance.

But an objector was arguing that the act of the nutritive soul and of the sensitive soul does not result from the soul which is in the embryo, but from a power whose existence in the embryo stems from the soul of the parent.

(2) On the contary, no finite agent acts through its own power except at a determinate distance, as is clear in forward motion. For when someone throws an object to a definite place, he throws in accordance with the mode of his power. But there are movements and operations of the soul in an embryo no matter how far away the father might be, and yet the father's power is finite. Consequently the operations of a soul are not in the embryo through the power of the father's soul.

(3) Futhermore, the Philosopher says, in his book *De Generatione Animalium,*[1] that an embryo is first an animal and then a human being. But an animal is that which has only a sensitive soul, whereas a human being exists because of a rational soul. Therefore a sensitive soul itself, and not only its power, is in the embryo prior to a rational soul.

(4) Furthermore, to live and to sense are operations which can proceed only from an intrinsic principle; they are, however, acts of a soul. Therefore, since an embryo first lives and senses before it has a rational soul, to live and to sense are not dependent upon the soul of the external parent but upon the soul which exists within the embryo.

(5) Furthermore, the Philosopher states, In Book II of his *De Anima*,[2] that a soul is the cause of a living body, not only as a form but also as an efficient and final cause. But it could not be the efficient cause of its body unless it were present to its body when the body is formed. Now a body is formed before the rational soul is infused. Consequently, before the infusion of the rational soul, there is a soul in the embryo and not merely a power of a soul.

But an objector was arguing that the formation of the body is caused, not by the soul that is in the embryo, but by the soul of the parent.

(6) On the contrary, living bodies move themselves by movements which are properly their own. But the generation of a living body is a proper motion, since its proper principle is the generative power. In this way, therefore, a living thing moves itself. But a self-mover is composed of something which produces movement and something which is moved, as is proved in Book VIII of the *Physics*.[3] Consequently the principle of generation that forms the living body is the soul that is in the embryo.

(7) Furthermore, it is evident that an embryo grows. Now growth is local motion, as is said in Book IV of the *Physics*.[4] Now since an animal moves itself locally, it will also move itself as it grows, and thus there must be in the embryo a principle of such a motion, and the embryo must not derive this motion from a soul extrinsic to it.

(8) Furthermore, the Philosopher says, in his book *De Generatione Animalium*,[5] that you cannot assert that there is no soul in the embryo. And first a nutritive soul exists in the embryo, afterward a sensitive soul.

But an objector was arguing that the Philosopher says this in the sense that the soul is in the embryo potentially but not actually.

(9) On the contrary, nothing acts except insofar as it is in act. Now there are in an embryo the actions of a soul. Consequently a soul is there in act, and so it follows that in the embryo there is more than one substance.

(10) Furthermore, it is impossible that one and the same thing be derived from an extrinsic and from an intrinsic source. But a rational soul issues from an extrinsic principle, while the nutritive and sensitive souls issue from an intrinsic principle, that is, from a principle existing in the semen, as is clear from what the Philosopher says in his book *De Generatione Animalium*.[6] Consequently in a human being the nutritive, sensitive and rational souls are not subtantially one and the same.

(11) Furthermore, it is impossible that what is a substance in one being be an accident in another being. Hence the Philosopher says, in Book VII of the *Metaphysics*,[7] that heat is not the substantial form

of fire, since it is an accident in other beings. But the sensitive soul is a substance in brute animals. Consequently it is not merely a power in a human being, since powers are properties and accidents of a soul.

(12) Furthermore, a human being is a nobler animal than any brute animal. But an animal is called an animal because of its sensitive soul; therefore the sensitive soul of a human being is nobler than that which belongs to brute animals. But in brute animals the sensitive soul is a substance and not merely a power of the soul. Therefore in a human being it is all the more a substance in its own right.

(13) Furthermore, it is impossible that one and the same thing be in its very substance both corruptible and incorruptible. But a rational soul is incorruptible, whereas sensitive souls and nutritive souls are corruptible. Therefore it is impossible that the rational, sensitive and nutritive souls be one and the same in substance.

But an objector was arguing that the sensitive soul in a human being is incorruptible.

(14) On the contrary, the corruptible and the incorruptible differ generically, as the Philosopher says in Book X of the *Metaphysics*.[8] But the sensitive soul in brutes is corruptible; consequently, if the sensitive soul in a human being is indeed incorruptible, the sensitive soul of a human being and that of a horse will not belong to the same genus. And hence, since an animal is called an animal because of its sensitive soul, a human being and a horse would not be in one and the same genus, 'animal,' and this is clearly false.

(15) Furthermore, it is impossible that one and the same thing be substantially rational and irrational, because a contradiction cannot be truly asserted of one and the same thing. But a sensitive soul and a nutritive soul are irrational. Therefore they cannot be substantially the same as a rational soul.

(16) Furthermore, a body is proportioned to its soul. But there are in the body diverse principles of the soul's operations, and these are called the principal members. Consequently there is not just one soul in a human being but several.

(17) Furthermore, the powers of a soul issue naturally from the soul's essence. Now only one thing comes naturally from one thing. Therefore, if there is only one soul in a human being, there could not issue from it both powers joined to organs and powers that are not so joined.

(18) Furthermore, genus is derived from matter; specific difference is derived from form. But the genus of a human being is 'animal,' whereas the specific difference is 'rational.' Therefore, since an animal is called animal because of the sensitive soul, apparently not only the body but also the sensitive soul is related to the rational soul as its matter. Therefore a rational soul and a sensitive soul are not one and the same substantially.

(19) Furthermore, a human being and a horse are alike in being animal. Now an animal is called an animal because of its sensitive soul; therefore a human being and a horse are alike in their sensitive souls. But the sensitive soul of a horse is not rational. Consequently neither is that of a human being.

(20) Furthermore, if the rational, sensitive and nutritive souls in a human being are substantially one and the same, it is necessary that in whatever part of the body one of them is, so is another. But this is false. For the nutritive soul is in the bones because they are nourished and grow, but the sensitive soul is not in the bones because they lack sensation. Therefore these souls are not substantially one and the same.

On The Contrary,

One can cite what is said in the book *De Ecclesiae Dogmatibus:*[9] "We do not say that there are two souls in a human being, as James and others assert, one an animal soul by which the body is animated and the other a rational soul which serves reason; but we declare that it is one and the same soul in a human being which both gives life to its body by being united to it and governs itself by its power or reason."

The Response:

There are diverse opinions on this question, not only among modern thinkers but also among the ancients. For Plato asserted that there were diverse souls in the body, and this conclusion did in fact follow from his principles. For Plato held that a soul is united to its body as a mover and not as a form, declaring that a soul is in its body as a sailor is in a ship.[10] But one must posit diverse movers where there is evidence of actions which are generically diverse. For example, on a ship one man steers and another man rows, and yet the fact that one of these men is not the other does not militate against the unity of the ship; because just as their actions are related to each other, so also the movers who are on the ship are related, one subordinated to the other. In like fashion it does not seem to militate against the unity of a human being or of an animal if in one body there are several souls as movers, subordinated to one another according to the hierarchy of the soul's operations.

But the conjunction of a mover with the body that it moves does not produce something that is essentially and unqualifiedly one. If then one accepts Plato's opinion, a human being would not be an essential and unqualified unity, nor would he be an animal; nor would there be generation and corruption in the absolute sense when a body acquires or loses its soul. Hence one must maintain that a soul is united to its body, not only as a mover, but as a form, and this is clear also from what was said in earlier questions.

But even if one accepts the fact that the soul is a form, it remains a consequence of Plato's principles that there are several souls in a human being and in an animal. For the Platonists maintained that universals are separate forms which are predicated of sensible realities because sensible things participate in them; for example, Socrates is called an animal because he participates in the idea of an animal, and is called a human being because he participates in the idea of a human being. Accordingly it follows that there is one essential form through which Socrates is called an animal and another form through which he is said to be a human being. Hence a further consequence is that the sensitive and the rational soul in a human being differ substantially.

But this position is untenable because, if various things are predicated of a given subject according to diverse forms, one of them is predicated of the other accidentally; for example, when Socrates is said to be white because of whiteness and musical because of music, 'musical' is predicated of 'whiteness' accidentally. Therefore, if Socrates is said to be a human being and an animal because of two distinct forms, it follows that this predication, "A human being is an animal," is accidental, and that a human being is not in truth what an animal is.

However, there can be an essential predication through diverse forms when these forms are mutually related, as when, for example, we say that something possessing a surface is colored; for color exists in the substance through the medium of the surface. But this mode of predication is not an essential one but rather the opposite when the predicate is not included in the definition of the subject. For 'surface' is included in the definition of 'color,' just as 'number' is included in the definition of 'even.' Now the sensitive soul in man is potential in relation to the rational soul. If then these two forms are diverse, and if there is essential predication between 'man' and 'animal' based on the relation between these two forms, it follows that 'animal' is not predicated essentially of 'man,' but rather 'man' is so predicated of 'animal.'

Another difficulty also follows from Plato's principles. For something unqualifiedly one does not arise from several things which exist in act unless there be something which unites them by binding them together in some manner. Therefore it follows that if Socrates were an animal and were rational because of diverse forms, then these two forms would need something that would make them one reality so that they might be united in the absolute sense. Now since it is impossible to assign such a cause of their unity, it will remain true that a human being will not be one except as an aggregate is one, for example, like a pile of stones, which is one in a qualified sense but is unqualifiedly many. And consequently it also follows that a human being will not be a being without qualification; for something is a being insofar as it is one.

Still another difficulty follows from Plato's principles. For since genus is a substantial predicate, it is necessary that the form on account of which an individual of a given substance receives its generic predication be its substantial form. Consequently it is necessary that the sensitive soul, on account of which Socrates is called an animal, be his substantial form; and as a result it is necessary that this soul give existence without qualification to its body and make it to be an entity. Therefore, if the rational soul is other than the sensitive soul in substance, it does not produce an individual entity nor does it give existence without qualification, but only existence of a certain kind, since it accrues to a thing which already subsists. Hence it will not be a substantial but an accidental form; and thus it will not give Socrates his specific nature, since species is also a substantial predicate.

We are therefore left with the conclusion that there is in a human being only one soul substantially, a soul which is rational, sensitive and nutritive. And this assertion is a consequence of what we have pointed out in earlier questions about the hierarchy of substantial forms, namely, that no substantial form is joined to matter through the medium of another substantial form, but rather a more perfect form gives to matter whatever a lower form gave it, and something more. Hence a rational soul gives to the human body whatever a nutritive soul gives to plants and whatever a sensitive soul gives to brute animals, and in addition something more. And therefore the soul in a human being is nutritive, sensitive and rational. Evidence of this truth is that when the operation of one power is unusually strong, another operation is hindered; and also that there is an overflowing of one power into another, something that would not happen unless all the powers were grounded in one and the same essence of the soul.

Replies to the Opposing Arguments:

(1) Granted that the substance of the soul which is in the human body be one only, different authorities have given diverse answers to this argument. For some say that in the embryo, there is no soul prior to the rational soul but only a power which is derived from the soul of the parent; and that from this power, which is called the formative

power, proceed those operations which appear in the embryo. Now this cannot be wholly true, because in the embryo there is perceptible not only the formation of the body, which could be attributed to the formative power, but also other operations, such as the operations of growth, sensation and the like, and these can be attributed only to a soul. Still this position could be defended if the active principle in the embryo of which we were just speaking were merely called a power of a soul, not a soul; because this principle is not yet fully a soul, just as an embryo is not fully an animal. But then the same uncertainty will remain.

For other authorities hold that although in an embryo the nutritive soul is prior to the sensitive soul, and the sensitive soul is prior to the rational soul, nevertheless there are not different souls. First the semen becomes actually a nutritive soul in virtue of an active principle which is in the semen; and this soul in the course of time is brought to a higher level of perfection through the generative process and itself becomes the sensitive soul; and this soul is further brought to a still greater perfection by an extrinsic principle and becomes a rational soul. But according to this position it follows that the substance of a rational soul is derived from an active principle which is in the semen, even though some perfections ultimately accrue to it from an extrinsic principle; and thus it follows that a rational soul is corporeal in its substance for what is circumscribed by a power that is in the semen cannot be incorporeal.

Consequently a different answer must be given, namely, that the generation of an animal is not merely a single and simple generation, but that many generations and corruptions follow each other; so it is said that an animal first of all has the form of semen, and secondly the form of blood, and so on until its generation is complete. And as a result, since corruption and generation do not take place without the loss and addition of a form, it is necessary that the less perfect form which was first present be lost and a more perfect form be induced; and that this process continue until the fetus possesses a fully developed form. And consequently it is said that the nutritive soul exists first, but that it is superseded in the process of generation, and that another soul takes its place, a soul that is not only nutritive but also sensitive; and this soul is superseded by yet another soul which at one and the same time is nutritive, sensitive and rational.

(2) The power in the semen which comes from the father is a power that is permanently intrinsic and does not proceed from an extrinsic source, as does the power of a mover which is in things that are thrown. Consequently, no matter how far away the father may be, the power which is in the semen operates. For the active power which is in the semen cannot be derived from the mother, even though

some teach this, because in generation a woman is not an active but rather a passive principle.

There is nevertheless a certain likeness between the two powers, as the objection states. For just as the power of a thrower, since it is finite, moves its object by local motion to a place that is a determinate distance away, so the power of the generator, through the movement of generation, moves the embryo to a determinate form.

(3) The power referred to has the nature of a soul, as has been said, and consequently an embryo can be called an animal because of this power.

(4-8) The fourth, fifth, sixth, seventh, and eighth objections are to be answered in the same way.

(9) Just as the soul is in act, but in incomplete act, in the embryo, so also the soul operates, but performs imperfect operations.

(10) Although the sensitive soul in brutes is derived from an intrinsic principle, in a human being the substance of that soul which is at one and the same time nutritive, sensitive and rational is derived from an extrinsic principle, as has already been said.

(11) The sensitive soul in a human being is not an accident but a substance, since it is substantially the same as the rational soul; however, a sensitive power is an accident in a human being just as it is in other animals.

(12) The sensitive soul is nobler in a human being than in other animals because in a human being it is not merely sensitive but also rational.

(13) The sensitive soul in a human being is incorruptible in substance since its substance is the substance of the rational soul; although it may be that its sensitive powers, because they are the acts of a body, do not remain after the soul's separation from the body, as some hold.

(14) If the sensitive soul which is in brutes and the sensitive soul which is in a human being were located by themselves in a genus or in a species, they would not belong to the same genus, unless perhaps one were to consider them in the logical order under some common intention. For what is in a genus or in a species in the proper sense is the composite, and the composite is corruptible in both instances.

(15) The sensitive soul in a human being is not an irrational soul, but is at one and the same time a sensitive and a rational soul. But it is true that some at least of the powers of the sensitive soul, which are irrational in themselves, nevertheless share in reason to the extent that they are subservient to reason. However, the powers of the nutritive soul are wholly irrational since they are not under the control of reason, as is clear from what the Philosopher says in Book I of the Ethics. [11]

(16) Although there are several principal members of the body in which the principles of various operations of the soul are manifested, nevertheless all of these depend upon the heart as the primary corporeal principle.

(17) From the human soul, insofar as it is united to its body, there issue powers united to organs: however, insofar as the soul by its power transcends the capacity of its body, there issue from it powers which are not united to organs.

(18) As is clear from preceding questions, matter receives, from one and the same form, diverse grades of perfection; and to the extent that matter is perfected by a lower grade of perfection, matter remains in potency to a higher degree of perfection. And consequently, inasmuch as a body is perfected in sensible being by the human soul, it still remain in potency with respect to further perfection. And for this reason 'animal,' which is the genus, is derived from matter; and 'rational,' which is the specific difference, is derived from form.

(19) Just as animal, precisely as animal, is neither rational nor irrational, but 'rational animal' is a human being, whereas 'irrational animal' is a brute; so also the sensitive soul precisely as sensitive is neither rational nor irrational; rather the sensitive soul in a human being is rational, whereas in brutes it is irrational.

(20) Although the sensitive soul and the nutritive soul are one and the same, still because of a diverse disposition of parts it is not necessary that wherever an operation of one soul is evident the operation of the other soul be apparent. For the same reason it also happens that not all the operations of the sensitive soul are carried out through one part, but sight takes place through the eye, hearing through the ears, and so on for the other operations.

Notes to Question Eleven

1. Aristotle, *De Generatione animalium*, II, 3 (736a 35 - b 5).
2. Aristotle, *De Anima*, II, 4 (415b 8-12).
3. Aristotle, *Physics*, VIII, 5 (257b 16-20).
4. Aristotle, *Physics*, IV, 4 (211a 14-17).
5. Aristotle, *De Generatione animalium*, II, 3 (736a 33-35).
6. Aristotle, *De Generatione animalium*, II, 3 (736b 21-30).
7. This idea, though not explicitly stated by Aristotle, is definitely implied in the following works: *De Generatione et corruptione*, II, 9 (335b 25-336a 14); *Physics*, I, 7 (190b 17-191a 5); I, 3 (186b 20-187a 10); IV, 9 (217a 25-217b 10); V. 1 (224b 1-10); V, 2 (225b 15-25); *Metaphysics*, IV, 4 (1007a 30 - 1007b).
8. Aristotle, *Metaphysics*, X, 10 (1058b 26-29).
9. Gennadius of Marseilles, *De Ecclesiasticis dogmatibus*, XV (PL 58: 984).
10. Plato, *Timaeus*, 69E - 70A; *Republic*, IX, 580D - 581C.
11. Aristotle, *Nicomachean Ethics*, I, 13 (1102b 30).

QUESTION TWELVE

Parallel texts: *In I Sent.*, dist. 3, q. 4, a. 2; *Quodl.*, VII, q. 2, a. 5; X, q. 3, a. 5; X, q. 3, a. 1; *Summa theol.*, I, q. 54, a. 3; q. 77, a. 1; q. 79, a. 1; *De Spir. creat.*, a. 11.

The twelfth question that is asked about the soul is this: Whether a soul is its own powers? And is seems that it is.

(1) For it is said in the book *De Spiritu et Anima*, "The soul has its own natural powers, and it is all of them; for its powers and forces are the same as itself. It has accidents, and is not its accidents; it is its powers, but it is not its virtues. For it is not its prudence, its temperance, its justice, its fortitude."[1] This text seems to state explicitly that the soul is its own powers.

(2) Furthermore, in the same book it is stated: "The soul is given various names because of its functions. For it is called soul while it lives and grows, sense while it senses, spirit while it knows, mind while it understands, reason while it makes distinctions, memory while it remembers, will while it wills. Now these activities do not differ in substance as they do in name; because they are all one and the same soul."[2] From this text the same conclusion can be reached as above.

(3) Furthermore, Bernard states, "I note three powers in the soul, memory, intelligence and will; and I regard these three as being the soul itself."[3] The same reasoning is also valid for the other powers of the soul. Therefore the soul is its powers.

(4) Furthermore, Augustine says, in Book IX of his *De Trinitate*,[4] that memory, intelligence and will are one life, one essence. But the essence meant is the essence of the soul. Therefore the powers of the soul are the same as its essence.

(5) Furthermore, no accident transcends its subject. But memory, intelligence and will transcend the soul. For the soul does not remember only itself, does not understand and will only itself, but also other things. Consequently these three powers are not accidents of the soul; therefore these powers are the same as the essence of the soul, and for the same reason so are the other powers.

(6) Furthermore, the image of the Trinity in the soul is conceived

by reference to these three powers. But a soul is an image of the Trinity through the soul's own reality and not merely with respect to its accidents. Therefore memory, intelligence and will are not accidents of the soul. Consequently they belong to its essence.

(7) Furthermore, an accident is that which can be present or absent without entailing the corruption of its subject. But the powers of a soul cannot be absent. Consequently they are not accidents of the soul, and so we have the same conclusion as in the previous argument.

(8) Furthermore, no accident is a principle of substantial difference, because a difference completes the definition of a thing, and the definition signifies what a thing is. But the powers of a soul are the principles of substantial differences; for a soul is called 'sensitive' because of the senses, and 'rational' because of reason. Consequently its powers are not accidents of a soul; but they are the soul itself, which is the form of its body, for form is the principle of substantial difference.

(9) Furthermore, a substantial form is more powerful than an accidental form. But an accidental form acts of itself and not through some intermediate power; consequently so does a substantial form. Therefore, since a soul is a substantial form, the powers by which it acts are nothing other than itself.

(10) Furthermore, the principle of being is the same as the principle of operating. Now a soul is of itself a principle of being, because by its very essence a soul is a form. Therefore its essence is a principle of operating. But a power is nothing other than a principle of operating. Therefore the essence of a soul is its power.

(11) Furthermore, insofar as the substance of a soul is in potency to intelligible objects, it is the possible intellect; but insofar as it is in act with respect to them, it is the agent intellect. But to be in act and to be in potency do not signify anything other than the very thing which is in potency and in act. Therefore the soul is the agent intellect and the possible intellect, and for the same reason the soul is its powers.

(12) Furthermore, the intellective soul is in potency to intelligible forms as prime matter is in potency to sensible forms. But prime matter is its own potency. Therefore the intellective soul is its own potency.

(13) Furthermore, the Philosopher, in his book *The Ethics,*[5] says that a human being is an intellect. But this is so only because of his soul. Therefore the soul is its intellect, and for the same reason the soul is its other powers.

(14) Furthermore, the Philosopher states, in Book II of the *De Anima*,[6] that a soul is first act in the way in which science is act. But science is the immediate principle of a second act, which is the act of thinking. Therefore the soul is the immediate principle of its operations. But an immediate principle is called a power. Consequently a soul is its powers.

(15) Furthermore, all parts of a whole are substantial parts, because a whole is made up of its parts. But the powers of a soul are its parts, as is clearly stated in Book II of the *De Anima*.[7] Therefore the powers of a soul are its substantial parts and are not accidents of a soul.

(16) Furthermore, a simple form cannot be a subject. But a soul is a simple form, as I have already shown. Therefore it cannot be the subject of accidents. Consequently the powers which are in a soul are not its accidents.

(17) Furthermore, if the powers of a soul are its accidents, they must issue from a soul's essence; for proper accidents are caused by the principles of a subject. But the essence of a soul, since it is simple, cannot be the cause of such a great diversity of accidents as that found in the powers of a soul. Therefore the powers of a soul are not its accidents. It follows, therefore, that the soul itself is its own powers.

On The Contrary,

Power is related to action as essence is related to being. Therefore, by an alteration of terms, potency and essence are related to each other as 'to be' is related 'to act.' But 'to be' and 'to act' are the same in God alone; therefore in God alone are potency and essence the same. Therefore the soul is not its own powers.

(2) Furthermore, no quality is a substance. But a natural potency is a species of quality, as is clear in the *Categories*.[8] Therefore the natural powers of a soul are not the very essence of a soul.

The Response:

There are diverse opinions with regard to this question. For there are those who say that the soul is its powers; but there are others who deny this, declaring that the powers of the soul are its properties. And to understand the reason for this disagreement, we should realize that a power is nothing other than a thing's principle of operation, whether this be action or passion. It is not of course a principle in the sense of the subject that acts or is acted upon, but is rather that in virtue of which an agent acts or a patient is acted upon. Thus the art of building is a power in the builder through which he builds a house; and heat is a power in fire which heats by means of it; and dryness is a power in wood because it enables wood to burn.

Therefore those who assert that the soul is its powers mean by this that the essence of the soul is the immediate principle of the soul's operations. They state that a human being understands, senses, and carries on other operations of this kind by means of the essence of the soul, and that the soul is given diverse names on account of the diversity of these operations. Thus the soul is called 'sense' insofar as it is the principle of sensing but 'intellect' inasmuch as it is the principle of understanding, and so for its other names; just as if we were to call the heat of a fire its 'liquefying' power, its 'warming' power, and its 'drying' power because fire performs all these operations.

Now this position cannot be upheld. First, with reference to active powers: everything acts inasmuch as it is actually that which it produces by its action. For fire warms, not insofar as it is something bright, but insofar as it is actually something hot. For this reason every agent produces something like itself. Hence we must arrive at an understanding of the principle by which some effect is produced from a consideration of that effect; for the two must be alike. (Hence it is stated in Book II of the *Physics* [9] that the form and the generator are specifically the same.)

Now when the effect which is produced does not belong to the substantial being of the agent, it is impossible that the principle by which the effect is produced be part of the agent's essence. This fact is seen most clearly in natural agents, which generate by changing matter to correspond to the form. This transformation takes place because matter is initially disposed to the form, and finally acquires this form because generation terminates in the replacment of one form by another. Hence, on the part of the agent, that which acts directly must be an accidental form that corresponds to the disposition of matter. But it is necessary that this accidental form act in virtue of the substantial form, as if it were its instrument; otherwise it would not induce a substantial form through its action. For this reason no principles of action are observable in the elements except active and passive qualities, but these act through the power of their substantial forms. And for this reason their action does not terminate only in accidental dispositions but in substantial forms. For in the production of artifacts too, the action of the artisan's tool terminates in the form that the artisan intended. But if there is any agent that by its action directly and immediately produces a substance, such an agent acts through its essence; and hence there will not be in it an active power distinct from its essence. We Christians say that God is such an agent, because by His creative action He produces the substances of things; and Avicenna makes this claim for his Agent Intelligence, from which, he says, substantial forms emanate into lower substances on this earth. [10]

Secondly, with reference to passive powers, it is clear that a passive power which is ordered to substantial act belongs to the genus of substance, and that passive power which is ordered to accidental act belongs to the genus of accident by reduction: as a principle, that is, and not as a complete species. The reason is that every genus is divided by potency and act: hence man in potency is in the genus of substance and white in potency is in the genus of quality. Now it is obvious that the powers of the soul, whether active or passive, are not predicated directly in relation to something substantial but in relation to something accidental: for example, to be actually understanding or to be actually sensing is not substantial being but rather accidental being, toward which the intellect and the senses are directed; and in like fashion to be large or small is accidental being to which the power of growth is ordered. The generative power and the nutritive power are indeed ordered toward producing or conserving a substance, but they do this through the transformation of matter. Hence this kind of action, like the other actions of natural agents is caused by a substance through the intermediacy of an accidental principle. Therefore it is obvious that the essence of a soul is not itself the immediate principle of a soul's operations, but rather it operates by the mediation of accidental principles. Hence the powers of a soul are not its very essence but are its properties.

This same conclusion can also be proved from the diversity of a soul's actions, which are generically diverse and cannot be reduced to a single immediate principle. For some of them are actions and others are passions, and they can be distinguished by other differences of this kind, which must be attributed to diverse principles. And so, since the essence of the soul is a single principle, it cannot be the immediate principle of all of its actions, but rather it must possess a number of diverse powers which correspond to the diversity of its actions. For a potency is so called with reference to an act, so that there must be a diversity of powers which correspond to the diversity of acts. This is why the Philosopher, in Book VI of the *Ethics*,[11] says that the scientific power, which deals with what is necessary, and the ratiocinative power, which treats of things that are contingent, are diverse powers because the necessary and the contingent differ generically.

Replies to the Opposing Arguments:

(1) Augustine is not the author of the book *De Spiritu et Anima;* but it is said to have been written by a Cistercian; nor do we need to be much concerened with what is said in that book. If, in spite of this, one takes the text seriously, one can say that the soul is its powers or its forces because they are its natural properties. Hence

in this same book it is asserted that all the powers of the soul are a single soul, the properties being diverse but the power one. This is like saying that the hot, the dry and the light are one fire.

(2-4) The same answer can be given to arguments two, three and four.

(5) An accident does not transcend its subject in being, but it does go beyond it in acting; for the heat of a fire heats things external to the fire. In this way the powers of a soul transcend the soul inasmuch as a soul understands and loves not only itself but also other things. Now Augustine makes use of this argument when he relates knowledge and love to the mind, not as to that which knows and that which loves, but rather as to that which is known and that which is loved. For if knowledge and love were related to the mind in this way, namely, as accidents are related to a subject, it would follow that a soul would know and love nothing but itself. Hence perhaps this is what he means when he said that they are one life, one essence, because actual knowledge is in a certain sense the thing known and actual love is in some sense the thing loved.

(6) The image of the Trinity in the soul is conceived by reference not only to the soul's powers but also to its essence; for in this way one essence belonging to three Persons is represented, even though in an inadequate way. Now if a soul were its powers, there would be only a verbal distinction of the powers in relation to one another; and hence the distinction of the Persons which exists in God would not be appropriately represented.

(7) There are three genera of accidents. Some accidents are caused by the principles of the species and are called proper accidents, as 'risible' for human beings. Other accidents are caused by the principles of an individual, and these are of two kinds. For either they have a cause that permanently resides in the subject, and these are inseparable accidents, for example, 'masculine,' 'feminine' and other accidents of this kind; or they have a cause which does not reside permanently in the subject, and these are separable accidents, for example, sitting and walking. Now it is a common feature of all accidents that they do not belong to the essence of a thing and consequently are not included in a thing's definition. Hence we understand what a thing is without understanding any of its accidents. But a species cannot be understood as being without those accidents which result from a principle of the species; however, a species can be understood apart from the accidents that belong to the individual, even in separable accidents. But not only the species but even the individual can be understood apart from the separable accidents. Now the powers of the soul are proper accidents; hence we can understand what the soul is without reference to these powers, but it is impossible that the soul

should exist without them, or that it should be understood as so existing.

(8) 'Sensitive' and 'rational,' insofar as they are essential differences, are not derived from sense or intellect but rather from the sensitive and intellective soul.

(9) The reason why a substantial form is not the immediate principle of action in lower agents has been made clear.

(10) A soul is a principle of operation, but it is the first and not the proximate principle. For its powers operate through the power of the soul, just as the qualities of the elements operate through the power of their substantial forms.

(11) The soul itself is in potency to intelligible forms. However, this potency is not the soul's essence any more than the potency to be a statue which is in copper is the essence of copper. For to be actual and to be potential do not belong to the essence of a thing when the act is not an essential one.

(12) Prime matter is in potency to substantial act, which is form; consequently potency itself is prime matter's very essence.

(13) A human being is said to be an intellect because intellect is what is preeminent in a human being, just as the ruler of a state is said to be the state; but a human being is not said to be an intellect in the sense that the essence of his soul is the actual power of the intellect.

(14) The likeness between a soul and science has to do with the fact that each of them is a first act, but it does not apply to them in every respect. Hence it is not necessary that a soul be the immediate principle of operation as a science is.

(15) The powers of a soul are not essential parts of a soul, as if they constituted its essence, but they are potential parts because the power of the soul is differentiated through these powers.

(16) A simple form which does not subsist, or, if it does, is pure act, cannot be the subject of an accident. Now a soul is a subsisting form and is not pure act, that is, if we are speaking of a human soul. Consequently it can be the subject of certain powers, for example, the intellect and the will. On the other hand, the powers of the sensitive and nutritive parts of the soul are in the composite as in a subject; because the potency too belongs to the subject which possesses the act, as is clear from what the Philosopher says in his book *De Somno et Vigilia.*[12]

(17) Although the soul is one in essence, still there is in it both potency and act; and it is diversely related to things, and even is related to its body in diverse ways. Because of this, diverse powers can issue from the single essence of the soul.

Notes to Question Twelve

1. Alcher of Clairvaux (Pseudo-Augustine), *Liber de Spiritu et anima,* XIII (PL 40: 789).

2. *Ibid.,* (PL 40: 788-789).

3. Pseudo St. Bernard, *Meditationes Piisimae,* I (PL 184: 487).

4. St. Augustine, *De Trinitate,* X, 11 (PL 42: 983).

5. Aristotle, *Nicomachean Ethics,* IX, 4 (1166a 16).

6. Aristotle, *De Anima,* II, 1 (412a 19-27).

7. Aristotle, *De Anima,* II, 2 (413b 13 - 414a 3).

8. Aristotle, *Categories,* 8 (9a 14-28).

9. Aristotle, *Physics,* II, 7 (198a 24-27).

10. Avicenna, *Metaphysics,* Tractatus VIII, cap. 7, p. 263 ff; Tractatus IX, cap. 5, p. 305 ff; ed. S. Bonaventure, N.Y., The Franciscan Institute, 1948.

11. Aristotle, *Nichomachean Ethics,* VI, 1 (1139a 6-15).

12. Aristotle, *De Somno et Vigilia,* I (454a 8).

QUESTION THIRTEEN

Parallel Texts: *In I Sent.,* dist. 17, q. 1, a. 4; *In II Sent.,* dist. 44, q. 2, a. 1; *Summa theol.,* I, q. 77, a. 3; *In II De An.,* lect. 6.

The thirteenth question that is asked about the soul has to do with the distinction between the powers of the soul, namely, whether the powers of the soul are distinguished by their objects. And it seems that they are not.

(1) Contraries are those things which are most unlike each other. But a contrariety of objects does not diversify powers; for the same power, sight, is directed toward both black and white. Therefore no difference located in the objects diversifies powers.

(2) Furthermore, things which differ substantially differ more than those things which differ accidentally. But a human being and a stone differ substantially; on the other hand what produces sound and what is colored differ accidentally. Consequently, since a human being and a stone are related to the same power, all the more so are that which produces a sound and that which is colored. And as a result no difference in objects produces a difference in powers.

(3) Furthermore, if a difference in objects were the cause of a diversity in powers, then the unity of an object would necessarily be the cause of the identity of powers. However, we observe that one and the same object is related to diverse powers; for it is the same object which is understood and desired, since the intelligible good is the object of the will. Therefore the difference between objects is not the cause of a diversity of powers.

(4) Furthermore, where there is the same cause, there is the same effect. Therefore, if diverse objects diversified certain powers, it would be necessary that they cause diversity everywhere in powers. We do not experience this, however; for some diverse objects are in fact related to diverse powers, for example, sound and color to hearing and sight; and also to a single power, namely, to the imagination and to the intellect. Therefore it follows that a difference in objects is not a cause of the diversity of powers.

(5) Furthermore, habits are the perfections of powers. Now things

capable of being perfected are distinguished by their proper perfections. Therefore powers are distinguished by habits and not by objects.

(6) Furthermore, whatever is in something is in it according to the mode of the recipient. But the powers of a soul are in the organs of its body; for they are the acts of the organs. Therefore powers are distinguished by the organs of the body and not by objects.

(7) Furthermore, the powers of a soul are not the very essence of the soul, but rather are its properties. Now the properties of a thing flow from its essence. But only one thing can proceed directly from one source. Therefore only one power of a soul flows first of all from the essence of the soul, and through the mediation of this power the soul's other powers flow, following a certain order. Therefore the powers of a soul differ because of their origin and not because of their objects.

(8) Furthermore, if a soul's powers are diverse, one of them must issue from another, because they cannot all issue directly from the soul's essence since it is one and simple. Now it seems impossible that one of the soul's powers should issue from another power, both because all the soul's powers exist simultaneously, and also because an accident arises from a subject. However, one accident cannot be the subject of another accident. Therefore there cannot be diverse powers of the soul because of the diversity of objects.

(9) Futhermore, the loftier a substance is, the greater is its power, and, as a result, its power is less manifold; because every unified power approaches more closely to the infinite than a manifold power, as is said in the *Liber de Causis*.[1] Now the soul occupies the highest place among the lesser beings of this world. Therefore its power is more fully one, although it is related to many thing. Consequently its power is not multiplied because of differences in objects.

(10) Furthermore, if the diversity of a soul's powers is consequent upon a difference in objects, then the order of its powers must correspond to the order of objects. This does not seem to be so, for the intellect, whose object is essence and substance, is dependent on sensation, whose objects are accidents, for example, color and sound. Furthermore, touch is prior to sight, even though the visible is prior to and more general than the tangible. Consequently the diversity of powers does not follow upon the difference in objects.

(11) Furthermore, every appetible object is sensible and intelligible. Now an intelligible object is the perfection of an intellect and a sensible object is the perfection of sense. Therefore, since each thing naturally desires its own perfection, it follows that intellect and sense naturally desire every appetible object. Consequently it is not necessary to posit an appetitive power in addition to sensitive and intellective powers.

(12) Furthermore, there is no appetite except the will and the irascible and concupiscible appetites. But the will is in the intellect, and the irascible and concupiscible appetites are in the senses, as is said in Book III of the *De Anima*.[2] Consequently there is no need to posit an appetitive power in addition to the sensitive and intellective powers.

(13) Furthermore, the Philosopher proves, in Book III of the *De Anima*,[3] that the principles of local motion in animals are sense or imagination, the intellect and appetite. But the motive power in animals is the same as their principle of motion. Therefore there is no motive power over and above the cognitive and appetitive powers.

(14) Furthermore, the powers of a soul are ordered to something higher than nature, otherwise there would be powers of the soul in all natural bodies. Now the powers of the soul which are attributed to a nutritive soul do not seem to be ordered to anything higher than nature. For these powers are directed toward the conservation of the species through generation, to the conservation of the individual through nourishment, and to the attaining of an individual's appropriate size through growth; and nature performs all these operations even in natural things. Therefore the powers of the soul are not to be directed toward such operations.

(15) Furthermore, the loftier a power is, the more numerous are those things to which it extends while remaining one. But a power of a soul is loftier than a power of nature. Therefore, since nature by one and the same power causes a natural body to exist, gives this body its appropriate quantity and conserves it in existence, it seems even more likely that a soul would perform these operations by means of a single power. Consequently the powers of generation, nutrition and growth are not diverse powers of the soul.

(16) Furthermore, a sense power is able to know accidents. But there are some accidents which differ from one another in a greater degree than do sound and color and accidents of this kind, which not only belong to the same genus, that of quality, but even belong to the same species, namely, the third species of quality.[4] Therefore, if powers are to be distinguished because of a difference of objects, the powers of the soul ought not to be distinguished because of this kind of accident, but rather according to accidents which are more unlike each other.

(17) Furthermore, in any given genus there is one contrary which is primary. Therefore, if the sensitive powers are diversified by reference to diverse genera of qualities by which the sense powers can be affected, its seems that wherever there are diverse contraries, there would be diverse sensitive powers. And in some instances this is so: thus sight perceives white and black, and hearing apprehends low and high sounds. But in other instances the fact is otherwise; for the objects

of touch are the hot and cold, the moist and dry, the soft and hard, and other qualities of this sort. Therefore powers are not distinguished in relation to their objects.

(18) Futhermore, memory does not seem to be a power distinct from the senses, for it is, according to the Philosopher, a passion of the primary faculty of sensation.[5] However, their objects differ; for the object of the senses is what is present, whereas the object of the memory is what is past. Consequently powers are not distinguished from each other in relation to their objects.

(19) Furthermore, all those things which are known by the sense are also known by the intellect, and the intellect knows many additional things. Consequently, if the sensitive powers are distinguished according to the plurality of objects, the intellect too must be divided into diverse powers, just as the senses are, and this is obviously false.

(20) Furthermore, the possible intellect and the agent intellect are diverse powers, as we established in earlier questions. But both of them have the same object. Therefore powers are not distinguished by reference to a difference in objects.

On The Contrary,

It is said in Book II of the *De Anima* [6] that powers are distinguished by their acts, and that acts are distinguished by their objects.

(2) Furthermore, things that can be perfected are distinguished by reference to the perfections to which they are ordered. But objects are the perfections of powers. Therefore powers are distinguished by reference to their objects.

The Response:

A power, taken in its essential sense, is named by reference to an act. Hence a power must be defined through an act, and powers must be diversified because of a diversity of acts. Now an act derives its specific nature from its objects: for if they are the acts of passive powers, their objects are active; but if they are acts of active powers, their objects have the nature of ends. Now the specific nature of an operation must be considered from both perspectives; for instance, to heat and to make cold are distinguished inasmuch as the principle of the former is heat and the principle of the latter is cold; although they terminate in similar ends. For an agent acts in order that it might induce a likeness of itself in another. Consequently we recognize that the distinction of the powers of the soul is based upon a distinction of objects.

The distinction of objects which concerns us here must, however, be understood of objects inasmuch as they are objects of the soul's actions, and not with reference to some other aspect. The reason is that the species in any genus are diversified only by the differences which essentially divide that genus; thus the species of 'animal' are differentiated by 'rational' and 'irrational,' not by 'white' and 'black.' Now one must consider that there are three levels in the actions of the soul; for the action of the soul transcends the action of nature as nature operates in inanimate things. But the soul's superiority is revealed in two ways: with respect, that is, to its mode of acting and also with respect to the action it performs. Now with regard to the mode of acting, every action of the soul must transcend the operation or the action of nature in an inanimate thing, because every action of the soul must result from an intrinsic principle of action. This is so because the action of the soul is a vital action, and a living thing is one that moves itself to its operation.

But with respect to the action it performs, not every action of the soul transcends the action of nature in inanimate things. Therefore, as inanimate bodies must possess their natural being and whatever else is necessary to sustain this being, so living bodies have the same. But in inanimate bodies this effect is brought about by an extrinsic agent, whereas in living bodies it is produced by an intrinsic agent; and it is to actions of this kind that the powers of the vegetative soul are ordered. For the generative power is ordered to the production of an individual in its being; the augmentative power assures that the individual achieve its proper size; and the nutritive power assures the individual be conserved in its being. Now these effects accrue to inanimate bodies solely from an extrinsic natural agent, and because of this the powers of the soul just mentioned above are called natural powers.

However, there are other loftier actions of the soul which transcend the actions of natural forms even with respect to their effects, inasmuch, that is, as all things, because of the nature of the soul, are able to exist in the soul with an immaterial existence. For the soul is in some way all things, inasmuch as the soul senses and understands; for there must be two distinct levels of this sort of immaterial being.

For there is one level insofar as things exist in the soul without the matter which is proper to them, but nevertheless with that singularity and with those individual conditions which result from matter. This level of immaterial being is that of the senses, which are capable of acquiring individual species, free of their matter, and yet acquire them in a bodily organ. Now a loftier and a more perfect level of immateriality is that of the intellect, which receives species that are totally abstracted from matter and from the conditions of matter, and receives them without a bodily organ. Now each thing, through its natural form, has a tendency toward something and has also a movement or action by which it seeks that toward which it tends; so too the tendency toward that thing follows upon a sensible or an intelligible form, grasped either by the senses or by the intellect; this tendency belongs to the appetitive power. And furthermore, in consequence of all this, there must be movement through which a living being might attain the thing which it desires, and this activity belongs to the power of movement.

Now for complete sense knowledge, which would be adequate for an animal, five things are indispensable. First, that a sense power receive a species from sensible things, and this activity belongs to a proper sense (one of the external senses). Secondly, that there be a sense to discriminate among the sensible qualities perceived and to distinguish them from one another; and this action must be performed by a power in which all sensible perceptions terminate, and this power is called the unifying sense. Thirdly, that the species of sensible thing which have been received be retained. For an animal needs to know sensible things not only when they are present, but also after they are no longer present. And it is necessary that this activity be attributed to another power, because in corporeal things the principle which receives and that which retains are distinct; for that which is very receptive is sometimes poorly retentive. Now this power is called imagination or fantasy. Fourthly, a sense is required which might apprehend intentions that the other senses do not perceive, such as the harmful, the useful, and other notions of this sort. Now a human being arrives at a knowledge of these intentions by investigation and deliberation; but other animals possess this kind of knowledge by natural instinct, as, for example, a sheep naturally flees a wolf as being harmful. Hence in animals other than human beings a natural estimative power is directed toward this end, whereas in a human being there is a cogitative power, which compares these particular intentions; hence this power is called both the particular reason and the passive intellect. Fifthly, complete sense knowledge requires that things which were previously apprehended by the external senses and have been retained in the interior senses be once again summoned up for actual consideration. And this activity belongs to the power of recollection, which in animals other than human beings operates without investigation, but in human beings operates through inquiry and endeavor. Hence there is in human beings not only memory but also reminiscence. Now it was necessary that the power which is ordered to this end be distinct from the other powers, because the activity of the other sensitive powers involves a movement from things to the soul, whereas the activity of the power of recollection involves a movement from the soul toward things.

Now diverse movement require diverse motive principles; and these principles of movement are called powers. But a proper sense which comes first in the order of sensitive powers is directly immuted by sensible things; hence it was necessary that the external senses be divided into diverse potencies according to the diversity of sensible immutations. For since a sense power is receptive of sensible species disengaged from matter, it is necessary to rank the level and order of the immutations by which the senses are immuted by sensible things by reference to the material immutations. Therefore there are some sensible things whose species, although they are immaterially received in a sense power, nevertheless produce also a material immutation in the animals which do the sensing. Now of this sort are the qualities which are the principles of transmutations even in material things, such as the hot, the cold, the dry and other qualities of this kind. Therefore, because sensible things of this sort cause immutations in us by acting simply as material agents, and because a material immutation takes place through contact, it is necessary that sensible things of this sort be sensed by touching. Because of this the sensitive power which apprehends such sensibles is called touch.

There are, however, certain sensible things that do not themselves cause a material immutation in us, although the immutation which they do produce has a material immutation connected with it; and this occurs in two ways. First, the accessory material immutation is located both in the sensible thing and in the one who senses; this is true of the sense of taste. For although flavor does not change the sense organ by making it flavorful, still this change does not take place without some transmutation both of the flavorful thing and also of the organ of taste, and moisture is the principal cause of these changes. Secondly, the conjoined material transmutation takes place only in the thing sensed. Now a transmutation of this kind takes place either through a dispersion and change in the sensible thing as in the sense of smell; or only through a change in place, as in hearing. Hence the auditory and olfactory senses operate through an extrinsic medium and not by contact with their objects, because these senses produce no material immutation in the one who senses, even though they involve a materal mutation in the sensible thing. Taste, however, operates only through contact with its object because it demands a material immutation on the part of the one sensing.

Now there are other sensible thing which change a sense power without a conjoined material immutation, such as light and color, which are the object of sight. Hence sight is loftier and more universal than any of the other senses, because the sensible things perceived by sight are common to corruptible and to incorruptible bodies.

Now there are likewise two divisions of the appetitive power which follows upon a sensory apprehension. For something is appetible either because it is pleasing to and appropriate to one of the senses, and the concupiscible power is concerned with this; or something is appetible because through it one possesses the power to enjoy things that please the senses. This pleasurable experience sometimes occurs in conjunction with an experience that is painful to the senses, as when ,an animal gains the power to enjoy the pleasurable object proper to one of its sense only by fighting and warding off whatever would hinder this enjoyment; and the irascible power is concerned with this. Now the motive power, since it is ordered to movement, is not diversified except with respect to the diversity of movements; these movements are adapted to diverse animals, for some animals are able to crawl, some to fly, some to walk, and some have other forms of movement. Or these movements are adapted to the diverse parts of one and the same animal, for the individual parts have their own natural movements.

Now the levels of intellective powers are also divided into cognitive and appetitive powers; for the motive power is common to both sense and intellect, since one and the same body, by one and the same movement, is moved by both of these powers. But intellectual cognition demands two powers, namely, the agent and the possible intellect, as is clear from what we said in earlier questions. And so it is clear that there are three levels of powers in a soul, namely, the level of the nutritive soul, that of the sensible soul and that of the rational soul. Now there are five genera of powers: nutritive, sensitive, intellective, appetitive, and motive with respect to place; and each of these powers has under it several powers, as has already been said.

Replies to the Opposing Arguments:

(1) Contraries are most unlike each other, but within the same genus. Now a diversity of objects within a genus is appropriate to a diversity of powers, because a genus too is somehow in potency. And therefore contraries are related to the same power, and so forth.

(2) Although sound and color are diverse accidents, still they differ essentially with respect to their immutation of a sense power, as has been stated; however, a man and a stone do not so differ, because a sense power is immuted in the same way by both of them. And therefore a man and a stone differ accidentally insofar as they are sensed, although they differ essentially insofar as they are substances. For nothing prevents a difference from being related essentially to one genus and being related to another genus accidentally, as white and black differ essentially in the genus of color but not in the genus of substance.

(3) The same thing is not related to the diverse powers of the soul under the same formality as an object, but under different formalities.

(4) The loftier a power is, the more numerous are the things to which it is related; hence it has a more universal formal object. And this is why some things which are united within the formal object of a higher power are distinguished from each other according to the formal object of lower powers.

(5) Habits are perfections of powers, not in the sense that powers exist for the sake of these perfections, but inasmuch as it is by means of habits that powers are to some extent related to their objects, for whose sake they exist. Hence powers are not distinguished by reference to their habits but by reference to their objects; just as artifacts are not distinguished by reference to their objects but by reference to their ends.

(6) Powers do not exist for the sake of organs but rather vice versa. Hence organs are distinguished by reference to their objects rather than the opposite.

(7) A soul has a principal end, for example, a human soul has as its principal end the intelligible good. However, a soul has other ends that are ordered to this ultimate end, for example, the fact that the sensible good is ordered to the intelligible good. And because a soul is ordered to its objects through its powers, it follows also that the sensitive power in a human being exists for the sake of the intellective power, and the same is true for the other powers. Hence there is no contradiction in saying that the powers of the soul can be distinguished both by reference to the powers themselves and by reference to their objects.

(8) Although an accident cannot be the subject of an accident, still a subject can be modified by one accident through the intermediary of another accident, as a body has the accident of color through the medium of its surface. And thus one accident arises from its subject through the mediation of another; and one power arises from the essence of the soul through the mediation of another power.

(9) By a single power the soul can act upon a greater number of objects than can a natural thing, as sight, for example, apprehends everything that is visible. But a soul, because of its nobility, has many more operations than does an inanimate thing; hence it must possess a greater number of powers.

(10) The order of a soul's powers is consequent upon the order among their objects. But order can be considered from two points of view: either with reference to the level of perfection, as intellect has a priority over sense; or with reference to the mode of generation, and in this way sense has a priority over intellect, because as generation

takes place an accidental disposition is induced prior to the substantial form.

(11) It is true that an intellect naturally seeks what is intelligible insofar as it is intelligible; for an intellect by its nature desires to understand, as sense desires to sense. But because a sensible thing or an intelligible thing is not only desired in order that it might be sensed or understood, but also for another reason, it follows that in addition to sense and intellect there must be an appetitive power.

(12) The will exists in the reason inasmuch as the will follows the apprehension of the reason. However, the operation of the will belongs to the same level of a soul's powers, but not to the same genus of powers. The same thing must be said about the irascible and concupiscible appetites with respect to the sense powers.

(13) Intellect and appetite bring about movement by commanding it. But there must be a motive power which carries out the movement, namely, a power according to which the members of the body execute the command of appetite, intellect or sense.

(14) Powers of a nutritive soul are called natural powers because they do only what nature does in bodies; but they are called powers of a soul because they carry out these operations in a loftier way, as was said above.

(15) An inanimate natural thing acquires simultaneously its specific nature and its appropriate quantity; this cannot happen in living things, for at the beginning of their process of generation they must be small in size because they are begotten from semen. And consequently they must have, in addition to the generative power, an augmentative power which brings them to their proper size. This growth must come about because something is changed into the substance that is to be enlarged and is thus added to its bulk. Now this change takes place because of heat, which both converts the food that the body takes in from outside and also digests that already inside it. Hence for the conservation of an individual, in order that what is lost may be constantly renewed, in order that what is needed for its appropriate size be added, and that what is required for the generation of semen be produced, it is necessary that there be a nutritive power which ministers to the augmentative and generative powers, and moreover keeps the individual in existence.

(16) Sound and color and things of this kind differ because of the diverse mode of immutation of the sense, but sensible things which belong to diverse genera do not differ in this way. And consequently the sensitive powers are not diversified in relation to these sensible objects.

(17) The contraries which are the object of the sense of touch cannot be reduced to a single genus, whereas the diverse contraries

that can be observed in the objects of the sense of sight are reduced to the single genus of color. It is for this reason that the Philosopher decides, in Book II of the *De Anima*,[7] that touch is not one sense but several senses. However, all these senses of touch are alike in that they do not sense through an extrinsic medium, and hence all of them are called 'touch,' so that there is one sense generically, divided into several species. However, it could be said that touch is one sense without qualification because all the contraries which are its object are known through one another and are reducible to a single genus, but this genus is unnamed; just as the proximate genus of 'hot' and 'cold' is unnamed.

(18) Since the powers of the soul are its various properties, the fact that memory is called 'the passion of the primary faculty of sensation' does not prevent its being a power distinct from the external senses; but the statement reveals the relation of memory to the external senses.

(19) A sense power receives the species of sensible things in bodily organs and is perceptive of particular things. On the other hand, an intellect receives the species of things without using a bodily organ and is perceptive of universals. Consequently a diversity of objects requires a diversity of powers in the sensitive part of a soul but does not demand a diversity of powers in the intellective part. For to receive and to retain follow upon different principles in material things; but in immaterial things they follows upon the same principle. So too the sense powers must be diversified according to the diverse modes of immutation; but there is no such necessity for the intellect.

(20) The same object, namely, an intelligible in act, is related to the agent intellect as being produced by it, but is related to the possible intellect as moving the possible intellect. Hence it is clear that the same thing is related to the agent intellect and to the possible intellect but not according to the same formality.

Notes to Question Thirteen

1. *Liber de Causis.* XVI; ed. Bardenhewer, p. 179, 1.
2. Aristotle, *De Anima,* III, 9 (432b 5-7).
3. Aristotle, *De Anima,* III, 10 (433a 9 ff.)
4. See Aristotle, *Categories,* VIII.
5. Aristotle, *De Memoria et reminiscentia,* I (451a 17-18).
6. Aristotle, *De Anima,* II, 4 (415a 16-22).
7. Aristotle, *De Anima,* II, 11 (422b 17-33); Cf. II, 7 (418a 13-14).

QUESTION FOURTEEN

Parallel texts: *In II Sent.*, dist. 19, a. 1; *In IV Sent.*, dist. 50 q. 1, a. 1; *Quodl.*, X, q. 3, a. 2; *Contra gent.*, II, 79-81; *Summa theol.*, I, q. 75, a. 6; *Compend. theol.*, cap. 84.

The fourteenth question that is asked about the human soul has to do with its immortality. And it seems that the human soul is corruptible.

(1) For Ecclesiastes III [1] says: "The death of a human being and of beasts is one, and the condition of both is equal." But when beasts die, their souls perish. Therefore, when a human being perishes, his soul is corrupted.

(2) Furthermore, corruptible and incorruptible are generically different, as is said in Book X of the *Metaphysics*. [2] But a human soul and an animal soul do not differ generically; because a human being does not differ in genus from an animal. Therefore a soul of a human being and a soul of an animal do not differ as the corruptible and the incorruptible do. But a soul of an animal is corruptible. Therefore a human soul is not incorruptible.

(3) Furthermore, Damascene [3] says that an angel receives immortality by grace and not by nature. But an angel is not inferior to a soul. Therefore a soul is not naturally immortal.

(4) Furthermore, the Philosopher proves, in Book VIII of the *Physics*, [4] that the Prime Mover is of infinite power because he moves in infinite time. Therefore, if a soul has the power to endure for an infinite time, it follows that its power is infinite. But there is no infinite power in a finite essence. Therefore it follows that the essence of a soul be infinite if it be incorruptible. Now this is impossible, because only the divine essence is infinite. Therefore a human soul is not incorruptible.

But an objector was arguing that a human soul in incorruptible, not by its own essence but through divine power.

(5) On the contrary, whatever does not belong to something through the thing's own essence is not essential to it. But 'corruptible' and 'incorruptible' are predicated essentially of whatever they are

predicated of, as the Philosopher says in Book X of the *Metaphysics*.[5] Consequently, if a soul is incorruptible, it must be incorruptible through its own essence.

(6) Furthermore, whatever exists is either corruptible or incorruptible. Therefore, if a human soul is not incorruptible according to its own nature, it follows that according to its own nature it is corruptible.

(7) Furthermore, whatever is incorruptible possesses the power to exist forever. Therefore, if a human soul is incorruptible, it follows that is possesses the power to exist forever. Consequently it does not possess being after non-being, and this is contrary to faith.

(8) Furthermore, Augustine[6] says that just as God is the life of a soul, so a soul is the life of its body. But death is the privation of life; hence by death a soul is deprived of life and destroyed.

(9) Furthermore, a form does not exist except in that in which it is a form. Therefore, if a soul is the form of a body, it cannot exist except in a body. Therefore, when its body is taken away, it perishes.

But an objector was arguing that this is true of a soul insofar as it is a form, not according to its essence.

(10) On the contrary, a soul is not the form of a body in an accidental way; otherwise, since a soul constitutes a human being insofar as it is the form of its body, it would follow that a human being is an accidental being. Now whatever does not belong to a being by accident belongs to it according to its essence. Consequently a soul is a form according to its essence. Therefore, if a soul is corruptible insofar as it is a form, then it is also corruptible according to its essence.

(11) When several elements come together to constitute a single existent, they are so related to one another that if one is corrupted, the other is corrupted. But soul and body come together to constitute a single existent, namely, an existing human being. Therefore, when the body is corrupted, the soul is corrupted.

(12) Furthermore, in a human being the sensitive soul and the rational soul are one in substance. But the sensitive soul is corruptible; therefore so is the rational soul.

(13) Furthermore, a form must be proportioned to its matter. But a human soul is in its body as form is in matter. Therefore, since the body is corruptible, a soul will also be corruptible.

(14) Furthermore, if a soul can be separated from its body, there must be some operation belonging to it that is independent of a body, for no substance is functionless. But a soul can have no operation without its body, not even understanding, which seems the likeliest possibility, because there is no act of understanding apart from a phantasm, as the Philosopher says.[7] Now there is no phantasm apart from a body. Therefore a soul cannot be separated from its body, but is corrupted when its body is corrupted.

(15) Furthermore, if a human soul be incorruptible, this will be only because it possesses intelligence. But it seems that to understand does not belong to a human soul; because whatever is highest in a lower nature imitates to some degree the action of a loftier nature, but does not quite attain this action; just as monkeys imitate to some degree the operation of a human being but do not quite attain this operation. In like fashion it seems that since a human being is the loftiest being in the realm of material things, a human being imitates in some degree the action of the separate intellectual substances, which is the action of understanding, but he does not quite reach this action. Therefore there does not seem to be any necessity for declaring that the soul of a human being is immortal.

(16) Furthermore, either all or nearly all of those who belong to a species achieve the essential operation of that species. But only a few human beings become actually intelligent. Therefore to understand is not the essential operation of a human soul. And consequently there is no necessity for the human soul to be incorruptible simply because it is intellectual.

(17) Furthermore, the Philosopher says, in Book I of the *Physics,*[8] that everything which is finite is finally reduced to nothing since something is always being taken away from it. But the natural good of a soul is a finite good. Therefore, since any sin whatsoever diminishes the natural good of a human soul, it seems that finally a soul will be entirely obliterated; and thus a human soul is corrupted at some time or other.

(18) Furthermore, when its body weakens, the soul too becomes weak, a fact that is clear from its operations. Therefore also when its body is corrupted, the soul is corrupted.

(19) Furthermore, whatever comes from nothing can return to nothingness. But a human soul is created from nothing. Hence it can return to nothingness. And thus it follows that a soul is corruptible.

(20) Furthermore, so long as a cause remains, its effect remains. But a soul is the cause of the life of its body. Therefore, if a soul always continues to exist, it is clear that its body would live forever; and this is clearly false.

(21) Furthermore, whatever subsists through itself is an entity, located in a genus or a species. But it seems that a human soul is not an entity and that it is not located in a species or a genus as an individual or species is, since a soul is a form. For to be in a genus or to be in a species belongs to a composite, not to matter or to form, except by reduction. Therefore a human soul is not self-subsistent, and consequently, when its body is corrupted, it cannot continue to be.

On The Contrary,

Wisdom II says, "God made man to be inexterminable, and He made him in the image of His own likeness." 9 From this one can draw the conclusion that man is inexterminable, that is, incorruptible, insofar as he is made to the image of God. Now it is with respect to his soul that a human being is made to the image of God, as Augustine states in his book *De Trinitate.* 10 Therefore a human soul in incorruptible.

(2) Whatever undergoes corruption has contraries or is composed of contraries. But a human soul wholly lacks contrariety; because even those things which are contraries in themselves are not contraries in a soul; for the notions of contraries which exist in a soul are not contrary. Therefore a human soul is incorruptible.

(3) Furthermore, the celestial bodies are said to be incorruptible because they do not have the same kind of matter as things which are generable and corruptible. But a human soul is wholly immaterial; this is clear from the fact that it receives the species of things in an immaterial way. Therefore a soul is incorruptible.

(4) Furthermore, the Philosopher 11 says that an intellect exists in separation as that which is everlasting is separate from the corruptible. Now the intellect is a part of a soul, as he himself says. Therefore a human soul is incorruptible.

The Response:

It must be stated that it is necessary that a human soul be totally incorruptible. To make this clear one must note carefully that whatever belongs to something essentially cannot be taken away from it; for example, one cannot separate animality from man, nor odd and even from number. Now it is obvious that being essentially follows upon form; for each thing has being in accordance with its proper form; hence being cannot in any way be separated from form. Therefore things which are composed of matter and form are corrupted because they lose the form upon which their being follows. However, a form itself cannot of itself be corrupted; but when the composite is corrupted, the form is corrupted accidentally because the being of the composite, which exists through the form ceases to exist. This is true with regard to a form of the kind that does not possess being, but is only that by which the composite exists.

Therefore, if there be a form which is in such a way that it possesses existence, it is necessary that such a form be incorruptible. For existence is not separated from something which possesses existence unless its form is separated from it. Hence, if that which possesses existence is the form itself, it is impossible that existence be separated from it. Now it is clear that the principle by which a human being understands is a form that possesses existence and is not merely that by which something exists. For to understand, as the Philosopher proves in Book III of the *De Anima,*[12] is not an act that is completed through a bodily organ. For it is impossible that there should be found a bodily organ which is capable of receiving all sensible natures, especially because a recipient must be free of the nature received, just as the pupil of the eye lacks color. Now every bodily organ has a sensible nature. On the other hand, the intellect by which we understand is capable of knowing all sensible natures. Hence it is impossible that the intellect's operation, which is to understand, be carried out through anything that is corporeal. Hence it is clear that the intellect has an essential operation in which its body does not share. Now each thing operates in accordance with what it is. For things which exist through themselves operate through themselves, whereas things which do not have existence through themselves do not have an operation through themselves; for heat does not through itself produce warmth, but something which is hot does. Accordingly, therefore, it is clear that the intellective principle by which a human being understands possesses an existence that transcends its body and is not dependent upon its body.

It is also evident that an intellective principle of this kind is not composed of matter and form, because species are received in it in a wholly immaterial way. This is made clear from the fact that the intellect is concerned with universals, which are considered in abstraction from matter and from material conditions. Therefore one can conclude that the intellective principle by which a human being understands is a form that possesses existence. Hence it necessarily follows that it is incorruptible, and this is what the Philosopher too says: that the intellect is something divine and everlasting.[13]

Now it has been pointed out in preceding questions that the intellective principle by which a human being understands is not a separate substance, but is something which formally belongs in a human being, which is the soul or a part of the soul. Hence we conclude from what has been said that a human soul is incorruptible.

Now all those who taught that the human soul is corruptible denied some of the points already made. For some of them, declaring that a soul is a body, taught that it is not a form but rather something composed of matter and form. Others, however, declaring that the intellect does not differ from the sense powers, taught as a consequence that the intellect does not have an operation except through a bodily organ; and consequently that the intellect does not have an existence that transcends its body; hence it is not a form that possesses existence. However, others held that the intellect by which a human being understands is a separated substance. All these positions have been shown to be false in earlier questions. Hence it follows that a human soul is incorruptible.

There are two sources of direct evidence in support of this assertion. First, from the side of the intellect: for things which of themselves are corruptible are incorruptible insofar as they are perceived by an intellect. For an intellect is able to grasp things in a universal way according to which they are not subject to corruption. Secondly, from the fact of natural appetite which cannot be in vain wherever it is found. For we observe that there exists in human beings a desire for everlastingness, and this is a reasonable desire; for since existence is of itself desirable, an intelligent being who grasps existence without qualification and not merely existence here and now must naturally desire to exist without qualification and for all time. Hence it seems that this appetite is not in vain, but that a human being is incorruptible with respect to his intellective soul.

Replies to the Opposing Arguments:

(1) Solomon, in the book *Ecclesiastes,* speaks as a preacher, sometimes playing the role of wise men, sometimes the role of fools. The text cited represents the role of the foolish. Or one can say that the death of a human being and of animals is one and the same with respect to the composite's corruption, which takes place for both through the separation of soul from body, although after its separation a human soul continues to exist while a soul belonging to an animal does not.

(2) If a human soul and the soul of an animal, considered merely in their essence, were located in a genus, they would as a result be in different genera, inasmuch as genus is here understood from the viewpoint of the philosophy of nature. For under this aspect, the corruptible and the incorruptible must necessarily be generically different, although they can be united under a common notion; and hence the human soul and the soul of an animal can also be in the same genus if genus is understood in its logical sense. In fact, however, a soul is not in a genus as a species is, but rather as a part of its species. Now each of these composites is corruptible, both that of which a human soul is a part as well as that of which the soul of a beast is a part. For this reason nothing prevents their belonging to a single genus.

(3) As Augustine says,[14] true immortality is true immutability.

Now both a soul and an angel possess by grace that immutability which results from the divine decision that they should be incapable of changing from good to evil.

(4) Existence is related to form as essentially following form, but not as an effect follows upon the power of an agent, as, for example, movement is consequent upon the power of the one that causes movement. Therefore, although the fact that something can cause movement in infinite time demonstrates the infinite power of that which causes the movement, still the fact that something is able to exist for an infinite period of time does not demonstrate the infinity of the form through which it exists; just as the fact that the number two is always even does not prove its infinity. Rather the fact that something exists in infinite time demonstrates the infinite power of that which causes existence.

(5) 'Corruptible' and 'incorruptible' are essential predicates because they belong to essence as a formal or as a material principle, but not as an active principle. Rather the active principle for the perpetuity of certain things is a principle which is extrinsic to them.

(6) And from this the solution to the sixth argument is clear.

(7) A soul possesses the power to exist always, but it did not always have this power; and therefore it is not necessary that a soul should always have existed, but rather that in the future it will never cease to be.

(8) A soul is said to be the form of its body insofar as it is the cause of life, just as form is the principle of existing. For in beings which are alive, their 'to live' is their 'to be,' as the Philosopher says in Book II of the *De Anima*.[15]

(9) A soul is the kind of form whose existence does not depend upon that of which it is the form; its operation makes this clear, as we have already said.

(10) Although a soul through its essence is a form, nevertheless something may belong to it insofar as it is the kind of form it is, namely, a subsistent form, which does not belong to it insofar as it is a form; just as to understand does not belong to a human being insofar as he is an animal, although a human being is an animal by his essence.

(11) Although a soul and its body unite to achieve a single act of existence of a human being, still that act of existence accrues to the body from the soul, so that a human soul communicates to its body the soul's own existence by which it subsists, as we have shown in earlier questions. Consequently, when its body is taken away, a soul continues to exist.

(12) The sensitive soul in beasts is corruptible; but in a human being, since the sensitive soul is the same substance as the rational soul, it is incorruptible.

(13) A human body is matter that is proportioned to a human soul with respect to a soul's operations; but it is subject to corruption and other defects because of the exigencies of matter, as we explained earlier. Or one can say that corruption befalls the body because of sin, not because of the original constitution of nature.

(14) When the Philosopher says that there is no understanding apart from a phantasm, the statement is to be understood in reference to the present state of life, in which a human being understands through his soul. There will be a different mode of understanding for a separated soul.

(15) Although a human soul does not achieve that mode of understanding by which loftier substances understand, it still achieves understanding in some degree; and this is certainly enough to establish its incorruptibility.

(16) Although only a few human beings achieve complete understanding, still all human beings achieve understanding to some degree. For it is clear that the first principles of demonstration are conceptions common to all, and these principles are grasped by the intellect.

(17) Sin totally removes grace, but it does not take away anything belonging to a thing's essence. Sin does, however, diminish the inclination toward or aptitude for grace; and to the extent that every sin introduces a contrary disposition, every sin whatsoever is said to diminish that natural good which is aptitude for grace. However, sin never wholly removes the good of nature, because there always remains the potency, with its contrary dispositions, even though the potency is more and more remote from act.

(18) A soul is not weakened when its body is weakened, not even the sensitive soul; this is clear from what the Philosopher says in Book I of the *De Anima*,[16] that if an old man were to receive the eye of a young man, he would see just as well as the young man does. From this it is obvious that inadequacy of action does not occur because of the weakness of the soul but that of the organ.

(19) Whatever arises from nothing can return to nothingness unless it be kept in existence by the hand which rules it. But it is not for this reason that something is said to be corruptible, but from the fact that something possesses an intrinsic principle of corruption. It is in this latter sense that 'corruptible' and 'incorruptible' are essential predicates.

(20) Although the soul, which is the cause of life, is incorruptible, still the body which receives its life from the soul is subject to change; and because of this the body loses that disposition by which it is suited to receive life. It is in this way that the corruption of a human being takes place.

(21) A soul, although it can exist of itself, does not of itself possess a specific nature, since it is part of the specific nature.

Notes to Question Fourteen

1. *Ecclesiastes,* 3: 19.
2. Aristotle, *Metaphysics,* X, 10 (1058b 26-29).
3. St. John Damascene, *De Fide orthodoxa,* II, 3 (PG 94: 868).
4. Aristotle, *Physics,* VIII, 10 (267b 24-26).
5. Aristotle, *Metaphysics,* X, 10 (1058b 36 - 1059a 10).
6. St. Augustine, *City of God,* XIX, 26 (PL 41: 656).
7. Aristotle, *De Anima,* III, 7 (431a 16).
8. Aristotle, *Physics,* I, 4 (187b 25-26).
9. *Wisdom,* 2: 33.
10. St. Augustine, *De Trinitate,* X, 12 (PL 42: 984).
11. Aristotle, *De Anima,* II, 2 (413b 24-27).
12. Aristotle, *De Anima,* III, 4 (429b 4).
13. Aristotle, *De Anima,* III, 5 (430a 23).
14. St. Augustine, *De Immortalitate animae,* I, 1, 1 (PL 32: 1021); Cf. also 2, 2; 3, 3; 4, 5 (PL 32: 1022, 1023, 1024).
15. Aristotle, *De Anima,* II, 4 (415b 13).
16. Aristotle, *De Anima,* I, 4 (408b 21-22).

QUESTION FIFTEEN

Parallel texts: *In III Sent.*, dist. 31, q. 2, a. 4; *In IV Sent.*, dist. 1, q. 1, a. 1; *De Ver.*, q. 19, a. 1; *Contra gent.*, II, 81, *Summa theol.*, I, q. 89, a. 1; I-II, q. 67, a. 2; *Quodl.* III, q. 9, a. 1.

The fifteenth question that is asked about the soul is this: Whether a soul that is separated from its body is able to understand? And it seems that it cannot.

(1) Because, as the Philosopher says in Book I of the *De Anima*,[1] to understand is either imagination or it does not occur apart from imagination. Now imagination does not exist apart from a body; therefore neither does understanding. Therefore a separated soul does not understand.

(2) Furthermore, the Philosopher says, in Book III of the *De Anima*,[2] that intellect is related to phantasms as sight is related to colors. But sight cannot see without colors. Therefore neither can intellect understand without phantasms, nor, consequently, without a body.

(3) Furthermore, the Philosopher says, in Book I of the *De Anima*,[3] that the activity of understanding is corrupted from within when some bodily element has been corrupted: that is, either the heart or the body's natural heat. But if the act of understanding does in fact cease, a soul separated from its body is not able to understand.

But an objector was arguing that a soul separated from its body does in fact understand, but not in the way it does now, that is, by abstracting from phantasms.

(4) On the contrary, form is united to matter not for the sake of matter but for the sake of form, for form is the end and the perfection of matter; thus form is united to matter so that form may achieve its own operation. Hence a form requires the kind of matter through which the operation of the form might be completed, as, for example, the form of a saw requires an ironlike matter to achieve its work of cutting. Now a soul is the form of its body; therefore it is united to the kind of body that enables the soul to accomplish its proper operation. Now its proper operation is to understand; therefore, if a soul can understand without its body, it would be united to its body for no purpose.

(5) Furthermore, if a soul separated from its body is able to understand, it understands in a nobler way apart from its body than when united to its body; for those beings which do not require phantasms in order to understand, namely, separate substances, understand in a nobler fashion than we who understand through phantasms. Now the good of a soul consists in understanding; for the fulfilment of any substance is its essential operation. Therefore, if a soul separated from its body is capable of understanding without phantasms, it would be injurious to a soul to be united to a body, and thus to be united to a body would not be natural to it.

(6) Furthermore, powers are diversified in relation to their objects. But phantasms are the objects of the intellective soul, as is stated in Book III of the *De Anima.*[4] Therefore, if a soul understands without phantasms when separated from its body, it would then have to have other powers than it has when united to its body; and this is impossible, since powers are natural to a soul, and they inhere in a soul so as to be inseparable from it.

(7) Furthermore, if a separated soul understands, it must understand by means of a power. Now there are only two intellective powers in a soul, namely, the agent intellect and the possible intellect. However, it seems that a separated soul can understand by neither one of these powers, because the operation of each of these intellects is related to phantasms. For the agent intellect causes phantasms to be actually intelligible, while the possible intellect is mindful of the intelligible species which have been abstracted from phantasms. Therefore it seems that a separated soul would not be able to understand in any way.

(8) Furthermore, a single being has only one proper operation, just as there is one perfection belonging to one perfectible thing. Therefore, if the operation of a soul consists in understanding through the reception of intelligible species from phantasms, it seems that its operation cannot be to understand without phantasms; and consequently, when a soul is separated from its body, it will not understand.

(9) Furthermore, if a separated soul understands, it necessarily understands by means of something; because the act of understanding takes place through a likeness of the thing understood in the one who understands. Now one cannot say that a separated soul understands through its own essence, for this is true only of God. For His essence, because it is infinite, antecedently contains in itself the sum total of perfection and is the likeness of all things. Nor can it be said that a soul understands through the essence of the thing which is understood; because if this were so, a soul would understand only those things which are in the soul through its own essence. Nor does it seem that a separated soul is able to understand through species of any kind,

neither by means of innate species nor through those that are con-created; for this would be to return to the doctrine of Plato,[5] who taught that all the sciences are naturally present within us.

(10) Furthermore, innate species of this kind would seem to be quite useless to the soul, since it could not understand by means of such species while it is in the body. Now intelligible species seem to have no other purpose than that the soul might understand through them.

But an objector was arguing that a soul, taken in its own right, is able to understand through innate species, but is prevented by its body from understanding through them.

(11) On the contrary, the more perfect a being is in its own nature, the more perfect it is in operating. But a soul united to its body is more perfect in its nature than when it is separated from its body, just as any part is more perfect when it exists within its whole. There-fore, if a soul can understand through innate species when it is sepa-rated from its body, it is all the more capable of understanding by means of such species when it is united to its body.

(12) Furthermore, nothing is completely obstructed in the exercise of its natural powers by something that belongs to its own nature. Now it belongs to the nature of a soul to be united to its body, since it is the form of the body. Therefore, if intelligible species are naturally implanted in a soul, a soul will not be prevented through its union with its body from understanding by means of them; and yet we experi-ence the contrary of this.

(13) Nor does it seem that one can say that the separated soul understands through species which it had formerly acquired while it was in its body. For many human souls which acquired no intelligible species will continue to exist separated from their bodies; this is obvi-ously true of the souls of small children, and even more true of the souls of those children who died in their mothers' wombs. Therefore, if separated souls cannot understand except through species acquired before the separation, it would follow that not all separated souls would understand.

(14) Furthermore, if a separated soul were not to understand except through species previously acquired, it seems to follow that it could understand only those things which it had previously under-stood while it was united to its body. However, this does not seem to be true; for the separated soul understands many things about punishments and rewards which it does not understand at present. Therefore a separated soul will not understand solely through species acquired prior to its separation from the body.

(15) Furthermore, an intellect is actualized through an intelligible species which exists within it. But an actualized intellect actually under-

stands. Therefore an actualized intellect understands all those things whose intelligible species are actually within the intellect. Therefore it seems that intelligible species are not retained in the intellect after it ceases to actually understand them; and consequently they do not remain in a soul after its separation from its body so that the soul might understand through them.

(16) Furthermore, acquired habits produce acts which are similar to those acts from which the habits were acquired, as is clear from what the Philosopher says in Book II of his *Ethics,*[6] that a man becomes a builder by building, and that once he has become a builder, he is able to build. But the intellect acquires intelligible species by the fact that it turns toward phantasms. Therefore the intellect can never understand through such species unless it turns to phantasms. Therefore it seems that when a soul is separated from its body, it cannot understand through acquired species.

(17) Nor can it even be claimed that a separated soul understands through species that some higher substance causes to flow into it; for each thing that is capable of receiving has a proper agent from which by nature it receives whatever it receives. It is the nature of the human intellect to receive species from the senses; therefore it does not receive them from higher substances.

(18) Furthermore, for those things whose nature it is to be caused by lesser agents, the action of a higher agent is not sufficient; for example, animals which by nature are generated from semen are not generated by the action of the sun alone. But the human soul by nature receives its species from sensible realities. Therefore, in order that a human soul acquire intelligible species, an influx from higher substances alone is not sufficient.

(19) Furthermore, an agent must be proportioned to its patient, and that which causes an influx, to the recipient of the influx. But the intelligence of higher substances is not proportioned to a human intellect, since these substances possess knowledge which is more universal than ours and incomprehensible to us. It seems, therefore, that a separated soul is unable to understand through species derived from higher substances; and consequently there is no way in which a soul can understand.

On The Contrary,

To understand is the loftiest operation of a soul. Therefore, if to understand does not belong to a soul which lacks its body, no other operation belongs to a soul either. But if no other operation belongs to a soul without its body, it is impossible that a soul exist separate from its body. However, we assert that a soul does exist in separation from its body. Consequently it is necessary to assert that a separated soul understands.

(2) Furthermore, those who are recorded in Scripture to have been brought back to life possessed after this event the same knowledge which they possessed prior to it. Consequently the knowledge of those things which a human beings possesses in this world is not taken away after a person's death. Therefore a soul can understand through species acquired prior to death.

(3) Furthermore, a likeness of lower beings is verified in loftier beings; thus it is that mathematicians through examining the likenesses of things which go on in this world as verified in the celestial bodies can foretell the future. Now a soul is loftier in nature than all bodily things. Therefore a likeness of all bodies exists in a soul, and it exists in an intelligible mode of being since a soul is an intellective substance. Consequently it is clear that a soul through its own nature would be able to understand all bodily things even when it will have been separated from its body.

The Response:

It must be stated that a problem arises in dealing with this question from the fact that in the present life our souls seem to have a need of senses [7] in order to understand. Hence the truth of this question must be viewed in different ways according to the various reasons that are given for the soul's dependence on the senses.

For some authorities, namely, the Platonists, asserted that senses are necessary in order that our souls might understand. They do not mean that science is essentially caused in us by the senses, but accidentally, inasmuch, that is, as our soul is somehow aroused by the senses to recall things it had previously known, the knowledge of which it possesses as a natural endowment. And to understand this position, we must realize that Plato [8] maintained that the species of things subsist as separate and actually intelligible; these species he called 'Ideas'; and said that it is through participation in the Ideas, or through some sort of influx from them, that our soul know and understands. He said further that before a soul is united to its body it can use that knowledge freely; but that from its union with the body the soul is so weighed down and almost permeated by the body that it seems to have forgotten things that it had previously known because it had connatural knowledge of them. But the soul is stimulated in some fashion by the senses to turn within itself and to recall those things which it understood in a prior state, and of which it possessed innate knowledge; as it sometimes happens that we too, as the result of our seeing certain sensible objects, recall vividly other sensible things that we seem to have forgotten.

Now this position of Plato on knowledge and on sensible things is in harmony with his position on the generation of natural things. For he asserted that the forms of natural things, through which each individual is fixed in its species, arise from a participation in the Ideas of which we have just spoken, so that lower agents have no other role than to make matter fit to participate in the separate species.

Now if one adopts this position, the question before us is easily solved. For according to the Platonists a soul does not need sensible things essentially but only accidentally in order to understand, and this need will be removed when the soul will have been separated from its body; for when the body no longer weighs upon the soul, the soul will not need to be aroused but will of itself be alert and ready to understand all things.

However, according to this position, it does not seem that one can assign a reasonable cause why a soul should be united to a body. It is not united for the good of the soul, since a soul not united to a body could carry out perfectly its proper operation, and because of its union to its body its proper operation is hindered. Likewise one cannot say that a soul is united to its body for the good of the body; for a soul does not exist for the sake of the body, but the body rather exists for the good of the soul, since a soul is nobler than a body. Hence it also seems inappropriate that a soul should sustain harm to its own operation in order to ennoble its body.

It also seems to be a consequence of this position that the union of a soul to its body is not natural; for whatever is natural to some thing does not hinder its proper operation. Consequently, if union with a body hinders the soul's intellectual understanding, it will not be natural for a soul to be united to a body but contrary to nature; and so it follows that a human being who is constituted by the union of soul and body will not be a natural being, and this seems to be absurd. Likewise it is obvious from experience that knowledge does not arise in us from participation in separate species but is acquired from the senses; for he who lacks one of the senses lacks knowledge of those sensible things which are grasped by that sense, as one who is born blind cannot possess knowledge of colors.

Now there is another position which maintains that the senses serve the human soul in understanding, not accidentally, as the Platonists hold, but essentially. This theory does not in fact hold that we acquire knowledge from the senses, but that the senses prepare the soul to obtain knowledge from some other source; and this is the doctrine of Avicenna.[9] For Avicenna holds that there is a separate substance, which he calls an 'agent Intellect' or an agent 'Intelligence,' from which there flow into our intellect intelligible species through which we understand; and further that through the operations of the sensitive part of the soul, namely, the imagination and other powers of this sort, our intellect is made ready to turn to the agent Intelligence and to receive from it an outpouring of intelligible species.

This position is also consistent with what he teaches about the generation of natural things. For he holds that all substantital forms flow from the Intelligence, and that natural agents do no more than prepare matter to receive forms from the agent Intelligence.

According to this position, as with that of the Platonists, it seems that the question now before us presents very little difficulty. For if the senses are necessary for understanding only insofar as they make the soul ready to receive species from the agent Intelligence by causing the soul to turn toward this Intelligence, then when the soul will finally have been separated from its body, it will turn of itself to the agent Intelligence and will receive intelligible species from it. At this point the senses will not be necessary to the soul for understanding, just as a ship which is necessary for crossing the sea is no longer necessary for a man once he has crossed.

But from this doctrine it seems to follow that a human being would instantaneously acquire all knowledge, both of things perceived by the senses as well as of other things. For if we understand through species which flow into us from the agent Intelligence, and if to receive an influx of this kind we need only turn our soul toward the Intelligence that has been described, then whenever our soul turns to the Intelligence, it will be able to receive the influx of all intellgible species whatever. For one cannot say that the soul is turned toward one species but not toward another; and consequently a person blind from birth will be able, by imagining sounds, to acquire a knowledge of colors or of any other sensible object, and this is obviously false. It is also clear that in order to understand, we need the sensitive powers not only to acquire knowledge, but also to use the knowledge we have acquired. For we cannot actively consider even those things which we know except by turning to phantasms, even though Avicenna teaches the contrary. For hence it is that when the organs of the sensitive powers which preserve and contain phantasms are injured, the vision of the soul is handicapped in considering even those things which it knows. It is also clear that we need some phantasms to understand things divinely revealed to us through the influence of higher substances. Hence Dionysius says,[10] in Chapter I of his *Celestial Hierarchy,* that it is impossible for the divine light to shine upon us unless it be clothed in a number of sacred veils; and this would not be so if the phantasms were not necessary to us except insofar as they served to turn us to the higher substances.

Consequently a different doctrine is demanded to explain that sensitive powers are necessary to a soul if it is to understand, not accidentally as merely arousing it, as Plato held, nor as merely preparing it, as Avicenna teaches, but as making present to the intellective soul its proper object; for as the Philosopher states, in Book III of the *De Anima,*[11] "Phantasms are related to the intellective soul as sensible realities are related to the senses." But just as colors are not actually visible except through light, so phantasms are not actually intelligible except through the agent intellect.

And this doctrine is in agreement with what we hold concerning the generation of natural things. For just as we teach that higher agents cause natural forms through the mediation of natural agents, so we hold that the agent intellect causes knowledge in our possible intellect through phantasms which are made actually intelligible by the agent intellect. Nor is it relevant to this issue whether the agent intellect is a separate substance, as some hold, or whether it is a light in which our soul participates after the fashion of higher substances.

Now is we accept this position, it is even more difficult to see how a separated soul is able to understand; for there will not be any phantasms, which require bodily organs if they are to be apprehended and retained. But if phantasms are taken away, it does not seem possible that the soul should understand, any more than the sense of sight can see in the absence of colors. Therefore, in order to escape this difficulty, one must note that since the soul is lowest in order of intellective substances, its participation in intellectual light or intellectual nature is of the lowest and weakest kind. For in God, the Primary Knower, the intellectual nature is so powerful that through one intelligible form, namely, His own essence, God understands all things. However, lower intellectual substances understand through many species, and the higher one of these substances is, the fewer forms it possesses and the more its power is capable of understanding all things through a small number of forms. But since a lower intellectual substance has not so great a power of understanding as does a higher substance, its knowledge would remain incomplete if it possessed forms of the same universality as those possessed by the higher substance. The reason is that it would then know things only in a universal way, and would not be able to proceed from its knowledge of those few forms to a knowledge of singulars.

Now the human soul is lowest among intellectual substances and has the least power of understanding. If then it were to receive forms at the level of abstraction and universality which is appropriate to separate substances, its knowledge would be very imperfect since it would know things in a universal and indistinct way. And consequently, in order that its knowledge be made perfect and distinct by reference to singulars, the soul must gather its knowledge of truth from singular things. But for this it is necessary that the light of the agent intellect exist so that things may be received in the soul in a higher mode of being than they have in matter. Consequently for the perfection of its intellectual operation it was necessary that the soul be united to a body.

There is, however, no doubt that because of changes in the body and the soul's preoccupation with the senses, a soul is hindered in receiving an influx from the separate substances; hence it is that people who are asleep or bereft of their senses receive revelations that are not given to those who are using their senses. Therefore, when a soul will have been totally separated from its body, it will be able more fully to perceive an influx from higher substances, in the sense that through an influx of this kind the soul will be able to understand without phantasms, something which it cannot do at present. But an influx of this kind will not cause knowledge which is as perfect and as determinate with respect to singulars as the knowledge which we acquire in this life through our senses. The exception would be those souls who will have, over and above this natural influx, another super-natural influx of grace, by which they can know all things fully and see even God Himself. Separated souls, too, will possess a determinate knowledge of things which they knew while here on earth and whose intelligible species are preserved within them.

Replies to the Opposing Arguments:

(1) The Philosopher is speaking about the operation of the intellectual soul insofar as it is united to its body; for in this state it does not understand without phantasms, as we have said.

(2) According to its present state, in which it is united to its body, a soul does not participate in intelligible species derived from higher substances, but only in intellectual light; and consequently the soul needs phantasms as objects from which it acquires intelligible species. However, after separation from the body, a soul will participate more fully even in intelligible species, and hence it will not need external objects.

(3) The Philosopher is speaking of the position of certain men who held that the intellect has a bodily organ just as a sense does; this is clear from what precedes the text referred to. For if this be granted, a separated soul will be totally unable to understand. Or one might say that he is speaking about understanding according to the mode of understanding by which we understand in this life.

(4) A soul is united to its body through its operation, which is

understanding, not in the sense that without a body the soul could not understand in any way at all, but because in the natural order it cannot understand adequately without a body, as we have explained.

(5) And through this last the answer to the fifth argument is clear.

(6) Phantasms are not objects of the intellect unless they are made to be actually intelligible through the light of the agent intellect. Hence the intelligible species that are received in the intellect, of whatever sort they may be and whatever their source, will have no other formality as an object than that according to which objects diversify powers.

(7) The operation of the agent intellect and of the possible intellect has to do with phantasms insofar as a soul is united to its body. But when a soul will have been separated from its body, it will receive through its possible intellect species flowing from higher substances, and through its agent intellect it will have the power to understand.

(8) The proper operation of a soul is to understand objects that are actually intelligible; and the kinds of intellectual operation are not diversified by the fact that the actual intelligible objects are derived from phantasms or from some other source.

(9) A separated soul does not understand things through its own essence, nor through the essence of the things understood, but through species which flow into the soul from higher substances. But it receives such species only after it is separated from its body, and not from the first moment of its existence, as the Platonists held.

(10) And through this last answer the reply to the tenth argument is clear.

(11) If a soul, when united to its body, possessed innate species, it would be able to understand through them just as it understands through species which it has acquired. But although a soul is more perfect in nature when united to its body, nevertheless on account of bodily changes and preoccupation with the senses, it is held back so it cannot so freely be joined to higher substances in order to receive their influence, as it will be able to after its separation from the body.

(12) It is not natural to a soul to understand through infused species while it is united to its body, but only after it has been separated from its body, as we have said.

(13) Separated souls will also be able to understand by species which they had acquired while in a body; not, however, through such species only, but also through infused species, as we have said.

(14) And through this last answer the reply to the fourteenth argument is clear.

(15) Sometimes intelligible species are in the possible intellect only potentially, and then a human being understands potentially and needs something to actualize him; this can be either teaching or his own investigations. Sometimes, on the other hand, intelligible species

are in the possible intellect in a fully actual way, and then the human being actually understands. Sometimes, however, the intelligible species are in the possible intellect in a way that is midway between potency and act, that is, as a habit, and when this is so, a human being can actually understand when he wishes to do so. And it is in this way that acquired intelligible species are in the possible intellect when someone is not actually understanding.

(16) As we have said, intellectual operations do not differ specifically whether the intelligible species which is the object of the intellect is derived from phantasms or from some other source. For the operation of a power is distinguished and specified by the object inasmuch as this latter has the formality of object, and not because of its material content. And consequently, if a separated soul would understand by means of intelligible species preserved in the intellect and derived from phantasms without turning to those phantasms, there would be no specific difference between the operation which is caused by these acquired species and the operation through which the species are acquired.

(17) The possible intellect is not by nature receptive of anything from phantasms except insofar as the phantasms are actualized by the light of the agent intellect, which is a kind of participation in the light of the higher substances. Consequently there is no objection to saying that the possible intellect can receive species from the higher substances.

(18) Knowledge is naturally caused in the soul by phantasms in the soul's present state of union with a body, and in this state knowledge cannot be caused solely by higher agents. However, this will be possible when a soul will have been separated from its body.

(19) From the fact that the knowledge of separate substances is not proportioned to our soul it does not follow that the soul cannot achieve any understanding as a result of an influx from these substances, but only that it cannot achieve an understanding that is full and clear, as we have explained.

Notes to Question Fifteen

1. Aristotle, *De Anima,* I, 4 (403a 8-9).

2. Aristotle, *De Anima,* III, 7 (431a 14-15).

3. Aristotle, *De Anima,* I, 4 (408b 24-25).

4. Aristotle, *De Anima,* III, 7 (431a 15); III, 8 (432a 8-9).

5. Plato, *Phaedo,* 75C-D.

6. Aristotle, *Nicomachean Ethics,* II, 1 (1103a 26 - b 2).

7. For this translation I have adopted the reading of the manuscripts which are not of the University of Paris tradition. The Parisian manuscripts read *sensibilibus* at this point and throughout this question; the other manuscripts read *sensibus.*

8. Plato, *Phaedo,* 73C - 77A; *Timaeus,* 52A - 53C.

9. Avicenna, *De Anima,* V, cap. 6, fol. 25vb ff., ed. Venetiis, 1508.

10. Pseudo-Dionysius, *De Coelesti hierarchia,* I, 2 (PG 3: 122).

11. Aristotle, *De Anima,* III, 7 (431a 14-15).

QUESTION SIXTEEN

Parallel texts: *De Ver.*, q. 10, a. 11; q. 18, a. 5, ad 7, ad 8; *In lib. Boet. De Trin.*, q. 6, a. 3; *Contra gent.*, II, 6; III, 42-46; *Summa theol.*, I, q. 88, a. 1; *In II Metaph.*, lect. 1.

The sixteenth question that is asked about the soul is this: Whether a soul, when it is joined to its body, can understand separate substances.[1] And it seems that it can.

(1) For no form is prevented from achieving its end by the matter to which it is naturally united. But it seems that the end of an intellective soul is to understand separate substances, which are intelligible to a very high degree. For the end of anything is to achieve fullness in its operation. Therefore a soul is not prevented from understanding separate substances because of the fact that it is united to the body which is its proper matter.

(2) Furthermore, the end of a human being is happiness. Now ultimate happiness, according to the Philosopher in Book X of the *Ethics*,[2] consists in the operation of a human being's loftiest power, namely, the intellect, with respect to its noblest object, which would seem to be nothing other than a separate substance. Therefore the ultimate end of a human being is to understand separate substances. Now it is not fitting that a human being should fail totally in achieving his end, for then his existence would be meaningless. Therefore a human being is able to know separate substances. But it is of the very nature of a human being that its soul be united to its body. Therefore a soul united to its body is able to understand separate substances.

(3) Furthermore, every act of generation arrives at a terminus, for no motion continues to infinity. Now there is a kind of generation that belongs to the intellect insofar as it is reduced from potency to act, that is, insofar as it becomes actually knowing. Therefore this motion does not go on to infinity but at some point it will arrive at a terminus; that is, when it is totally actualized as a knower. Now this cannot occur unless the intellect understands all intelligible objects, and among these the separate substances hold the primary rank. Therefore the human intellect is able to attain an understanding of separate substances.

(4) Furthermore, it seems to be more difficult to separate from matter things which are not separate and then to understand them than to understand things which of themselves are separate from matter. But our intellect, even when united to its body, separates from matter things which of themselves are not separate when it abstracts from material things the intelligible species through which it understands material things. Therefore our intellect will be even more capable of understanding separate substances.

(5) Furthermore, sensible objects that are in the highest degree perceptible are for this very reason not well perceived by the senses because they destroy the harmony of the sense organ. However, if there were a sense organ which was not injured by such a sensible object, then the more intensely perceptible were the object, the more acutely would the sense power perceive it. Now an intellect is in no fashion injured by an intelligible object but is rather perfected by it. Therefore an intellect understands better those objects which are more intelligible. But separate substances, which of themselves are actually intelligible inasmuch as they are immaterial, are more intelligible than material substances, which not intelligible except potentially. Therefore, since an intellective soul while united to its body understands material substances, it is all the more able to understand separate substances.

(6) Furthermore, an intellective soul even while united to its body abstracts the quiddity from things which have a quiddity. And since there cannot be a regress to infinity, it is necessary that the intellect arrive in its abstractive process at a quiddity which is not a thing possessing a quiddity, but a quiddity only. Therefore, since separate substances are nothing other than subsistent quiddities, it seems that an intellective soul united to its body can understand separate substances.

(7) Furthermore, it is natural for us to know causes through their effects. Now there must exist some effects of separate substances in sensible and material things since all corporeal realities are governed by God through the ministry of angels, as is clear from Augustine in Book III of the *De Trinitate*.[3] Therefore a soul united to its body can, through sensible things, understand separate substances.

(8) Furthermore, a soul united to its body understands itself; for mind understands and loves itself, as Augustine says in Book IX of the *De Trinitate*.[4] But a soul belongs to the nature of separate intellectual substances. Therefore, while united to its body, it can understand separate substances.

(9) Furthermore, the intellect is related to intelligible objects as sight is to visible objects. But our power of sight can know all visible objects, even those which are incorruptible, although our sense of sight

itself is corruptible. Therefore our intellect, even on the supposition that it were corruptible, would be able to understand incorruptible separate substances, since they are of themselves intelligible.

On The Contrary,

A soul understands nothing apart from a phantasm, as the Philosopher says in Book III of the *De Anima*.[5] But separate substances cannot be understood through phantasms. Therefore a soul united to a body cannot understand separate substances.

The Response:

It must be stated that Aristotle promised, in Book III of the *De Anima*,[6] to resolve this question although he does not in fact do so in those books of his which have come down to us. Hence there was an opportunity for Aristotle's followers to proceed along diverse lines in the solutions they proposed.

For some maintained that our soul, even while united to its body, can achieve an understanding of separate substances. Further, they hold that to understand separate substances is the ultimate happiness for human beings; but they differ in their explanation of the way in which we understand these substances. For some of them held that our soul can arrive at an understanding of separate substances, not indeed in the same way in which we attain an understanding of other intelligible objects, about which we learn in the speculative sciences through definitions and demonstrations, but rather through a 'continuation'[7] of the agent intellect with us. For they maintain that the agent intellect is a separate substance which by nature understands separate substances. Hence, when this agent intellect will have been united to us in such a way that we understand by and through it, as we now understand through habitual scientific knowledge, the consequence would be that we would understand separate substances. And they give the following explanation of the way in which their agent intellect might be joined to us so that we might understand through it.

For it is clear from what the Philosopher says in Book II of the *De Anima*[8] that when we are said to be something or to do something, two factors are involved: one of these factors is comparable to form, the other to matter; for example, we are said to become healthy by means of health and in our body, so that health is related to the body as form is to matter. It is also evident that we understand through the agent intellect and through 'speculated'[9] intelligible objects; for we arrive at a knowledge of conclusions through principles which are naturally known and through the agent intellect. Consequently it is necessary that the agent intellect be related to immediately cognized intelligible objects in the way in which a principal cause is related to an instrument, and as form is related to matter, or act to potency; for the more perfect of two things is always related to the other as the act of the other.

Now whatever receives within itself that which is like matter also receives that which is like form; for example, when a body acquires a surface, it also acquires color, which is a kind of form with respect to the surface, or when the pupil of the eye acquires color, it also acquires light, which is the act of color, since color is made actually visible by light. In this way, then, the possible intellect receives a part of the agent intellect in proportion to the number of immediately cognized intelligible objects it receives from that intellect. Therefore, when the possible intellect will have acquired all immediately cognized intelligible objects, it will at that moment totally receive the agent intellect within itself; and thus the agent intellect will become as it were the form of the possible intellect, and will consequently be one with us. Hence, just as at present we understand through the possible intellect, so at that time we shall understand through the agent intellect not only all natural objects but also all separate substances.

But on this point there is a diversity of opinions among those who follow this teaching. For some, who maintain that the possible intellect is corruptible, state that the possible intellect can in no way understand the agent intellect or separate substances. However, when we are in the state of continuation with the agent intellect, we shall understand the agent intellect itself and other separate substances by mean of the same agent intellect inasmuch as it will be united to us as a form. But other exponents of this doctrine, asserting that the possible intellect is incorruptible, state that the possible intellect can understand the agent intellect and other separate substances.

This position, however, is untenable, groundless and contrary to what Aristotle meant. It is untenable because it asserts two premises which are impossible, that the agent intellect is a substance separate from us in existence, and that we understand through the agent intellect as through a form. For we operate by means of some principle as a form to the extent that by it we cause something actually to exist: for instance, something which is hot heats by means of its hotness insofar as it is actually hot; for nothing acts except insofar as it is in act. Consequently that by which something acts or operates must be formally united to the agent in respect to its existence. Hence it is impossible that one of two substances which are separate in existence should operate formally through the other. And so if the agent intellect is a substance separate from us in existence, it is impossible that we should formally understand by means of it. It would, however, be possible that we should understand by means of its activity, just as we are said to see by the sun's illumination.

The position we have described is groundless as well as impossible because the arguments which are advanced to support it do not of necessity lead to their conclusions; this is obvious for two reasons. First, because if the agent intellect is a separate substance, as they maintain, the relation of the agent intellect to immediately cognized intelligible objects will not be comparable to the relation of light to colors, but rather to the sun inasmuch as it is the source of light. Hence the possible intellect, from the fact that it receives immediately cognized intelligible objects, will not be joined to the substance of the agent intellect but rather to an effect of the agent intellect; just as the eye by the fact that it receives colors is not united to the substance of the sun but to the light of the sun. Secondly, let us even concede, for the sake of argument, that the possible intellect is somehow joined to the very substance of the agent intellect because it receives immediately cognized intelligible objects from it. It does not follow, however, from this that the possible intellect would be completely joined to the substance of the agent intellect by receiving all those intelligible objects which are known by abstraction from phantasms and acquired by means of the principles of demonstration. This conclusion would follow only if it could be proved that the totality of intelligible objects that are known in this way were equal to the power and substance of the agent intellect. But this proposition is obviously false; because if the agent intellect is a separate substance, it exists at a higher level of being than all the things in the realm of nature which are made intelligible through its agency.

Therefore it is clear that these men did not understand the error in their argument. For although they held that through one or two immediately cognized intelligible objects the agent intellect is united to us, it does not follow according to them that for this reason we should understand all other immediately cognizable intelligible objects. For it is clear that separate substances surpass those intelligible objects which they call 'immediately known' to a far greater degree than all those object taken together would surpass any one or two separate substances. For all of these objects belong to the same genus and are intelligible in the same way; whereas separate substances belong to a higher genus and are understood in a higher way. Hence, even if there were a continuation of the agent intellect with us inasmuch as it is a form and an agent which produces these intelligibles, it does not therefore follow that there is a continuation of the agent intellect with us because it understands separate substances.

It is also clear that this position is contrary to the meaning of Aristotle, who says, in Book I of the *Ethics*,[10] that happiness is a common good which can be attained by all those who are not totally incapacitated for acquiring virtue. Now to understand all those things they call immediately cognized intelligible objects either is impossible for any human being or is so rare that in this life no human being ever achieved such perfection except Christ, who was God and man. Hence it is impossible that this kind of understanding be required for human happiness. Now ultimate human happiness consists in understanding the noblest intelligible objects, as the Philosopher states in Book X of the *Ethics*.[11] If, therefore, human happiness consists in understanding separate substances, the noblest of intelligible objects, it is not necessary that a person, in order to gain this knowledge, should also understand all the objects that are immediately and directly intelligible.

It is also clear that the position we have been treating is contrary to Aristotle's meaning in another way. For it is said in Book I of the *Ethics*[12] that happiness consists in an operation which is in accordance with complete virtue. And therefore, as Aristotle himself says at the end of Book I of the *Ethics*,[13] he found it necessary to deal specifically with each of the virtues in order to make clear in what happiness precisely consists. Some virtues he calls 'moral' virtues, such as fortitude, temperance, and others of this kind; but some he calls 'intellectual' virtues, of which there are five according to him: wisdom, understanding, science, prudence and art. Among these he assigns first place to wisdom, and he states in Book X[14] that ultimate happiness consists in the activity of wisdom. Now from what he says at the beginning of his *Metaphysics*,[15] it is clear that wisdom is first philosophy itself. Hence it follows that the ultimate human happiness which can be possessed in this life, according to the teaching of Aristotle, is that knowledge of separate substances that can be gained through the principles of philosophy, and is not a knowledge gained through that 'continuation' of the agent intellect with us which is the fanciful invention of some philosophers.

Hence there was still another opinion among the followers of Aristotle, according to which a human soul can arrive at an understanding of separate substances themselves by means of the principles of philosophy. In order to establish this point they argued as follows: It is clear that a human soul can abstract from natural things their quiddities and can understand these quiddities. This process occurs whenever we understand what a material thing is. Therefore, if that abstracted quiddity is not a pure quiddity but rather something which has a quiddity, then our intellect must once again abstract that quiddity. And since one cannot proceed to infinity, one will finally arrive at an understanding of a simple quiddity; and in contemplating such a quiddity our intellect will understand separate substances, which are nothing other than simple quiddities.

But this argument is wholly inadequate. First, because the quiddities of material things belong to a different genus than separate quiddities, and they have a different mode of existing. Hence from the fact that our intellect understands the quiddities of material things it does not follow that it understands separate quiddities. Further, diverse quiddities grasped by the intellect differ in species. Hence it is that even someone who understands the quiddity of one material thing does not understand the quiddity of another; for one who understands what is a rock is does not therefore understand what an animal is. Hence, even if one grants that separate quiddities were the same kind of intelligible object as material quiddities, it would not follow that he who understands the quiddities of material things would understand separate substances; unless, of course, one were to follow the teaching of Plato, [16] who held that separate substances are the species of these sensible things.

And therefore we must take a different position and say that a human soul, because of its union with its body, has its sight directed toward phantasms. Consequently it does not acquire the form through which it understands something except through species derived from phantasms. And the statement of Dionysius in Chapter I of *The Celestial Hierarchy* [17] agrees with this position. For he says that it is impossible for the divine light to shine upon us unless it be clothed in a number of sacred veils. Therefore a soul, while united to its body, can rise to only such a knowledge of separate substances as that to which it can be led through species received from phantasms. Now in this fashion a soul is not able to understand what separate substances are, since such substances are utterly disproportionate to intelligible objects derived from phantasms; but we can in this way and in some fashion know that separate substances exist. In the same way we can proceed from lowly effects to a knowledge of higher causes, so that we know only that these causes exist; and at the same time that we know that these causes are superior, we know that they cannot be of the same order as the effects we observe. And this is rather to know what they are not than to know what they are. And in this sense it is to some extent true that insofar as we understand quiddities which we abstract from material things, our intellect, in turning toward those quiddities, can understand separate substances, so that it underststands them to be immaterial, like those quiddities themselves which are abstracted from matter. And thus through the reflective activity of our intellect we are led to a knowledge of separate intelligible substances. Nor is it remarkable that in this life we are not able to know separate substances in the sense of understanding what they are, but rather what they are not, for this is the same way in which we know the quiddity and nature even of celestial bodies. Even Aristotle makes this same point in Book I of his *De Caelo et Mundo,* [18] when he proves that celestial bodies are neither heavy nor light, neither able to be generated nor corrupted, and that they do not possess contrariety.

Replies to the Opposing Arguments:

(1) The end to which the natural power of a human soul reaches is to know separate substances in the way stated above; and it is not hindered from achieving this end because it is united to a body. And likewise the ultimate happiness of a human being consists in that kind of knowledge about a separate substance at which a human being can arrive through natural things.

(2) Thus the answer to the second argument is obvious.

(3) The possible intellect is continually being brought from potency to act because it understands more and more, but the final stage of actualization or generation of this kind will be to understand the highest intelligible reality, and this is the divine essence. However, the intellect cannot achieve this end through what belongs to nature, but only through grace.

(4) It is more difficult both to separate from matter and to understand than it is to understand things which are separate from matter, if one is dealing with things of the same kind; but if one is dealing with things of different kinds, this is not necessarily so. For there can be greater difficulty in simply understanding some things which are separate than in separating from matter and understanding other things.

(5) With respect to sense objects that are perceptible in the highest degree, one of the senses can be subject to a two-fold deficiency: in one way, because the sense power cannot comprehend the object since the object is disproportionate to the sense power; secondly, because after perceiving such lofty sensible objects a sense power does not perceive lesser sense objects because the sense organ has been damaged. Therefore, although the intellect does not have an organ which can be injured by a lofty intelligible object, nevertheless a lofty intelligible object can transcend the the power of our intellect to understand. Such an intelligble object is a separate substance, which transcends the power of our intellect, whose nature it is to be perfected by species abstracted from phantasms because it is united to its body. Nevertheless, if our intellect were to understand separate substances, it would be more rather than less capable of understanding other things.

(6) Quiddities abstracted from material things are not adequate so that through them we might be able to know what separate substances are, as we have already shown.

(7) A similar answer can be given to the seventh argument; for remote effects, as we have already explained, do not suffice so that through them we can know what their cause is.

(8) Our possible intellect does not understand itself directly by apprehending its own essence, but rather through a species derived from phantasms. Hence the Philosopher says, in Book III of the *De Anima*,[19] that the possible intellect is intelligible just as other things are. And this is so because nothing is intelligible insofar as it is in potency but only because it is in act, as is said in Book IX of the *Metaphysics*.[20] Hence, since the possible intellect belongs only potentially to intelligible being, it cannot be understood except through its own form by which it is made to be actual, and this form is a species abstracted from phantasms; just as everything else is understood through its form. And it is a characteristic common to all the powers of the soul that acts are known through their objects, and powers are known through their acts, and the soul is known through its powers. In like fashion, therefore, the intellective soul is known through its intelligible being. A species received from phantasms is not the form of a separate substance; hence a separate substance cannot be known by such a form in the way in which the possible intellect is known to some degree through such a form.

(9) This argument has no validity whatever for two reasons. First, because intelligible beings do not exist for the sake of the intellects which know them, but are rather the ends and the perfections of intellects. Hence, if an intelligible substance should not be understood by some other intellect, it does not follow that for this reason such a substance is without a purpose; for that is said to be 'without a purpose' which pertains to the end which something fails to reach. Secondly, because although separate substances are not understood by our intellect inasmuch as it is united to its body, nevertheless they are understood by separate substances.

(10) The species of which sight is receptive can be the likenesses of bodies of any sort, whether corruptible or incorruptible. But species abstracted from phantasms, of which the possible intellect is receptive, are not the likenesses of separate substances; and hence the two situations are not alike.

Notes to Question Sixteen

1. Separate substances or angels belong to a higher level of being than do human beings. In the doctrine of St. Thomas they are pure intelligences, each specifically different from another. Their knowledge is co-created with them and is not derived from things. They are not, however, fully actual; even in them there is a distinction between essence and existence.

2. Aristotle, *Nicomachean Ethics,* X, 7 (1177a 11-18).

3. St. Augustine, *De Trinitate,* III, 4 (PL 42: 873)

4. St. Augustine, *De Trinitate,* IX, 4 (PL 42: 963).

5. Aristotle, *De Anima,* III, 7 (431a 16).

6. Aristotle, *De Anima,* III, 7 (431b 19).

7. 'Continuation' a literal rendering of the Latin *continuatio* signifies the uniting in some way of the separate agent intellect with the human soul. Followers of Avicenna and Averroes tried to explain in various ways how the purely immaterial and separate intellect could be joined in some fashion to the human soul in order to account for human acts of understanding. Hereafter I shall usually translate *continuatio* as 'conjunction.'

8. Aristotle, *De Anima,* II, 2 (414a 4-14).

9. St. Thomas seems to indicate that he is borrowing this term from the Arabian thinkers. The term is *intelligibilia speculata.* By this I believe he means "intelligible objects that are immediately seen" or "immediately cognized." This is how I shall normally translate this phrase.

10. Aristotle, *Nicomachean Ethics,* I, 9 (1099b 18-20).

11. Aristotle, *Nicomachean Ethics,* X, 7 (1177a 11-18).

12. Aristotle, *Nicomachean Ethics,* I, 7 (1098a 16-17).

13. Aristotle, *Nicomachean Ethics,* I, 13 (1102a 5-6; 1103a 4-6).

14. Aristotle, *Nicomachean Ethics,* X, 7 (1177a 10 - 1177b 1).

15. Aristotle, *Metaphysics,* I, 2 (982b 7-10).

16. Plato, *Timaeus,* 52 A.

17. Pseudo-Dionysius, *De Coelesti hierarchia,* I, 2 (PG 3: 122).

18. Aristotle, *De Caelo,* I, 2 (269b 30); I, 3 (270a 12-22).

19. Aristotle, *De Anima,* III, 4 (429b 7-9).

20. Aristotle, *Metaphysics,* IX, 9 (1051a 29-33).

QUESTION SEVENTEEN

Parallel texts: *Contra gent.*, III, 45; *Summa theol.*, I, q. 89, a. 2; *Quodl.*, III, q. 9, a. 1.

The seventeenth question that is asked about the soul is this: Whether a separated soul understands separate substances. And it seems that it does not.

(1) For a more perfect operation belongs to a more perfect substance. But a soul united to its body seems to be more perfect than when it is separated from its body, since any part is more perfect when united to the whole of which it is part than when separated from it. Therefore, if a soul cannot understand separate substances when united to its body, it seems that it will not be able to do so when separated from its body.

(2) Furthermore, our soul is able to know separate substances either naturally or solely by grace. If our soul can know separate substances naturally, then since it is natural for a soul to be united to its body, it would not be hindered from knowing separate substances because of its union with its body. However, if it knows them through grace alone, then since not all souls separated from their bodies possess grace, it follows at least that not all separated souls know separate substances.

(3) Furthermore, a soul is united to its body in order that the soul might be perfected in the body by sciences and by virtues. Now the highest perfection of a soul consists in knowledge about separate substances. Therefore, if a soul knows separate substances only because it is separated from its body, then a soul is united to its body to no purpose.

(4) Furthermore, if a soul when separated from its body were to know a separate substance, it would have to know the separate substance either through the essence of the separate substance or through a species of it. But a soul does not know a separate substance through its essence because the essence of a separate substance is not one with a separated soul. Nor does a soul know a separate substance through a species because there can be no abstraction of the species of separate

substances, since they are simple. Therefore a soul separated from its body does not know separate substances in any fashion.

(5) Furthermore, if a soul when separated from its body knows a separate substance, it knows that substance either by its senses or by its intellect. Now it is obvious that a soul does not know a separate substance through its senses, because separate substances cannot be sensed. Nor does it know a separate substance through its intellect, because its intellect does not deal with singulars and separate substances are singular substances. Therefore a separated soul has no way of knowing separate substances.

(6) Furthermore, the possible intellect of our soul differs more from an angel than our imagination differs from our possible intellect, because the imagination and the possible intellect are rooted in the self-same substance of the soul. But the imagination can in no way understand the possible intellect. Therefore our possible intellect can in no way apprehend a separate substance.

(7) Furthermore, just as the will is related to the good, so is the intellect related to truth. But the will of some separated souls, namely, those of the damned, cannot be ordered to the good. Therefore neither can their intellect be in any way ordered to truth, which an intellect achieves most fully in coming to know a separate substance. Therefore not every separated soul is able to know a separate substance.

(8) Furthermore, as we have already said, the philosophers say that ultimate happiness consists in understanding separate substances. Now if the souls of those who are damned understand separate substances, which we cannot understand in this life, it would seem that the damned are closer to happiness then we are; and this is not fitting.

(9) Furthermore, one intelligence understands another intelligence through the mode of its own substance, as is said in the *Liber de Causis*.[1] But it seems that a separated soul cannot know its own substance, because the possible intellect does not know itself except through a species that has been abstracted or derived from phantasms, as is said in Book III of the *De Anima*.[2] Consequently a separated soul is unable to know separate substances.

(10) Futhermore, there are two ways of knowing.[3] One way consists in going from what is posterior to what is prior; and in this way we know things which are more knowable without qualification by means of things which of themselves are less knowable. In the second way, one proceeds from what is prior to what is posterior; and in this way we have prior knowledge of things which are more knowable in themselves. Now the first way of knowing cannot exist in souls separated from their bodies; for this mode of knowing belongs to us insofar as we derive knowledge from our senses. Therefore a separated soul understands in the second way, that is, by proceeding

from what is prior to what is posterior; and thus it knows first the things which are more knowable without qualification. But that which is most knowable is the divine essence. Therefore, if a separated soul by its natural powers knows separate substances, it seems that by its natural powers alone a separated soul could see the divine essence, and to do this is eternal life; and this is contrary to the Apostle who says, Romans VI, "The grace of God is life eternal."[4]

(11) Furthermore, a separate substance of a lower order understands another insofar as an impression of the higher substance is present in the inferior one. But the impression of a separate substance is present in a separated soul in a far more imperfect way than it is in a separate substance. Therefore a separated soul cannot understand a separate substance.

On The Contrary,

Like is known by like. But a separated soul is a separate substance. Therefore it can understand separate substances.

The Response:

It must be said that according to the tenets of faith it seems appropriate to hold that separated souls know separate substances. For separate substances are called angels and demons, and it is to their company that the separated souls of human beings, both the good and the wicked, are assigned. Now it does not seem probable that the souls of the damned would not be aware of demons, to whose company they are assigned, and who are said to be terrifying to these souls. It seems even much less probable that the souls of the good do not know the angels in whose society they rejoice.

Moreover the fact that souls separated from their bodies should know separate substances wherever they may be is in accord with reason. For it is clear that a human soul united to its body has its sight directed toward things which are lower than the soul because of the soul's union with its body. Consequently a soul is not perfected in knowledge except by what it receives from things which are lower than it, that is, through species abstracted from phantasms. Hence the soul cannot arrive either at a knowledge of itself or at a knowledge of other things unless it be led to such knowledge from species of this kind, as we said in an earlier question.

But when a soul will finally have been separated from its body, its sight will not be oriented toward lower things in order to acquire knowledge from them. It will be freed from its body, able to receive an influx from loftier substances without turning to phantasms, which at that moment will no longer exist; and through an influx of this kind the soul will be actualized. And thus it will know itself directly, by gazing upon its own essence, and not by proceeding from the knowledge of things less knowable in themselves, as it must do now. Now its own essence belongs to the genus of separate intellectual substances and has the same mode of subsisting, although the soul is the lowest substance in this genus; for all of them are subsistent forms. Now any separate substance knows another separate substance by gazing on its own substance, because there exists in it a likeness of that other which is the object of its knowledge; this likeness results from the influx it receives either from the other substance or from some higher substance which is the common cause of them both. In the same way, therefore, a separated soul too will know separate substances by gazing directly on its own essence because of an influx it will receive either from the separate substances or from a higher cause, God. However a soul does not, by natural knowledge, know separate substances as perfectly as these separate substances know each other, because a soul is the lowest of separate substances and receives only a weak emanation of intelligible light.

Replies to the Opposing Arguments:

(1) A soul united to its body is in one respect more perfect than when separated from its body, that is, in relation to its specific nature. But with respect to its activity of understanding a soul possesses a perfection when it is separated from its body which it cannot possess while united to its body. Nor does this situation pose any difficulty because intellectual operation belongs to a soul insofar as a soul exceeds its relation to its body; for the intellect is not the act of any bodily organ.

(2) We are speaking in this argument about a separated soul's knowledge that belongs to it naturally; for if we speak of the knowledge which belongs to a separated soul through grace, a soul will be like the angels in its manner of knowing. Now this knowledge by which a soul knows separate substances in the way we have explained is natural to a soul, not without qualification, but insofar as a soul is separated from its body. Consequently, insofar as a soul is united to its body, such knowledge is not appropriate to it.

(3) The ultimate perfection for a human soul in the order of natural knowledge is to understand separate substances. But it can achieve this knowledge more perfectly by the fact that while in the

body it can be disposed to this end through study and more especially through merit. Consequently it is not united to its body to no purpose.

(4) A separated soul does not know a separate substance through that substance's essence, but through a species and a likeness of it. It must, however, be recognized that the species through which something is known is not always abstracted from the thing known, but only in the instance when the knower receives the species from the thing. And in this instance the received species is in the knower in a more simple and immaterial way than in the thing which is known. However, if the opposite were so, that is, that the thing known were more immaterial and simpler than the knower, then the species of the thing known, located in the knower, is not called 'abstract,' but rather 'impressed' or 'infused.' And it is this latter kind of species that is meant in our reply to this objection.

(5) That which is singular is not incompatible with the knowledge of our intellect except insofar as it is individuated by this particular matter; for the species belonging to our intellect must be abstracted from matter. But if there exist singulars in which the specific nature is not individuated through matter, but each of them is a specific nature which subsists immaterially, then each of them is of itself intelligible; and separate substances are singulars of this kind.

(6) The imagination and the human possible intellect are more alike, as being in a subject, than the human possible intellect and an angelic intellect; yet these latter are more alike in species and definition, since both of them are instances of intelligible being. Now action follows upon a form according to its specific nature and not with respect to its subject. Hence, with respect to similarity in action, a greater likeness is to be expected between two forms belonging to the same species found in diverse substances than between two forms differing in species found in the same subject.

(7) The damned are turned away from their ultimate end; hence their will is not directed to the good with respect to this order. However their will tends toward some good because even the demons, as Dionysius says in Chapter IV of *The Divine Names*,[5] desire what is good and best: to be, to live, to understand. But they do not direct this good toward the highest good, and therefore their will is perverse. Hence there is nothing to prevent the souls of the damned from understanding many true things, but not that first truth, namely, God, the vision of Whom would make them blessed.

(8) The ultimate happiness of a human being does not consist in the knowledge of a creature but solely in the knowledge of God. Hence Augustine says in his *Confessions*,[6] "Happy is he who knows You, even if he is ignorant of other things," that is, creatures; "unhappy is he, however, who knows other things and does not know You. But

he who knows both You and other things is not happier because he knows them, but is happy only because he knows You." Therefore, although the damned know some things of which we are ignorant, nevertheless they are further removed from true happiness than we are, for it is possible for us to achieve happiness whereas they cannot.

(9) A human soul will know itself in a different way when it will have been separated from its body than it does in this life, as we have explained.

(10) Although that mode of knowing by which one more fully knows those things which are unqualifiedly more knowable is proper to a separated soul, still it does not follow that a separated soul or any other created separate substance can, through its own natural powers, behold the divine essence. For just as separate substances have a different mode of being than do material substances, so also God has a mode of being that is different from that of all separate substances.

For in material substances one must consider three factors, all of them distinct, that is, the individual, the specific nature and existence. For we cannot say that this human being is his humanity, because humanity is constituted solely by the principles of the species; but this human being, over and above the principles of the species, contains also individuated principles, insofar as the specific nature is received and individuated in this particular matter. In like fashion humanity is not the act of existence itself that belongs to a human being. In separate substances, because they are immaterial, the specific nature is not received in any individuating matter, but the nature itself is self-subsistent. Hence in them there is no distinction between the quiddity itself and that which possesses the quiddity. However, God is His own subsistent existence. Hence just as we cannot know separate substances by knowing material quiddities, so neither can separate substances know the divine essence through a knowledge of their own substance.

(11) Because the impressions made by separate substances on a separated soul are received in an imperfect way, it does not follow that a separated soul can in no way know separate substances, but that separated souls know them imperfectly.

Notes to Question Seventeen

1. *Liber de Causis,* VIII, 16-20; ed. Bardenhewer, p. 172.

2. Aristotle, *De Anima,* III, 4 (429a 23-24; 429b 5-9; 430a 3-9; 431a 14-16; 432a 3-8).

3. St. Thomas distinguishes between demonstration *quia* and demonstration *propter quid;* in a *quia* demonstration one begins with data and then argues to a cause of the data, that is, one is arguing from effect to cause; in a *propter quid* demonstration one begins from data and argues to the effect of that data, that is, from cause to effect.

4. *Epistle to the Romans,* 6: 23.

5. Pseudo-Dionyius, *De Divinis nominibus,* IV, 23 (PG 3: 725).

6. St. Augustine, *Confessions,* V, 4, 7 (PL 32: 708).

QUESTION EIGHTEEN

Parallel texts: *In IV Sent.*, dist. 45, q. 3, a. 1, ad 1, ad 2; dist. 50, q. 1, a. 4, ad 1; *De Ver.*, q. 8, a. 4; a. 11, ad 12; q. 9, a. 6, ad 5; *Contra gent.*, II, 101; *Summa theol.*, I, q. 89, a. 3, a. 8; II-II q. 83, a. 4, ad 2; *De Anima*, q. 20, ad 3.

The eighteenth question that is asked about the soul is this: Whether a separated soul knows all natural things. And it seems that it does not.

(1) Because, as Augustine says,[1] demons know many things through experience over a long period of time, experience which a soul in fact does not possess since it is separated from its body after so short a time. Now demons possess greater intellectual capacity than a soul, because the natural cognitive powers that have been given them remain clear and lucid in them, as Dionysius says in Chapter IV, *On the Divine Names*.[2] It seems, therefore, that a separated soul does not know all natural things.

(2) Furthermore, when souls are united to their bodies, they do not know all natural things. Therefore, if souls know all natural things when separated from their bodies, it seems that they acquire such knowledge after separation from their bodies. But some souls have acquired knowledge of some natural things in this life. Therefore, after separation from their bodies, they will possess a two-fold knowledge of the same things, one knowledge acquired in this life and the other hereafter. Now this seems to be impossible, for there cannot be two forms of the same species in one and the same subject.

(3) Furthermore, no finite power can extend to an infinite number of things. But the power of a separated soul is finite because its essence is finite; therefore it cannot extend to an infinite number of things. But the number of natural things that can be understood is infinite; for the species of numbers and figures and relations are infinite. Therefore a separated soul does not know all natural things.

(4) Furthermore, all knowledge comes about through an assimilation of the knower to the thing known. But it seems impossible that a separated soul, since it is immaterial, can be assimilated to natural

things, since they are material. Therefore it seems impossible that a separated soul should know natural things.

(5) Furthermore, the possible intellect exists in the order of intelligible beings in the same way as prime matter does in the order of sensible beings. But prime matter, inasmuch as it is ordered only to act, can receive only one form. Now the separated possible intellect is ordered to only one object, since it is not distracted toward a variety of things by the senses. It seems, therefore, that it can receive only one intelligible form; and thus it cannot know all natural things, but only one.

(6) Furthermore, things which belong to diverse species cannot be similar to one and the same thing according to their specific nature. Now knowledge occurs when the knower takes on the likeness of another's species. Therefore a separated soul cannot know all natural things since they are diverse in species.

(7) Furthermore, if separated souls know all natural things, they must possess in themselves forms which are the likenesses of natural things. But these likenesses are either of genera and species only, or of individuals as well. If the first is true, separated souls will not know individuals and consequently not all natural things, because things that exist in nature seem to be primarily individuals. If the second be true, since individuals are infinite, it would follow that there are infinite likenesses in a separated soul; and this seems to be impossible. Therefore a separted soul does not know all natural things.

But an objector was arguing that in a separated soul there are likenesses only of genera and species, but that by applying these likenesses to singulars, a separated soul is able to know singulars.

(8) On the contrary, an intellect can apply the knowledge of the universal which it possesses only to those particulars which it already knows. For if I know that every female mule is sterile, I cannot apply this knowledge except to this mule which I know. For the knowledge of the particular precedes the natural application of the universal to the particular. Now an application of this sort cannot be the cause of the knowledge of particulars, and consequently particulars will remain unknown to a separated soul.

(9) Furthermore, wherever there is knowledge, the knower is ordered to the thing known. But the souls of the damned do not possess any order. For it is said, *Job* X,[3] that "there," that is, in hell, "there dwells no order, but everlasting horror." Therefore at least the souls of the damned do not know all natural things.

(10) Furthermore, Augustine says, in his book *De Cura pro Mortuis Agenda*,[4] that the souls of those who have died cannot know in any way what is going on here below. Now natural events are those that take place here below. Therefore the souls of the dead do not possess knowledge of natural things.

(11) Furthermore, whatever is in potency is actualized by that which is in act. Now it is clear that while a human soul is united to its body, it is in potency with respect to all or to most of the things which can be known naturally; for it does not actually know all things. Therefore, if it knows all natural things after separation from its body, it must be actualized by something. Now it seems that this can be nothing other than the agent intellect, "by which all things are made," as is said in Book III of the *De Anima*. [5] But a soul cannot be actualized by the agent intellect with respect to all the intelligibles which the soul did not previously understand. For in Book III of the *De Anima* [6] the Philosopher compares the agent intellect to light and phantasms to colors. Now light is not adequate to make visible objects actually seen unless colors are present. Therefore neither can the agent intellect actualize the possible intellect with respect to all intelligible objects, since phantasms cannot be present to a separated soul because they exist only in bodily organs.

But an objector was arguing that a separated soul is actualized with respect to all things that are naturally knowable not by the agent intellect, but by a higher substance.

(12) On the contrary, whenever something is actualized by an external agent that does not belong to the same genus, that actualization is not natural. For example, if something that can be cured is healed by art or by divine power, the healing will be the result of medical art or be miraculous; the healing will be natural only when it results from an intrinsic principle. Now the proper and connatural agent with respect to the human possible intellect is the agent intellect. Therefore, if the possible intellect were actualized by some higher agent and not by the agent intellect, this will not be natural knowledge, and it is of this that we are speaking. And consequently this knowledge will not be present to all separated souls, since all these separated souls are alike only in what is natural.

(13) Furthermore, if a separated soul were actualized with respect to all that is naturally intelligible, it would be so actualized either by God or by an angel. Now it does not seem that an angel can produce this effect because an angel is not the cause of the very nature of a soul; hence it does not seem that the soul's natural knowledge results from the action of an angel. Furthermore it seems inappropriate that the souls of the damned should receive from God, after their death, such great perfection that they would know all natural things. Therefore it seems that separated souls would not know all natural things in either of these ways.

(14) Furthermore, the ultimate perfection of whatever exists in potency is to be actualized with respect to all those things to which it is in potency. But the human intellect is naturally in potency only

with respect to all those things which are naturally intelligible: those, that is, which can be understood by natural knowledge. If, therefore, a separated soul understands all natural things, it seems that every separated soul, from the mere fact of being separated, possesses its ultimate perfection, which is happiness. Therefore, if separation from its body alone can provide happiness for a soul, all those other aids employed to achieve happiness are useless; and this seems incongruous.

(15) Furthermore, delight follows upon knowledge. Consequently, if all separated souls know all natural things, it seems that the souls of the damned would enjoy a maximum of delight, and this does not seem fitting.

(16) Furthermore, in reference to the text of *Isaiah,*[7] "Abraham did not know us," the *Gloss* runs: "Those who are dead, even the saints, do not know what the living do, not even what their children do."[8] But what is done in this world by the living, are natural events. Consequently separated souls do not know all natural things.

On the Contrary,

(1) A separated soul understands separate substances. But in the separate substances are the species of all natural things. Consequently a separated soul understands all natural things.

But an objector was arguing that it is not necessary that he who sees a separate substance should see all the species existing in its intellect.

(2) On the contrary, we have the statement of Gregory,[9] "What is it that he does not see who sees Him who sees all things?" Therefore they who see God see all the things which God sees. Therefore, and for the same reason, those who see the angels see all the things which the angels see.

(3) Furthermore, a separated soul knows a separate substance to the degree that it is intelligible; for it does not see the separate substance through bodily vision. Now just as a separate substance is intelligible, so also are the species which exist in its intellect. Therefore a separated soul not only understands a separate substance but also the intelligible species existing in it.

(4) Furthermore, that which is actually understood is the form of the one who understands it and is one with the one who understands it. Therefore, if a separated soul understands a separate substance which understands all natural things, it seems that this soul would understand all natural things.

(5) Furthermore, whoever understands loftier intelligibles also understands lesser intelligibles, as is stated even in Book III of the

De Anima.[10] Consequently, if a separated soul understands separate substances, which, as we have already said, are intelligible in the highest degree, it seems to follow that a separated soul would understand all other intelligible objects.

(6) Furthermore, if something is in potency to many things, it is actualized with respect to all of these by something which is actually all of them; for example, matter which is potentially hot and dry is made to be actually hot and dry by fire. But the possible intellect of a separated soul is in potency to all intelligibles. Now the active principle from which this possible intellect receives an influx, that is, a separate substance, is in act with respect to all of these intelligibles. Therefore it brings the soul from potency to act either with respect to all intelligibles or with respect to none. But obviously the active principle does not totally fail to actualize the intellect; because separated souls understand some things which even in this life they did not understand. Therefore, it is actuated with respect to all intelligibles. Consequently in this way a separated soul understands all natural things.

(7) Furthermore, Dionysius says, in the Fifth Chapter of his book *On the Divine Names,*[11] that loftier beings are exemplars of lower beings. Now separate substances are loftier than natural things. Therefore they are the exemplars of natural things. And thus it seems that separated souls would know all natural things by gazing upon separate substances.

(8) Furthermore, separated souls know things through infused forms. Now infused forms are said to be the forms of the order of the whole world. Consequently separated souls know the total order of the universe, and in this way they know all natural things.

(9) Furthermore, whatever exists in a lower nature exists in full in a higher nature. But a separated soul is higher than natural things. Therefore all natural things are in some fashion in the soul. But a soul knows itself. Therefore it knows all natural things.

(10) Furthermore, as Gregory says,[12] what is related in *Luke,* Chapter XVI, about Lazarus and the rich man is not a parable but something which happened; this is clear because the person involved is given his proper name. And in the text it is stated that the rich man in hell recognized Abraham, whom he had not known in his prior life. In similar fashion, therefore, separated souls, even those of the damned, know certain things which they did not know in this life. And thus it seems that they would know all natural things.

The Response:

It must be said that a separated soul understands all natural things in a qualified sense but not absolutely. In order to see this point one must take into account that the order among things is such that whatever is found in a lower nature is found more perfectly in a higher nature. For example, the qualities found in earthly bodies, which are generated and corrupted, exist in a loftier way in the celestial bodies as in their universal causes. For hot and cold and other accidents of this kind exist in the lower bodies as particular qualities and forms; whereas in the celestial bodies they exist as universal powers which are the source from which earthly bodies derive their qualities. In like fashion also all things which exist in corporeal nature exist more nobly in an intellectual nature. For the forms of corporeal things exist in corporeal things themselves in a material way and in a particular way; but in intellectual substances these forms exist immaterially and universally. Hence it is said in the *Liber de Causis* [13] that every intelligence is full of forms. Furthermore, all things that exist in the world of creation are in God in a higher way. For in creatures the forms and natures of things exist in multiple and distinct ways; but in God they exist in a simple and unified way. And this three-fold mode in which things exist is referred to in *Genesis*, Chapter I, where, in describing the production of things, the sacred text uses three different expressions. For first of all God said, "Let there be the firmanent," by which is understood the being which things have in the Word of God. Secondly, it is said, "And God made the firmament," by which is understood the being of the firmament in the angelic intelligence. Thirdly, it is said, "And thus it was done," by which is understood the being of the firmament in its own nature, as Augustine explains; [14] the same is true for other things. For just as things flowed forth from God, from the divine Wisdom, so that they might subsist in their proper nature, so also from the divine Wisdom there flowed forth into intellectual substances the forms of things by which these substances might understand them.

Hence it must be kept in mind that something belongs to the order of intelligible perfection according to the way in which it shares in the perfection of nature. For singulars do not share in the perfection of nature for their own sake but for another reason, that is, that the species which nature intends might be preserved in them. For nature intends to generate a human being and not this human being, except insofar as a human being cannot exist except as a particular human being. Thus the Philosopher say, in his book *On the Generation of Animals*, [15] that in assigning causes for the accidents that belong to a species, we must go back to the final cause, but that accidents of the individual are explained by the efficient or material cause; just as though only that which belongs to the species is intended by nature. Hence to know the species of things belongs to intelligible perfection, but not the knowledge of individuals, except perhaps by accident.[16]

Therefore this intelligible perfection, although it is present in all intellectual substances, is not present in the same way in all of them. For in the higher intellectual substances the intelligible forms of things are more unified and universal; in lower intellectual substances these forms are more numerous and less universal, to the extent that they are at a greater distance from the one first and simple principle and come closer to the particularity of things. But because in the loftier substances the intellective power is stronger, the higher substances achieve intelligible perfection through a few universal forms so that they know the natures of things down to their ultimate species. But lower substances have a weaker intellective power. If then they possessed forms of the same universality as those in higher substances, they would not obtain from these forms ultimate intelligible perfection, so that they would know things down to their individual species. Their knowledge of things would remain instead in a kind of confused universal state that is characteristic of imperfect knowledge. For it is clear that the more powerful an intellect is, the more it is able to grasp many meanings from a few instances. An example of this is that things must be explained one by one to ignorant persons and slow learners, and particular examples used for each single instance.

For it is clear that the human soul is the lowest of intellectual substances. Hence its natural capacity is to receive the forms that are appropriate to material things. And this is why a human soul is united to a body, so that it might acquire from material things the intelligible species that are appropriate to its possible intellect. Nor does it possess a greater natural power for understanding than it needs in order to be perfected in intelligible knowledge through such limited forms. Hence the intelligible light in which a soul participates, which is called the agent intellect, has as its operation to make intelligible species of this kind to be actual.

Therefore, as long as a soul is united to its body, it has as a result of this very union a vision turned to lower things, from which it acquires intelligible species proportionate to its own intellective power, and in this way its knowledge is perfected. But when a soul will have been separated from its body, it has its vision directed solely to higher beings from which it receives an influx of universal intelligible species. And although these species are received in the soul in a less universal way than the way in which they exist in higher substances, the strength of its intellective power is still not sufficient so that through this kind of intelligible species it is able to achieve perfect knowledge, that is, by understanding each thing in a special and determinate way; but rather the soul knows them in a kind of confused universality, in the way that things are known in their universal principles. Moreover, separated souls acquire this knowledge all at once by way of infusion, and not in stages by way of instruction, as Origen says.[17]

Thus one must say that separated souls know all natural things through natural knowledge in a universal way but do not know each thing individually. As to the knowledge which the souls of the saints possess through grace, another explanation is to be given, for with respect to such knowledge souls are made equal to angels inasmuch as they see all things in the Word.

Replies to Both Series of Arguments:

Consequently, I must reply to both sets of arguments, both those for and those against my position.

(1) According to Augustine,[18] demons know things in three ways: some things they know through a revelation made by the good angels, that is, those things which transcend their natural knowledge, as, for example, the mysteries of Christ and of the Church and other things of this kind. But other things they know through the keenness of their own intellect, that is, things which are naturally knowable; finally, they know some things through their experience extending over a long period of time, that is, future contingent events having to do with singulars, which of themselves do not belong to intelligible knowledge, as we have said. Hence discussion of them is irrelevant at present.

(2) Souls who in this life will have acquired a knowledge of some things which are naturally knowable will have determinate knowledge extending to the individual with respect to the things which they will have come to know in this life; but their knowledge of other things will be universal and confused. Hence it will not have been useless for them to have acquired knowledge. Nor is there any difficulty in the fact that both kinds of knowledge be present to the same soul, since the two knowledges are formally distinct.

(3) The argument is not relevant, because we do not hold that a separated soul knows all natural things individually. Hence the infinity of species found in numbers, figures and relations is not opposed to the soul's knowledge. Now because this same argument could in the same way be used as an argument against angelic knowledge, one must say that the species of figures, numbers and things of this sort are not actually but only potentially infinite. And it is not even inappropriate that the power of a finite intellectual substance extend to infinite objects of this sort, for an intellective power is in a certain sense infinite, insofar as it is not limited by matter. Hence it can know a universal, which is in a sense infinite, inasmuch as a universal, by its nature contains potentially an infinite number of particulars.

(4) The forms of material things are in immmaterial substances in an immaterial way; and thus one becomes like the other with respect to their nature as forms, but not with respect to their mode of existing.

(5) Prime matter is related to form in two ways only, either in pure potency or in pure act; this is so because natural forms, as soon as they are in matter, possess their own operations unless there be some impediment; and this is so because a natural form is related to one thing only. Hence just as soon as the form 'fire' is in matter, it causes the matter to move upward. On the other hand, the possible intellect is related to intelligible species in a three-fold way: sometimes, as before one learns, as pure potency; sometimes, however, as when one actually considers something, as pure act; and sometimes when one possesses habitual knowledge that he is not actually using, it is related in a way that is intermediate between potency and act. Therefore a form that is understood is related to the possible intellect as a natural form is related to prime matter but only inasmuch as the intelligible form is actually known, but not as it is habitually present in the intellect. And hence it is that just as prime matter cannot be actuated at one and the same time by more than one form, so the intellect understands only one intelligible object; however, an intellect can habitually know many intelligible objects.

(6) Something can be made to be like a knowing substance in two ways. first, according to its natural being, and in this way things which are specifically diverse cannot be made like a knowing substance, since this substance is one in being. Secondly, something can be like a knowing substance according to the thing's intelligible being, and in this way things which are specifically diverse can be made to be like a knowing substance insofar as that knowing substance possesses diverse intelligible species, even though this knowing substance is one in species.

(7) Separated souls do not understand only species but also individuals, not however all of them but only some. And therefore it is not necessary that there are infinite species in a soul.

(8) The application of universal knowledge to singulars is not the cause of the knowledge of singulars but a result of such knowledge. How a separated soul knows singulars will be treated in a subsequent question.

(9) Since the good consists in mode, species and order, according to Augustine in his book *On the Nature of the Good*,[19] order is found in anything in proportion to the good that is in it. Now in the damned there is no good in the order of grace but there is the good of nature. Hence in them there is no order of grace, but the order of nature; and this order is adequate for the kind of knowledge under discussion.

(10) Augustine is speaking of singular events which occur in this

world, and we have said that these do not pertain to intelligible knowledge.

(11) The possible intellect cannot be actualized to a knowledge of all natural things through the light of the agent intellect alone, but through a higher substance which actually possesses a knowledge of all natural things. And if one looks at this matter correctly, the agent intellect, according to what the Philosopher has to say about it, is not directly an active principle in relation to the possible intellect but rather in relation to the phantasms which it makes actually intelligible; and it is through them that the possible intellect is actualized when its gaze is turned to lower things because of the intellect's union with its body. And for the same reason, when its gaze is turned toward higher things because of separation from its body, it becomes actualized through species which are actually intelligible and which are located in higher substances as in a proper agent; and consequently such knowledge is natural.

(12) Hence the reply to the twelfth objection is obvious.

(13) Separated souls acquire perfection of this kind from God through the angels as intermediaries. For although the substance of a soul is directly created by God, nevertheless intelligible perfections come from God through the mediation of angels, not only natural intelligible perfections but even those which pertain to the mysteries of grace, as is clear from what Dionysius says in Chapter IV of his book *On the Celestial Hierarchy*. [20]

(14) When a separated soul possesses universal knowledge of things which are naturally knowable, it is not perfectly actualized, because to know something universally is to know it imperfectly. Hence such a soul does not attain even its natural happiness. Consequently it does not follow that other aids, by which such a soul can achieve happiness, are unnecessary.

(15) The damned are saddened by the very good of the knowledge they possess because they know that they are deprived of the highest good, to which they were ordered through other goods.

(16) This statement from the *Gloss* speaks of particular things, which, as we have said, do not pertain to intelligible perfection.

Now a reply must be given to the contrary arguments.

(1) A separated soul does not perfectly comprehend a separate substance and therefore it is not necessary that such a soul know all those things which are present by likeness in such a substance.

(2) The text of Gregory is true with respect to the power of that intelligible object which is God, an object which of itself is the likeness of all intelligible things. However it is not necessary that whoever sees God should know all the things which God knows, unless he were to comprehend Him as He Himself comprehends Himself.

(3) The species which are in the intellect of an angel are intelligible to that intellect of which they are the forms, not, however, to the intellect of a separated soul.

(4) Although that which is understood is the form of the substance which performs the act of understanding, it is not, however, necessary that a separated soul, when it understands a separate substance, should understand what the separate substance understands, because it does not comprehend the separate substance.

(5) Although a separated soul in some fashion knows separate substances, it is not therefore necessary that it know all other things perfectly, because it does not know these substances perfectly.

(6) A separated soul is actualized by a higher substance to know all intelligible objects, not perfectly, but rather universally, as we have said.

(7) Although separate substances are in some fashion the exemplars of all natural things, it still does not follow that when they are known, all things are known; unless these separate substances were themselves perfectly comprehended.

(8) A separated soul knows through infused forms, but these are not forms of the order of the universe in all its particulars, as they are in the higher substances, but only of the order of the universal in general, as we have said.

(9) Natural things are in some fashion both in separate substances and in a soul; but in separate substances they are present in act, whereas in a soul they are in potency insofar as a soul is in potency to all natural forms that can be understood.

(10) The soul of Abraham was a separated substance; hence too the soul of the rich man was able to know it, just as it could know other separate substances.

Notes to Question Eighteen

1. St. Augustine, *De Divinatione daemonum,* III (PL 40: 584).

2. Pseudo-Dionysius, *De Divinis nominibus,* IV, 23 (PG 3: 725).

3. *Job,* 10: 22.

4. St. Augustine, *De Cura pro mortuis gerenda,* XIII-XIV (PL 40: 604-606).

5. Aristotle, *De Anima,* III, 5 (430a 10).

6. Aristotle, *De Anima,* III, 5 (430a 14-17) 7 (431a 15-17)

7. *Isaiah,* 63: 16.

8. *Glossa interlinearis,* IV, 102v.

9. St. Gregory, *Dialogues,* IV, 33 (PL 87: 376); *Moralia,* XII, 21 (PL 85: 999).

10. Aristotle, *De Anima*, III, 4 (429b 3-4)

11. Pseudo-Dionysius, *De Divinis nominibus*, V, 9 (PG 3: 823).

12. St. Gregory, *In Evang, hom.* II, 40 (PL 76: 1302, 1304).

13. *Liber de Causis*, IX; ed. Bardenhewer, p. 173.

14. St. Augustine, *De Genesi ad litteram*, II, 8 (PL 34: 269).

15. Aristotle, *De Generatione animalium*, V, 1 (778a 30- b 1).

16. The object of the senses is a particular, material thing; the proper object of the human intellect is the intelligible content present in the particular. The intellect disengages this intelligible content from the phantasms present in the imagination, abstracting this content and expressing it in universal concepts. Both for the origin and for the use of intellectual knowledge, the intellect depends upon the phantasms.

17. Origen, *Peri Archon*, I, 6 (PG 11: 169).

18. St. Augustine, *De Divinatione daemonum*, III-VI (PL 40: 584-587).

19. St. Augustine, *De Natura boni*, III (PL 42: 553)

20. Pseudo-Dionysius, *De Coelesti hierarchia*, IV, 2 (PG 3: 180).

QUESTION NINETEEN

Parallel texts: *In IV Sent.*, dist. 44, q. 3, a. 3; q. 1, a. 1, 2; dist. 50, q. 1, a. 1; *Quodl.*, X, q. 4, a. 2; *Contra gent.*, II, 81; *Summa theol.*, I, q. 77, a. 8; I-II, q. 67, a. 1; *De Virtut. card.*, a. 4, ad 13.

The nineteenth question that is asked about the soul is this: Whether the sensitive powers remain in a separated soul. And it seems that they do.

(1) Because the powers of a soul either are located in it essentially or they are a soul's natural properties. But the essential principles of something cannot be separated from a thing while the thing continues to be, nor can its natural properties be separated from it. Therefore the sensitive powers remain in a separated soul.

But an objector was arguing that the powers remain in the soul as in their root.

(2) On the contrary, to exist in something as in its root is to exist in it potentially, that is, to be in something virtually and not actually. However, the essential principles of a thing and its natural properties must be in that thing actually and not only virtually. Therefore the sensitive powers do not remain in a separated soul only as in their root.

(3) Furthermore, Augustine says, in the book *De Spiritu et Anima*,[1] that when a soul departs from its body, it takes with it sense and imagination, the concupiscible and irascible appetites, which are located in the sensitive part. Therefore sensitive powers remain in a separated soul.

(4) Furthermore, a whole is not an integral whole if any of its parts is missing. But the sensitive powers are parts of a soul. Therefore, if they are not in a separated soul, a separated soul would not be an integral whole.

(5) Furthermore, just as a human being is such because of reason and intellect, so an animal is such because of sense powers; for 'rational' is the constitutive difference of a human being and 'sensible' is the constitutive difference of an animal. Therefore, if the sense powers are not the same, the animal will not be the same. But if the sensitive powers do not remain in a separated soul, then the sense powers which

are in a human being who rises from the dead will not be the same sense powers as now; for whatever lapses into nothingness cannot be brought back into being as numerically the same. Therefore a human being who rises from the dead will not be the same with respect to his soul, and thus will not be the same human being; and this is contrary to what is said in *Job,* XXIX, ² "Whom I myself shall see," and so forth.

(6) Furthermore, Augustine says, in Book XII of his *Super Genesim ad Litteram,*³ that the punishments which souls undergo in hell are like things seen by those who are asleep, that is, they are experienced through the likenesses of corporeal things. Now the things of this kind seen by those who are asleep are located in the imagination, which pertains to the sensitive part of a soul. Therefore there are sensitive powers in a separated soul.

(7) Furthermore, it is obvious that joy is located in the concupiscible appetite and anger, in the irascible appetite. But there is joy in the separated souls of those who are good and sorrow and anger in the souls of the wicked; for in that state there is weeping and gnashing of teeth. Therefore, since the concupiscible and irascible appetites are in the sensitive part of a soul, as the Philosopher says in Book III of the *De Anima,*⁴ it is clear that there are sensitive powers in a separated soul.

(8) Furthermore, Dionysius says, in Chapter 4 of his book, *On the Divine Names,*⁵ that the wickedness of a demon is an irrational rage, mindless concupiscence and a wanton imagination. But these movements pertain to sensitive powers. Therefore, there are sensitive powers in demons; consequently all the more so in a separated soul.

(9) Furthermore, Augustine says, in his book *Super Genesim ad Litteram,*⁶ that a soul senses some things without a body, that is, joy and sadness. But whatever pertains to a soul without its body is found in a separated soul. Therefore there are sense powers in a separated soul.

(10) Furthermore, in the *Liber de Causis*⁷ it is stated that there are sensible things in every soul. But sensible things are sensed only because they are in a soul. Therefore a separated soul senses sensible things, and so there are sense powers in it.

(11) Furthermore, Gregory says⁸ that what the Lord relates in *Luke* XVI about the wealthy man at his banquet is not a parable but something which happened. Now it is stated in this account that the rich man, who was situated in hell (and this could have been only through his separated soul), saw Lazarus and heard Abraham speaking to him. Therefore a separated soul saw and heard and thus sense powers exist in it.

(12) Furthermore, when there are two things which are the same

in existence and substance, one cannot be without the other. But the sensible soul and the rational soul in a human being are the same in existence and substance. Therefore it is not possible that sense powers would not remain in a separated rational soul.

(13) Futhermore, whatever lapses into nothingness cannot return to being as numerically the same thing. But if sensitive powers do not remain in a separated soul, they must lapse into nothingness. Therefore at the resurrection they will not be numerically the same. And thus, since the sensitive powers are the acts of their organs, neither will the organs be numerically the same, nor will the whole human being be numerically the same; and this is incongrous.

(14) Furthermore, reward and punishment correspond to merit and guilt. But for the most part merit and guilt for a human being consist in the acts of the sensitive powers, when we either yield to our passions or curb them. Therefore justice seems to require that there be acts of the sensitive powers in separated souls, which are rewarded or punished.

(15) Furthermore, a power is nothing other than a principle of action or of being acted upon. Now a soul is the principle of sensitive operations. Therefore sensitive powers are in a soul as in a subject. And so it cannot be that they do not remain in a separated soul, since accidents which lack contraries are not corrupted unless their subject is corrupted.

(16) Furthermore, according to the Philosopher,[9] memory is in the sensitive part of the soul. But there is memory in a separated soul; this is clear through what is said to the rich banqueteer by Abraham: "Remember that you received good things in your lifetime."[10] Therefore there are sensitive powers in a separated soul.

(17) Furthermore, virtues and vices remain in separated souls. Now some virtues and vices are located in the sensitive part of a soul; for the Philospher says, in Book III of the *Ethics,*[11] that temperance and fortitude belong to the irrational parts of a soul. Therefore sensitive powers remain in a separated soul.

(18) Furthermore, in stories told about those who have been raised from the dead, we read in many histories of the saints that they recounted having seen certain things which can be imagined, such as houses, fields, rivers and things of that sort. Therefore separated souls make use of the imagination, which is in the sensitive part of a soul.

(19) Furthermore, sense powers assist intellective cognition, for he who lacks a sense also lacks one kind of knowledge. But intellective cognition will be more perfect in a separated soul than in a soul joined to its body. Therefore sense powers will also be more present.

(20) Furthermore, the Philosopher says in the *De Anima,*[12] that

if an old man were to acquire the eye of a young man, he would see just as a young man sees. From this it seems to be true that when the sense organs are weakened, the sensitive powers are not weakened. Therefore neither are the sensitive powers destroyed when the organs die. And thus it seems that sensitive powers remain in a separated soul.

On the Contrary,

(1) The Philosopher says, in Book II of the *De Anima,*[13] where he is speaking about the intellect, that it alone is capable of existing apart as that which is perpetual is apart from that which is corruptible. Therefore sensitive powers do not remain in a separated soul.

(2) Furthermore, in Book XVI of the *De Animalibus,*[14] the Philosopher says that when certain principles are the source of operations that cannot take place apart from a body, then these principles themselves cannot be apart from a body. But the operations of the sensitive soul cannot take place apart from a body; for they employ bodily organs. Therefore sensitive powers cannot be apart from a body.

(3) Furthermore, Damascene[15] says that nothing is deprived of its proper operation. Therefore, if sensitive powers were to remain in a separated soul, they would have their proper operations; and this is impossible.

(4) Furthermore, a power which is not actualized is purposeless. However, in the operations of God nothing is purposeless. Therefore sensitive powers do not remain in a separated soul, in which these powers could not be actualized.

The Response:

It must be said that the powers of a soul do not belong to the essence of the soul but are natural properties which flow from its essence, as one can learn from earlier questions. Now an accident can be corrupted in two ways: either by its contrary, as the cold is corrupted by the hot; or through the corruption of its subject, for an accident cannot remain when its subject has been corrupted. Consequently those accidents or forms which do not have a contrary are not destroyed except through the destruction of their subject.

Now it is obvious that the powers of the soul have no contrary, and consequently if they should be corrupted, they are corrupted only through the corruption of their subject. Therefore, in order to examine whether the sensitive powers are corrupted when the body is corrupted or whether they remain in the separated soul, the starting point of the investitation must be to consider what is the subject of the sense powers of which we have been speaking.

Now it is clear that the subject of a power must be that which is said to be potent by reference to that same power; for every accident gives its name to its subject. Now it is one and the same thing that has the power to act or to be acted upon and that is agent and patient. Hence the subject of a power must be the subject of the action or passion of which that power is the principle. And this is what the Philosopher says in his book *De Somno et Vigilia*,[16] that an action belongs to the one to which the power belongs.

Now there have been diverse opinions about the operation of the senses. For Plato [17] held that a sensitive soul had of itself a proper operation. For he held that a soul, even a sensitive soul, is a self-mover, and that it does not move its body except insofar as it moves itself. Consequently there is a two-fold operation in sensing: one by which a soul moves itself and another by which it moves its body. Hence the Platonists define sense as a movement of a soul throughout its body. For this reason too some of the proponents of this position distinguish two kinds of operations in the sensitive part of a soul: some are interior operations, by which a soul senses insofar as it moves itself; and some are exterior operations insofar as a soul moves its body. They say too that there are two kinds of sensitive powers. Some of these are in the soul itself as the principle of its interior acts, and these powers remain in the separated soul when its body and the acts of its body are destroyed. But other powers are principles of external actions; these powers exist in soul and body together, and they perish when the body perishes.

Now this position cannot be maintained. For it is clear that everything operates inasmuch as it is a being. Hence things which possess being through themselves operate through themselves, for example, individuals. The forms of substances, however, cannot exist of themselves, but are called 'beings' because it is by them that things exist. These forms do not have an operation of themselves, but are said to operate because their subjects operate through them. For just as heat is not that which is hot, but is that by which something is hot; so heat does not heat something, but is that by which something which is hot heats. Therefore, if a sensitive soul were to have an operation of itself, it would follow that it would possess subsistence of itself; and thus it would not be corrupted when its body is corrupted. Hence even the souls of brute animals would be immortal; and this is impossible, although Plato is said to have asserted it.

Therefore it is clear that no operation of the sensitive part can belong to the soul alone as that which is operating, but rather belongs to the composite through the soul, as that which is hot performs the action of heating through heat. Therefore it is the composite which sees and hears and in general senses, but through the soul; hence, too, it is the composite which has the power to see and to hear and to sense, but through the soul. Therefore it is clear that the powers of the sensitive part of a soul are in the composite as in a subject, but come from the soul as from a principle. Consequently when its body is destroyed, the sensitive powers of the soul are destroyed, but they remain in the soul as in a principle. And this is what the second position holds, that is, that the sensitive powers remain in a separated soul only as in their root.

Replies to the Opposing Arguments:

(1) Sensitive powers do not belong to the essence of a soul but are natural properties, belonging indeed to the composite as to their subject, but to the soul as to their principle.

(2) Powers of this kind are said to remain in a separated soul as in a root, not because they are within the soul actually, but because such is the power of a separated soul that if it were united to a body, it can once again cause these powers in the body, just as it can cause life.

(3) It is not necessary for us to accept this authority because in its title this book names the wrong author; for the book is not written by St. Augustine but by someone else. Still this text could be explained to mean that a soul takes powers of this kind with it, not in act but virtually.

(4) The powers of a soul are not essential nor integral parts but potential ones; but even as potential, some of them belong to the soul in itself, while others belong to the composite.

(5) The term 'sense' can be understood in two ways. In one way, 'sense' means the sensitive soul which is the principle of sensitive powers, and thus an animal is animal through sense as through its proper form; for 'sensible,' inasmuch as it is the constitutive difference of 'animal,' is derived from 'sense' understood in this way. 'Sense' also means a sensitive power itself; and since these power are natural properties, as we have said, sense taken thus does not constitute the species but follows upon it. Therefore sense, understood in the second way, does not remain in a separated soul; but sense understood in the first way does remain. For in a human being the essence of the sensible soul is identical to the essence of the rational soul; hence nothing prevents a human being who rises from the dead from being numerically the same animal as before his death. For that something be numerically the same it is sufficient that its essential principles be numerically the

same; but it is not necessary that its properties and accidents are numerically the same.

(6) Augustine seems to have retracted this position in his book *Retractationes*.[18] For in Book XII of *Super Genesim ad Litteram*[19] he adds the comment that the punishments of hell consist in an imaginary vision, and that the place called hell is not corporeal but imaginary. Hence he was forced to explain why, if hell is not a corporeal place, the infernal regions are said to be 'under the earth.' And he himself condemns his earlier position saying: "I now think that I ought to have taught that the infernal regions are under the earth rather than to attempt to explain why they are believed and said to be there, as if in fact they were not." Now since he retracted what he had said about the location of hell, it seems that all the other things related to this topic were retracted.

(7) In a separated soul there is neither joy nor anger insofar as these are acts of the irascible and concupiscible appetites which belong to the sensitive part of a soul, but insofar as these terms designate a movement of the will which belongs to the intellective part.

(8) Human evil involves three movements, that is, wanton imagination (which in fact is the starting point of error), mindless concupiscence and irrational rage. For this reason Dionysius describes the wickedness of a demon by comparing it to human evil; but we are not thereby to understand that demons have an imagination or irascible and concupiscible appetites which belong to the sensitive parts of a soul, but only something analogous to these which befits an intellective nature.

(9) The words cited from Augustine are not to be understood as meaning that a soul senses something without a corporeal organ, but rather that it senses some things without sensible bodies themselves, as, for example, fear and sadness; but it senses other things through the bodies themselves, as, for example, hot and cold.

(10) All that is in something is in it according to the mode of the recipient. Hence sensible things are in a separated soul not through a sensible mode of being, but through an intelligible mode of being.

(11) There is no reason why in an account of things that happened something cannot be said metaphorically. For although what is said in the *Gospel* about Lazarus and the rich man is something which took place, still it is by way of metaphor that Lazarus is said to have seen and heard; just as it is also said metaphorically that he had a tongue.

(12) The substance of the sensible soul remains in a human being after death; however the sensitive powers do not.

(13) The term 'sense,' as it denominates a power, is not the form of the entire body; but the sensitive soul is this form, whereas sense is a property of the composite. So, too, the power of sight is not the

act of an eye as the sensitive soul is the act of the whole body. Now the power of sight is a property flowing from the soul. Hence it is not necessary that there be a different eye in one who rises from the dead although the sensitive power is different.

(14) A reward is not something that must be given for each meritorious act; but merit is related to reward as that for which someone can claim recompense. Hence it is not necessary that all the acts for which something is merited be brought back into being when a reward is given. Otherwise it would be necessary that the martyrs be slain a second time, and this is absurd.

(15) A soul is the principle of sensing, not as being the one who senses, but as that by which the one who senses does sense. Hence the sensitive powers are not in a soul as in a subject, but are from the soul as from a principle.

(16) A separated soul recalls the past, not through that memory which belongs to the sensitive part of the soul but that which is in its intellective part: the memory, that is, which Augustine [20] makes a part of God's image in the soul.

(17) Virtues and vices which belong to the irrational parts of the soul do not remain in a separated soul except as in their principles; for the seeds of all the virtues are in the will and the reason.

(18) As is clear from what we have already said, a soul which is separated from its body does not possess the same mode of knowing that it had when it was in its body. A separated soul retains knowledge of things that it knows in a way proper to it, that is, without phantasms; but after it returns to its original state by being once again united with a body, it now knows these things in a way suitable to the union, that is, by turning to phantasms. And therefore those things which souls have seen intelligibly, they speak about imaginatively.

(19) An intellect requires the help of the senses because of its state of imperfect knowledge, that is, according as it acquires knowledge from phantasms, but not according to a more perfect mode of knowledge which is appropriate to a separated soul; just as a human being requires milk in childhood but not when grown up.

(20) When sense organs become weakened, the sensitive powers do not become weakened essentially but only accidentally. Hence they are also accidentally corrupted when their organs are corrupted.

Notes to Question Nineteen

1. Alcherius Claravallensis (Pseudo-Augustine), *Liber de spiritu et anima,* XV (PL 40: 791).
2. *Job,* 19: 27.
3. St. Augustine, *De Genesi ad litteram,* XII, 32 (PL 34: 480).
4. Aristotle, *De Anima,* III, 9 (432b 5-7).
5. Pseudo-Dionysius, *De Divinis nominibus,* IV, 23 (PG 3: 725).
6. St. Augustine, *De Genesi ad litteram,* XII, 32 (PL 34: 480).
7. *Liber de Causis,* XIII; ed. Bardenhewer, p. 176, 8.
8. St. Gregory, *In Evang. hom.* II, 40 (PL 76: 1302, 1304).
9. Aristotle, *De Memoria et reminiscentia,* I (450a 14).
10. *Luke,* 16: 25.
11. Aristotle, *Nicomachean Ethics,* III, 9 (1117b 22-23).
12. Aristotle, *De Anima,* I, 4 (408b 21-22).
13. Aristotle, *De Anima,* II, 2 (413b 24-27).
14. Aristotle, *De Generatione animalium,* II, 3 (736b 22-24).
15. St. John Damascene, *De Fide orthodoxa,* II, 23 (PG 94: 949).
16. Aristotle, *De Somno et vigilia,* I (454a 8).
17. Plato, *Phaedrus,* 245C - 246A.
18. St. Augustine, *Retractationes,* II, 24 (PL 32: 640).
19. St. Augustine, *De Genesi ad litteram,* XII, 33 (PL 34: 481).
20. St. Augustine, *De Trinitate,* XIV, 8; 12 (PL 42: 1044; 1048).

QUESTION TWENTY

Parallel texts: *In IV Sent.*, dist. 50, q. 1, a. 3; *De Ver.*, q. 19, a. 2; *Contra gent.*, II, 100; *Summa theol.*, I, q. 89, a. 4.

The twentieth question that is asked about the soul is this: Whether a separated soul knows singulars. And it seems that it does not.

(1) Because among the powers of a soul only the intellect remains in a separated soul. But the object of an intellect is a universal and not a singular; for science is concerned with universals whereas sense is concerned with singulars, as is stated in Book I of the *De Anima*.[1] Therefore a separated soul does not know singulars but only universals.

(2) Furthermore, if a separated soul knows singulars, it knows them either through forms which were previously acquired while the soul was in its body or through infused forms. But it does not know singulars through forms previously acquired. For of the forms which a soul acquired through its senses while it is in its body, some are individual intentions which are retained in the powers of the sensitive part; and consequently they cannot remain in a separated soul since powers of this kind do not remain in it, as we have shown. Other previously acquired forms are universal intentions, which are in the intellect; hence only these are able to remain. But singulars cannot be known by means of universal intentions. Therefore a separated soul cannot know singulars either by means of species which it acquired in its body, or by means of infused species, because species of this kind are related to all singulars in exactly the same way. Therefore it follows that a separated soul would know all singulars, and this does not seem to be true.

(3) Furthermore, the cognition of a separated soul is hindered by spatial distance. For Augustine says, in his book *De Cura pro Mortuis Agenda*,[2] that the souls of the dead are in a place where they cannot know events that happen here on earth. However, spatial distance does not interfere with knowledge which occurs through infused species. Consequently a soul does not know singulars through infused species.

(4) Futhermore, infused species are related similarly to present and to future events; for the infusion of intelligible species is atemporal. Therefore, if a separated soul knows singulars by means of infused species, it seems that it would know not only present and past events but even future ones. And this cannot be, it seems, since to know the future is proper to God alone; for it is said in *Isaiah* XLI,[3] "Proclaim the things which are to come in the end, and I shall say that you are gods."

(5) Futhermore, singulars are infinite. But infused species are not infinite. Therefore a separated soul is not able to know singulars by means of infused species.

(6) Furthermore, that which is indistinct cannot be a principle of distinct knowledge. However, knowledge of singulars is distinct. Therefore, since infused forms are indistinct because they exist as universals, it seems that a separated soul would be unable to know singulars by means of infused species.

(7) Furthermore, everything that is received in something is received in it according to the mode of the recipient. But a soul is immaterial; therefore infused forms are received in it immaterially. But what is immaterial cannot be a principle for a knowledge of singulars which are individuated by matter. Therefore a separated soul cannot know singulars through infused species.

But an objector was arguing that singulars can be known through infused species, although these forms are immaterial, because they are likenesses of those ideal reasons by which God knows both universals and singulars.

(8) On the contrary, God knows singulars through these ideal reasons insofar as they are shapers of matter, which is the principle of individuation. But the infused forms belonging to a separated soul are not shapers of matter because they are not creative; for this activity belongs to God alone. Therefore a separated soul is unable to know singulars by means of infused forms.

(9) Furthermore, the likeness of a creature to God cannot be univocal but only analogous. But knowledge which results from an analogous likeness is very imperfect; for instance, if one thing is known through another because they are both beings. Therefore, if a separated soul knows singulars by means of infused species insofar as these are like the ideal reasons, it seems that it would know singulars in a very imperfect way.

(10) Furthermore, we have said in earlier questions that a separated soul does not know natural things by means of infused species except in a confused, universal state. But to know in this way is not to know singulars. Therefore a separated soul does not know singulars by means of infused species.

(11) Furthermore, these infused species by means of which a soul is alleged to know singulars are not immediately caused by God; because according to Dionysius [4] it is the law of divinity to actuate what is lowest by means of intermediaries. Nor are these species caused by an angel, because an angel is unable to cause species of this kind: it cannot cause them by creating, for an angel is not the creator of any thing; nor can it cause them by a process of change because this necessitates that there be something to serve as a medium for transmission. It seems, therefore, that a separated soul does not possess infused species through which it might know singulars.

(12) Furthermore, if a separated soul knows singulars by means of infused species, this can take place in only two ways: either the soul applies these species to singulars, or it turns to these species themselves. If it knows by applying species to singulars, it is clear that an application of this sort is not made by receiving something from singulars, since a separated soul does not possess sensitive powers which are naturally structured to receive species from singulars. It remains therefore that the soul makes this application by asserting something about singulars; and in this way it would not know the singulars themselves but only what it asserts about them. But if a separated soul knows singulars through these species by turning to them, it follows that it will know singulars only insofar as they are in the species themselves. But singulars are in these species only universally. Therefore a separated soul will not know singulars except universally.

(13) Furthermore, nothing finite can extend itself to what is infinite. But singulars are infinite. Therefore, since the power of a separated soul is finite, it seems that a separated soul would not know singulars.

(14) Furthermore, a separated soul can know something only by an intellectual vision. But Augustine says, in Book XII *Super Genesim ad Litteram,* [5] that neither bodies nor likenesses of bodies are known by intellectual vision. Therefore, since singulars are bodies, it seems that they cannot be known by a separated soul.

(15) Furthermore, where there is the same nature, there is also the same mode of operating. But a separated soul has the same nature as a soul joined to its body. Therefore, since a soul joined to a body cannot know singulars through its intellect, it seems that neither can a separated soul.

(16) Furthermore, powers are distinguished by their objects. But that which causes an effect in another is always greater than that effect. Therefore objects are more distinct than powers. But a sense power will never become an intellect. Therefore a singular which is sensible will never become intelligible.

(17) Furthermore, the cognitive power of a higher order is less

diversified with respect to the same knowable objects than is the cognitive power of a lower order. For the unifying sense is able to know all the things which are apprehended by the five external senses. And in a similar way an angel, by a single cognitive power, that is, its intellect, knows universals and singulars, which a human being apprehends by sense and intellect. But a cognitive power of a lower order is never able to apprehend the object of another power which is different from it; for example, sight is never able to apprehend the object of hearing. Therefore a human intellect can never apprehend a singular, which is the object of sense, although the intellect of an angel knows both of them.

(18) Furthermore, in the *Liber de Causis* [6] it is stated that an intelligence knows things either because it is the cause of them or because it governs them. But a separated soul neither causes nor governs singulars. Therefore it does not know them.

On The Contrary,

Only an intellect is able to form propositions. But a soul, even when joined to its body, formulates a proposition whose subject is singular and whose predicate is universal, as when I say, "Socrates is a human being." Now a soul would not be able to do this unless it knew the singular and its relation to the universal. Therefore a separated soul too knows singulars through its intellect.

(2) Furthermore, a soul is by nature inferior to all the angels. But angels of the lower hierarchy receive illuminations concerning singular effects; and in this way they are distinguished from angels belonging to the intermediate hierarchy, who receive illuminations by way of the universal reasons of these effects, and from angels of the supreme hierarchy who receive illluminations by way of these universal reasons as they exist in their cause. Since therefore knowledge is more particular to the exent that the knowing substance belongs to a lower order, it seems that a separated soul would know singulars much more perfectly than angels do.

(3) Furthermore, whatever a lower power can do, a higher power can do. But a sense power, which is lower than the intellect, can know singulars. Therefore a separated soul can also know singulars.

The Response:

It is necessary to say that a separated soul knows some, but not all, singulars. Now it knows some singulars of which it previously acquired knowledge while it was united to its body. For otherwise it would not remember the things which it did in this life, and as a result there would be no worm of conscience in a separated soul. It also knows some singulars of which it acquired knowledge after its separation from its body. For otherwise it would not be affected by the fire of hell and by other bodily punishments which are said to be in hell. However, it is clear that a separated soul does not know all singulars through natural knowledge, because the soul of those who are dead do not know the things that are happening here on earth, as Augustine says.[7]

Consequently this question poses two difficulties, one general, and one special to it. The general difficulty arises from the fact that our intellect does not seem to be capable of knowing singulars but only universals. Hence, since God, angels and separated souls have no other cognitive power that the intellect, it seems difficult to admit that they possess knowledge of singulars. This difficulty led some people into the gross error of denying that God and the angels know singulars. But that assertion is utterly impossible; for if it were true, divine providence would be excluded from natural events and God's judgment on human actions would be eliminated. Human beings would also be denied the ministry of angels who we believe are concerned with the salvation of human beings, according to the text of the Apostle:[8] Are not all of them ministering spirits, sent for the sake of those who shall receive the inheritance of salvation?"

Consequently others said that God, and also angels and separated souls, know singulars through a knowledge of the universal causes of the total order of the universe; for there is no singular which is not derived from these universal causes. And they give this example: if someone were to know the total order of the heavens and the stars, their size and their movements, he would know intellectually all future eclipses, both their number and where they would take place and at what times they would occur in the future. Such knowledge, however, is not adequate for a true knowledge of singulars. For it is clear that no matter how many universals are conjoined, no singular ever results from them; for example, if I say a human being is white, musical, and if I add any number of accidental qualities of this sort, there will still not be a singular. For it is possible that all of these qualities, even though they are found together, should belong to a number of individuals. Hence he who knows all causes universally will never for this reason properly know a singular effect; nor does he who knows the total order of the heavens know this eclipse as it exists here and now. For even if he would know that an eclipse will occur, and all details about it that can be observed in eclipses, such as the precise location of sun and moon and the exact time of year at which it will occur, it is still possible that an eclipse of this same sort could occur several times. And therefore, in order to assign a true knowledge of singulars to angels and separated souls, others said that they acquire knowledge of this kind from singulars themselves. But this position is wholly inadmissible. For since intelligible being and sensible material being differ so greatly, the form of a material thing is not directly received by an intellect but is brought to the intellect through many intermediaries. For example, the form of a sensible thing is first in some medium where it is more spiritual than it is in the sensible thing; afterwards it is in the sense organ; thence it is brought to the imagination and the other lower powers; and finally, at last, it is brought to the intellect. However, it is not even possible to imagine that these media are to be found in angels or in a separated soul.

And consequently we must state the matter differently. The forms of things through which an intellect knows have a two-fold relation to things: some of them produce things, while others are received from things. And those which are productive of things lead to a knowledge of a thing to the same extent as these forms are the causes of that thing. Hence an artisan who gives to his artifacts a form or a disposition of matter knows the artifact with respect to that element in it of which he is the cause. And because no human art is the cause of matter, which is the principle of individuation, but accepts matter as already pre-existing, it follows that an artisan, for example, a builder, knows a house universally through the form of his art, but not this house as it is here and now, except insofar as he gains knowledge of it through the senses.

However, God through His intellect not only produces form, from which the universal notion is derived, but also the matter, which is the principle of individuation; hence through His art He knows both universals and singulars. For just as material things flow forth from the divine art so that they might subsist in their proper natures, so also the intelligible likenesses of things flow forth from that same art into separate substances, likenesses by which they know things insofar as these things are produced by God. And consequently separate substances know not only universals but even singulars insofar as the intelligible species which are in them, and which emanate from the divine art, are likenesses of things with respect to both form and matter.

Nor is it inconsistent that a form which produces a thing, although it is immaterial, should be the likeness of the thing both with respect to form and with respect to matter; for something always exists more unifiedly in that which is higher than in a lower nature. Hence, although form and matter are distinct in sensible nature, nevertheless, the principle that is higher than matter and form and that, itself a unity, is their cause, is related to both of them. Because of this, higher substances know material things in an immaterial way and they know in a unified way things that are distinct, as Dionysius says in Chapter VII of his book *On the Divine Names.*[9] However, intelligible forms derived from things are received by an abstraction from things. Hence they do not lead to knowledge of a thing with respect to that element in the thing from which abstraction is made, but only with respect to that element which is abstracted. And consequently, since the forms received in our intellect from things are abstracted from matter and from the conditions of matter, they do not lead to a knowledge of a singular but only to knowledge of a universal. This therefore is the reason why separated substances can know singulars through their intellect whereas our intellect can know only universals.

But there is a difference between the intellect of an angel and the intellect of a separated soul with respect to the knowledge of singulars. For we said in previous questions that the efficacy of the intellective power which is in angels is proportioned to the universality of the intelligible forms which exist in them; and therefore through universal forms of this kind angels know all those things to which these forms are related. Hence, just as they know all the species of natural things which exist under their genera, so they also know all the singulars in the realm of natural things which are contained under their species.

However, the efficacy of the intellective power of a separted soul is not proportioned to the universality of infused forms, but is rather proportioned to forms received from things because it is natural for a soul to be united to a body. And therefore we said in earlier questions that a separated soul does not know all natural things, even with respect to their species, in a determinate and complete fashion, but rather in a universal sense and unclearly. Hence not even infused species are adequate to cause in them a knowledge of singulars so that they might be able to know all singulars as angels do. But infused species of this kind are limited in the soul itself to a knowledge of some singulars to which the soul has a special order or inclination, as, for example, to things from which it suffers, or to those things by which it is affected, or those things whose impressions and traces remain within the soul. For whatever is received is in the recipient in accordance with the mode of the recipient. And hence it is clear that a separated soul know singulars, not all of them, however, but some.

Replies to the Opposing Arguments:

(1) At the present time our intellect knows through species received from things, species which are abstracted from matter and

from all the conditions of matter; and consequently it is not able to know singulars whose principle is matter but only universals. But the intellect of a separated soul possesses infused forms through which it can know singulars, for the reason already stated.

(2) A separated soul does not know singulars through species acquired while it was united to its body, but through infused species; however it does not follow that it knows all singulars, as has been shown.

(3) Separated souls are not prevented from knowing things that happen in this life because of spatial distance, but rather because there is not in them adequate efficacy of intellectual power so that they are able to know all things by means of infused species.

(4) Not even the angels know all future contingents. For angels know singulars by means of infused species insofar as singulars participate in their species. Hence future events which, because they are future, do not yet participate in a species are not known by them, but only insofar as they are present in their causes.

(5) Angels who know all natural singulars do not possess as many intelligible species as there are singulars known by them; but rather they know many things by means of a single species, as we have shown in earlier questions. Separated souls, however, do not know all singulars; hence the argument is irrelevant with respect to them.

(6) An infused species, although it is immaterial and indistinct, is nevertheless a likeness of the thing, both with respect to form and with respect to matter, as has been shown.

(7) The same answer may be given to this objection.

(8) Although intelligible forms do not create things, they are nevertheless like creative forms, not indeed in having the power of creating but in having the power of representing created things. For an artisan is able to communicate to someone his art of making something, even though the one to whom he communicates the art does not possess the power to make that thing.

(9) Infused forms are not like the ideal reasons which exist in the divine mind except analogically; consequently these ideal reasons cannot be known perfectly by means of forms of this kind. However, it does not follow that the things of which these are ideal reasons are imperfectly known by means of infused forms. For things of this kind are not more excellent than infused forms but are rather less excellent. Hence things can be fully comprehended through infused forms.

(10) Infused forms are limited to producing the knowledge of certain singulars in a separated soul because of the disposition of the soul itself, as we have already said.

(11) Infused species are caused by God in a separated soul through the mediation of angels. Nor does it matter that some separated souls

are superior to some angels. For we are not at present speaking of the knowledge of glory, with respect to which a soul can be equal to or even superior to angels; rather we are speaking of natural knowledge in which a soul falls short of an angel. For forms of this kind are caused in a separated soul by an angel, not by way of creation, but rather just as that which is actual causes something in its own genus to go from potency to act. And since action of this kind does not require location in space, it is not necessary in this instance to look for a spatial medium of transmission; but in this instance the order of nature operates in the same way as the order of place operates in bodily things.

(12) A separated soul knows singulars through infused species insofar as they are the likenesses of singulars in the way we have just explained. However, application and conversion, which were referred to in the objection, accompany knowledge of this kind, rather than cause it.

(13) Singulars are not actually infinite but only potentially so. Neither the intellect of an angel nor that of a separated soul is prevented from knowing an infinite number of singulars one after another, since even the senses can do this; and our intellect knows the infinite species of numbers in this way. For in this way the infinite is known only successively and as its potential members are actualized, in the same way as an infinite is said to exist in material things.

(14) Augustine did not mean that bodies and the likenesses of bodies are not known by the intellect but rather that the vision of the intellect is not moved by bodies as a sense power is, nor by the likenesses of bodies as the imagination is, but by intelligible truth.

(15) Although a separated soul possesses the same nature as a soul joined to its body, nevertheless, on account of its separation from its body, it is free to turn its gaze toward higher substances in order that by means of them it might be able to receive an influx of intelligible forms through which it might know singulars; and this it is not able to do while it is united to its body, as we have shown in earlier questions.

(16) A singular, insofar as it is sensible, that is, as subject to bodily change, never becomes intelligible, but becomes such inasmuch as an immaterial or intelligible form can represent it, as we have shown.

(17) A separated soul acquires intelligible species through its own intellect in the manner of a higher substance, which knows by a single power what a human being knows through two powers, that is, sense and intellect; and consequently a separated soul is able to know both.

(18) Although a separated soul does not govern things nor cause them, it nevertheless possesses forms which are like those possessed by one who causes and governs; for one who causes and governs does not know what is governed and caused except insofar as he posssesses a likeness of that thing.

Now it is necessary even to reply to the "On The Contrary" arguments because they lead to false conclusions.

(1) When a soul is joined to its body, it knows the singular by means of its intellect, not indeed directly, but by a kind of reflection; inasmuch, that is, as by apprehending its intelligible object it turns back to consider its act and the intelligible species which is the principle of its operation and the source of its species. And in this way it proceeds to a consideration of phantasms and of the singulars to which the phantasms belong. But the intellect can carry out this reflective activity only by making use of the cogitative power and the imagination, and these powers do not exist in a separated soul. Hence a separated soul does not know singulars in this way.

(2) Angels of the lower hierarchy are illuminated concerning the reasons of singular effects not by means of singular species, but by universal reasons by means of which these angels are able to know singulars because of the efficacy of their intellective power, by which they surpass a separated soul. And although the reasons perceived by them are unqualifiedly universal, nevertheless they can be called particular in comparison to the more universal reasons which the higher angels perceive.

(3) What a lower power can do, a higher power can also do; however, not in the same way but in a more excellent way. Hence the intellect knows immaterially and universally the same things that a sense power perceives materially and singularly.

Notes to Question Twenty

1. Aristotle, *De Anima*, II, 5 (417b 22-23; 27-28).
2. St. Augustine, *De Cura pro mortuis gerenda*, XIII-XIV (PL 40: 604-606).
3. *Isaiah*, 41: 23.
4. Pseudo-Dionysius, *De Ecclesiastica hierarchia*, V, 4 (PG 3: 504); *De Coelesti hierarchia*, IV, 3 (PG 3: 182).
5. St. Augustine, *De Genesi ad litteram*, XII, 24 (PL 34: 474).
6. *Liber de Causis*, VII; ed. Bardenhewer, p. 170, 25-27; XXII, p. 183, 23; p. 184, 1.
7. Cf. Objection 3.
8. *Epistle to the Hebrews*, 1: 14.
9. Pseudo-Dionysius, *De Divinis nominibus*, VII, 2 (PG 3: 869).

QUESTION TWENTY-ONE

Parallel texts: *In II Sent.,* dist. 6, q. 1, a. 3; *In IV Sent.,* dist. 44, q. 26, a. 1; *Contra gent.,* IV, 90; *Summa theol.,* I, q. 64, a. 4, ad 1; *De Spir. creat.,* a. 1, ad 20; *De Anima,* q. 6, ad 7; *Quodl.,* III, q. 10, a. 1; q. 9, a. 21; II, q. 7, a. 1; *Compend. theol.,* cap. 180.

The twenty-first question that is asked about the soul is this: Whether a separated soul can suffer pain from corporeal fire. And it seems that it cannot.

(1) For nothing suffers except insofar as it is in potency. But a separated soul is not in potency except with respect to its intellect, because the sensitive powers do not remain in it, as we have shown. Therefore a separated soul cannot be acted upon by corporeal fire except with respect to its intellect, that is, by understanding fire. Now this is not painful but rather delightful. Therefore a soul cannot suffer pain from corporeal fire.

(2) Furthermore, agent and patient have matter in common, as is said in Book I of the *De Generatione.*[1] But a soul, since it is immaterial, does not have matter in common with corporeal fire. Therefore a separated soul cannot be acted upon by corporeal fire.

(3) Furthermore, that which does not touch does not act. But corporeal fire is not able to touch a soul, neither with respect to the last degree of quantity, since a soul is incorporeal, nor even by a contact of power, since the power of a body cannot make an impression on an incorporeal substance, but rather the opposite is true. Consequently there is no way in which a separated soul can be acted upon by corporeal fire.

(4) Furthermore, something is said to be acted upon in two ways, either as a subject, as wood is acted upon by fire, or as a contrary, as hot is acted upon by the cold. Now a soul cannot be acted upon by corporeal fire as the subject of a passion, because it would be necessary that the form of fire be produced in the soul; and thus it would follow that a soul would become hot and be on fire, and this is impossible. Nor can one say that a soul is acted upon by corporeal fire as one contrary is acted upon by its contrary: first, because there is no

contrary to a soul; secondly, because it would follow that a soul would be destroyed by corporeal fire, and this is impossible. Therefore a soul cannot be acted upon by corporeal fire.

(5) Furthermore, there must be some proportion between agent and patient. But there does not seem to be any proportion between a soul and corporeal fire, since they belong to diverse genera. Therefore a soul cannot be acted upon by corporeal fire.

(6) Furthermore, everything that is acted upon is moved. Now a soul is not moved since it is not a body. Therefore a soul cannot be acted upon.

(7) Furthermore, a soul is of greater excellence than the body of the fifth essence.[2] But the body of the fifth essence is totally incapable of material change. Therefore a soul is even more impervious to change.

(8) Furthermore, Augustine states, in Book XII of *Super Genesim ad litteram,*[3] that an agent is nobler than a patient. But corporeal fire is not nobler than a soul. Therefore fire cannot act upon a soul.

But an objector was arguing that fire does not act through its own essential and natural power but insofar as it is an instrument of divine justice.

(9) On the contrary, it is a trait of a wise workman to make use of instruments that are appropriate to his end. But corporeal fire does not seem to be an appropriate instrument for punishing a soul, since this role does not belong to fire by reason of its form, and it is through its form that an instrument is adapted to its effect, as an axe is adapted to chopping and a saw is adapted to sawing. Now an artisan would not be acting wisely if he were to use a saw for chopping and an axe for sawing. Therefore much less does God, who is supreme in wisdom, use corporeal fire as an instrument for punishing a soul.

(10) Futhermore, since God is the author of nature, He does nothing contrary to nature, as a gloss on *Romans* XI states.[4] But it is contrary to nature that something corporeal should act upon what is incorporeal. Therefore God does not do this.

(11) Furthermore, God cannot make contradictories to be simultaneously true. Now this would occur is something which belongs to a thing's essence is taken away from it; for example, if a human being were not rational, it would follow that a human being were simultaneously human and not human. Therefore God cannot bring it about that a thing lack that which is essential to it. But to be incapable of material change is essential to a soul; for this belongs to a soul insofar as it is immaterial. Therefore God cannot bring about that a soul be acted upon by corporeal fire.

(12) Furthermore, each thing possesses a power of acting that is appropriate to its own nature. Therefore a thing cannot acquire

a power of acting which is not appropriate to it but rather is appropriate to another being, unless it be changed from its essential nature to a different nature; as water does not cause heat unless it has been changed by fire. But it is not appropriate to the nature of corporeal fire to have the power of acting upon spiritual things, as we have pointed out. Consequently, if fire receives from God the power to act upon a separated soul because fire is an instrument of divine justice, it seems that then it is not corporeal fire but something possessing a different nature.

(13) Furthermore, that which is done by the divine power is done according to the essential and true principles of the thing which exists in nature. For when a blind man regains sight through divine power, he receives sight in accordance with the true, essential and natural principle of sight. Therefore, if a soul is acted upon through divine power by fire inasmuch as fire is an instrument of divine justice, it follows that a soul is truly acted upon in accordance with the proper nature of passion. Now to be acted upon has two meanings: in one way 'to be acted upon' means merely to receive, as an intellect is acted upon by something intelligible and a sense power is acted upon by something sensible. 'To be acted upon' also means that something is taken away from the substance of that which is acted upon, as when wood is acted upon by fire. Therefore, if a separated soul is acted upon by corporeal fire through divine power insofar as the nature of passion consists merely in reception, then since what is received is in the receiver according to the receiver's mode of being, it would follow that a separated soul would be affected by corporeal fire in an immaterial and incorporeal way in accordance with a soul's mode of being. Now to acquire something in this way does not punish a soul but perfects it; therefore a soul will not be punished in this way. Nor can a soul be acted upon by corporeal fire in the sense that being acted upon involves taking something from a substance, because in that way the substance of the soul would be corrupted. Consequently it is not possible that a soul be acted upon by corporeal fire even inasmuch as fire is an instrument of divine justice.

(14) Furthermore, no instrument acts as an instrument except by exercising its proper function, as a saw acts instrumentally by cutting in order that a chest might be built. But fire cannot act upon a soul by means of its own essential and natural action, for fire is unable to cause a soul to become hot. Consequently it is not able to act upon soul as an instrument of divine justice.

But an objector was arguing that fire acts upon the soul by another proper action, namely, insofar as fire holds the soul firmly, as something fettered to it.

(15) On the contrary, if a soul is bound to fire and is held fast

by it, it must be united to fire in some way. Now a soul is not united to fire as a form, because in that way a soul would give life to fire. Nor is a soul united to fire as a mover, because in that way fire would be acted upon by the soul, rather than the other way around. Therefore a separated soul cannot be fettered by corporeal fire nor be restrained by it. Now there is no other way in which an incorporeal substance could be united to a body. Therefore a separated soul cannot be fettered by corporeal fire nor be restrained by it.

(16) Furthermore, that which is fettered to something cannot be separated from it. But the spirits of the damned are at times separated from the corporeal fire of hell. For it is said that demons inhabit the murky air here on earth, and the souls of the damned have also sometimes appeared to certain people. Therefore a soul is not acted upon by corporeal fire by being fettered to it.

(17) Furthermore, whatever is fettered to something and confined by it is hindered by it from exercising its essential operation. But the essential operation of a soul is to understand; and a soul cannot be hindered in this operation by being bound to something corporeal, because it possesses its intelligble objects within itself, as is said in Book III of the *De Anima*.[5] As a result it is not necessary that a soul seek these objects outside itself. Therefore a separated soul is not punished by being fettered to corporeal fire.

(18) Furthermore, if fire is able to restrain a soul in this way, other bodies will be able to do the same, and even more effectively because they are more dense and heavier than fire. Therefore, if a soul is punished only by restraint and by being bound, its punishment ought not to be attributed to fire only, but even more so to other bodies.

(19) Furthermore, Augustine says, in Book XII of *Super Genesim ad litteram*,[6] that we ought not to believe that the substance of the infernal regions is corporeal, but that it is spiritual. Damascene[7] also says that the fire of hell is not material. Therefore it seems that a soul is not acted upon by corporeal fire.

(20) Furthermore, as Gregory says in his *De Moralibus*,[8] a wicked servant is punished by his master in order that he might be reformed. But those who are condemned to hell are incorrigible. Consequently they ought not to be punished by the corporeal fire of hell.

(21) Furthermore, punishments are assigned in terms of contraries. But the soul sinned by yielding its affection for corporeal things. Therefore it ought not to be punished by means of what is corporeal but rather by separation from bodily things.

(22) Furthermore, as the divine justice punishes sinners, so it rewards the just. But the just are not given corporeal rewards but only spiritual ones. Hence if Scripture recounts that certain corporeal rewards are to be given to the just, these should be understood in

a metaphorical sense, for example, in *Luke* XXII,[9] "You shall eat and drink," and so forth. Therefore corporeal punishments are not inflicted upon sinners but only spiritual punishments, and all the things that are said in the Scriptures about corporeal punishments are to be understood metaphorically. And consequently a soul is not acted upon by corporeal fire.

On the Contrary,

(1) The fire by which the bodies of the damned and by which demons are punished is the same, as is clear from what it said in *Matthew* XXV:[10] "Depart ye wicked into the fire," and so on. Now it is necessary that the bodies of the damned be punished by corporeal fire. Therefore, for the same reason, separated souls are punished by corporeal fire.

The Response:

It must be said that men have spoken in a variety of ways with respect to the suffering of a soul through fire. For some have said that a soul will not suffer punishment by a bodily fire, but that its spiritual suffering is designated metaphorically in the Scriptures by the name of fire; this was the teaching of Origen.[11] But still this does not seem to be an adequate answer; because, as Augustine says, in Book XXI of his *City of God,*[12] it is necessary that the fire by which the bodies of the damned will be tormented must be understood as corporeal; and it is this same fire by which both demons and separated souls are afflicted, according to the sentence of the Lord cited above.

And therefore it seemed to others that this fire is corporeal but that a soul does not suffer pain directly from this fire but rather from its likeness as seen in the imagination; just as it happens that those who are asleep are truly tormented by the terrors which, in their dreams, they see themselves suffering, although the things by which they are afflicted are not genuine bodies but are the likenesses of bodies.

But this position cannot be maintained, because it has been pointed out in previous questions that the powers of the sensitive part of a soul, among which is the imagination, do not remain in a separated soul. And therefore one must say that a separated soul suffers from corporeal fire itself; but how it suffers does not seem easy to explain.

For some have maintained that a separated soul suffers the pain of fire in the very power by which it sees the fire; Gregory touches upon this point in Book IV of his *Dialogues*[13] when he says: A soul

suffers from fire by the very act of seeing it. But since seeing is the
perfection of the one who sees, all vision as such is delightful. Hence
nothing is painful insofar as it is seen, but insofar as it is apprehended
as harmful.

And consequently others stated that a soul, seeing this fire and
recognizing it as harmful to itself, is by this fact tormented; and
Gregory touches upon this in Book IV of his *Dialogues* [14] when he says
that a soul perceives itself to be on fire when it is being burned. But
then one must still consider whether *the* fire is, in point of fact, harmful
to a soul or not. And if this fire in point of fact is not harmful to a
soul, it would follow that a soul would be deceived in the judgment
by which it apprehends the fire as harmful. And this seems to be untenable, especially with respect to demons, who, because of their keenness
of intellect, have a highly developed knowledge of the natures of things.
Therefore one must say that according to the truth of the matter corporeal fire is harmful to a soul. Hence in Book IV of his *Dialogues* [15]
Gregory concludes by saying, "We are able to conclude from the words
of the Evangelists that a soul suffers not only from seeing fire but also
by experiencing it."

Therefore, in investigating how corporeal fire can be harmful
to a soul or to a demon, one must bear in mind that something does
not incur injury because it acquires that by which it is perfected, but
because it is hindered by what is contrary to it. Hence the suffering
inflicted on the soul by fire does not come about only because the
soul is a recipient, as the intellect is acted upon by the intelligible
object and the senses by sensible objects. But the soul suffers as something that is acted upon by another by way of contrariety and impediment; and this happens in two ways. For something is hindered in
one way by its contrary with respect to its very existence which it
possesses through an inhering form. And in this way something is
acted upon by its contrary through alteration and corruption, as wood
is burned up by fire. Secondly, something is hindered by another which
opposes it or which is contrary to it with respect to its proper tendency;
for example, it is the natural tendency of a rock to be borne downward,
but this natural tendency can be impeded by something that opposes
it with contrary force, so that the rock is forced to be at rest or to
move upwards. But neither of these modes of undergoing punishment
is found in a thing which lacks knowledge; for pain and punishment
cannot be properly ascribed to something which is incapable of experiencing grief and sadness. But in a being which possesses knowledge,
pain and punishment can be a consequence of both modes of suffering,
but in diverse ways; for the passion which occurs through alteration
by a contrary results in pain and punishment which can be sensed,
as when a sensible object of great intensity destroys the harmony of

a sense organ. Therefore the intensity of sensible objects, especially those of the sense of touch, produce sensible pain; but when the sense objects are moderate, they produce delight because of their proportion to the sense. But passion of the second kind does not produce a punishment involving sensible sorrow but rather involving interior sadness, which arises in a human being or in an animal from the fact that something is apprehended by an interior power as being repellent to the will or to some other appetite. Hence things which are contrary to the will or to an appetite inflict suffering, and sometimes even more than things which are painful to the senses; for some would choose to be flogged and to suffer serious sensible pain rather than be subject to insults or other things of this kind which are repellent to the will.

Therefore a soul cannot undergo punishment by corporeal fire according to the first mode of suffering; for it is not possible that a soul be changed or destroyed by the fire. And therefore it is not tormented by the fire in such a way that it experiences sensible pain. However, a soul can be acted upon by corporeal fire according to the second mode of suffering, insofar as through fire of this kind a soul is hindered in its tendency or in its will; and the following explanation shows how this can occur. For a soul and any other incorporeal substance, so far as its own nature is concerned, is not restricted to a particular place but transcends the entire realm of bodily things. Therefore that it should be bound to something and restricted to a particular place by some necessity is contrary to its nature and contrary to its natural appetite. And I insist that this is so except insofar as a soul is united to the body of which it is the natural form and in which it attains a certain perfection.

Now that a spiritual substance be bound to a body does not result from the power of a body that is able to restrain an incorporeal substance, but rather from the power of a higher substance which binds a spiritual substance to such a body, as by divine permission and the power of higher demons certain spirits are bound through magical arts to bodies such as rings, statues, or other things of this kind. And it is in this way that souls and demons are fettered by the divine power to corporeal fire for their punishment. Hence Augustine says, in Book XXI of *The City of God*, [16] "Why shall we not say that even incorporeal spirits can be afflicted with the punishment of corporeal fire in true yet wondrous ways, if the spirits of human beings, also truly incorporeal, can in this life be confined to bodily members, and will in the life to come be able to be everlastingly bound to the fetters of their bodies? Therefore demons, although incorporeal, will cling to bodies, to be tormented by fires; and they will receive punishment from these flames rather than give life to them."

And in this way it is true that this fire, insofar as through the divine power it holds the soul bound fast, acts upon the soul as an instrument of divine justice. And inasmuch as a soul apprehends this fire as harmful to itself, it is afflicted with an interior sadness, and this sadness is indeed extreme since the soul which was by nature to enjoy union with God finds itself subject to things lower than itself. Therefore the greatest sorrow of the damned will be that they are separated from God, but secondly that they are subject to corporeal things in the lowest and most miserable place.

Replies to the Opposing Arguments:

Through what has just been said the answers to the first seven objections are clear. For we do not maintain that a soul is acted upon by corporeal fire, either by simply receiving something or through alteration brought about by a contrary, and these arguments are based on that premiss.

(8) An instrument does not act by its own power, but by the power of the principal agent. And consequently, since fire acts upon a soul as an instrument of divine justice, what is to be noted is not the worthiness of fire but the worthiness of divine justice.

(9) Bodies are appropriate instruments for punishing the damned. For it is fitting that those who were unwilling to be subject to their superior, that is, God, be subjected to lower things by way of punishment.

(10) Even though God does not act contrary to nature, He nevertheless operates in a way that is higher than nature when He does what nature cannot do.

(11) Because of the nature of its essence, the soul cannot be acted upon by something material in a way that causes alteration. However, it does not suffer in this way by divine power, but in the way we have just explained.

(12) Fire does not possess the power of acting upon a soul as if it acted by its own power, as do things which act in a natural way, but only instrumentally. And therefore it does not follow that it is changed with respect to its nature.

(13) A soul is acted upon by corporeal fire in neither of these ways, but rather in the way we explained above.

(14) Corporeal fire, even though it does not cause a soul to become hot, still has another operation or relationship to a soul which bodies by nature have to a spirit, that is, that bodies may be united to them in some fashion.

(15) A soul is not united as a form to the fire which is punishing it since it does not give life to it, as Augustine says.[17] Rather it is

united to it in the way in which spirits are united to bodily places by a contact of power, even though these spirits are not movers of these bodies.

(16) As we have already said, a soul is afflicted by corporeal fire because it apprehends the fire as harmful to it, as binding it and restricting it. Now this apprehension can be tormenting, even when a soul is not actually fettered, from the very fact that a soul apprehends itself as condemned to such confinement. And in this sense demons are said to carry hell with them wherever they go.

(17) Although a soul, by a fettering of this kind, is not hindered in its intellectual operation, it is restricted in its natural liberty, which consists in being free from all confinement to a corporeal place.

(18) The punishment of hell is not only for souls but also for bodies; for this reason fire is said to be particularly a punishment of hell since fire is especially painful to bodies. Nevertheless there will also be other punishments, according to the verse of the *Psalm,*[18] Fire, sulphur, and so on. It is also appropriate to inordinate love, which is the starting point of sinning, that just as the empyrean heaven corresponds to the fire of charity, so the fire of hell should correspond to inordinate desire.

(19) Augustine makes this statement, not as if he were giving a definitive answer, but by way of inquiry. Or if he did state it as something he held, he later expressly retracted it, in Book XXI of *The City of God.*[19] Or one can say that the substance of the infernal regions is said to be spiritual with respect to its proximate pain, which is fire apprehended as harmful by way of restricting and binding.

(20) Gregory introduces this statement by way of an objection made by those who believed that all the punishments inflicted by God were corrective and that none were eternal; now this view is in fact false. Some punishments are inflicted by God, either in this life or after this life, in order to correct and to cleanse; but some punishments are inflicted for final damnation. Nor does God inflict such torments because He delights in punishments, but because of the fact that He delights in justice, in accordance with which punishment is due to sinners. In the same way also among human beings some punishments are inflicted in order to correct the one who is being punished, as when a father whips his son; but some are inflicted as a final penalty, as when a judge hangs a thief.

(21) Punishments occur through a contrary with respect to the sinner's intention, for a sinner seeks to satisfy his own will; but punishment is contrary to his will. But sometimes the divine wisdom brings it about that that in which someone seeks to fulfil his will is changed into its contrary. And thus it is said in the *Book of Wisdom*[20] that a person will be punished by the very objects through which he sinned.

Hence, because a soul sins through bodily things, it is appropriate to divine wisdom that the sinner be punished through bodily things.

(22) A soul is rewarded through that which is higher than it, and it is punished by being made subject to things which are lower than itself. And consequently the rewards of souls are appropriately understood only in a spiritual sense; however, punishments are understood as involving bodies.

Notes to Question Twenty-One

1. Aristotle, *De Generatione et corruptione,* I, 7 (324a 34-35).
2. Aristotle's "quintessence" is the fifth essence or body of which the incorruptible heavenly bodies are composed. This is to distinguish them from earthly bodies which are composed of the 4 elements of classical physics. Cf. Aristotle, *De Caelo,* I, 2 (269a 30 - 269b 17).
3. St. Augustine, *De Genesi ad litteram,* XII, 16 (PL 34: 467).
4. *Glossa ordinaria, Ad Romanos,* 11: 24 (PL 114: 508).
5. Aristotle, *De Anima,* III, 4 (429a 27-28; 429b 5-9).
6. St. Augustine, *De Genesi ad litteram,* XII, 32 (PL 34: 481).
7. St. John Damascene, *Dialogus contra Manichaeos,* 36 (PG 94: 1542).
8. St. Gregory, *Moralia,* XXXIV, 19 (PL 76: 738)
9. *Luke,* 22: 30.
10. *Matthew,* 25: 41.
11. Origen, *Peri Archon,* II, 10 (PG 11: 236).
12. St. Augustine, *City of God,* XXI, 10 (PL 41: 724-725).
13. St. Gregory, *Dialogues,* IV, 29 (PL 77: 368).
14. *Ibid.*
15. *Ibid.*
16. St. Augustine, *City of God,* XXI, 10 (PL 41: 724-725).
17. St. Augustine, *City of God,* XXI, 2 (PL 41: 710).
18. *Psalms,* 10: 7.
19. St. Augustine, *City of God,* XXI 10 (PL 41: 724-725).
20. *Wisdom,* 11: 17.

BIBLIOGRAPHY

Primary Sources

I. Texts of St. Thomas Aquinas

1. SAINT THOMAS AQUINAS, *Opera Omnia*. ed. E. Frette P. Mare. Paris, Vivès, 34 vol., 1871-1882.

2. — *Opera Omnia*. Parma, P. Fiaccadori, 25 vol., 1852-1872.

3. — *Opera Omnia*. Iussu impensaque Leonis XIII. P.M. Edita. Rome, 1882.

4. — *Summa Theologiae*. cura et studio Instituti Studiorum Med. Ottaviensis. Ottawa, 5 vol., 1941-45.

5. — *Summa Contra Gentiles*. Editio Leonina Manualis. Rome, 1934.

6. — *Scriptum super Libros Sententiarum Magistri Petri Lombardi*. ed. P. Mandonnet and M.-F. Moos. Paris, Lethielleux, 4 vol., 1929-1947.

7. — *Quaestiones Disputatae*. ed. R. Spiazzi, *et al.* 8th ed. Turin-Rome, Marietti, 2 vol., 1949.

8. — *Tractatus De Spiritualibus Creaturis*. ed. Leo W. Keeler. Rome, 1946.

9. — *Quaestiones Quodlibetales*. ed. R. Spiazzi. 8th ed. Turin-Rome, Marietti, 1949.

10. — *Opuscula Omnia*. ed. P. Mandonnet. Paris, Lethielleux, 5 vol., 1927.

11. — *Opuscula Omnia necnon Opera Minora*. Tomus Primus, *Opuscula Philosophica*. ed. J. Perrier. Paris, Lethielleux, 1949.

12. — *Tractatus De Unitate Intellectus contra Averroistas*. ed. Leo W. Keeler. Rome, 1946.

13. — *In Duodecim Libros Metaphysicorum Aristotelis Expositio*. ed. M.-R. Cathala. rev. ed. R. Spiazzi. Turin-Rome, Marietti, 1950.

14. — *In Decem Libros Ethicorum Aristotelis ad Nicomachum Expositio*. ed. R. Spiazzi. Turin-Rome, Marietti, 1949.

15. — *In Aristotelis Librum De Anima Commentarium*. 2nd ed. A. M. Pirotta. Turin, Marietti, 1936.

II. Texts of Other Authors:

16. Peter Abelard. *Petri Abealardi, Sic et Non*. PL 178, 1339-1610.

17. St. Albert the Great. *Opera Cania*. ed. A. Borgnet. Paris, Vivès, 38 vol., 1890-99.

18. Aristotle. *Aristoteles Graece*, 2 vol., *ex recensione I. Bekkeri*, ed. Academia Regia Borussica. Berlin, 1831.

19. — *The Works of Aristotle.* Trans. into English under the editorship of J.A. Smith and W.D. Ross. 12 vol., Oxford, Clarendon Press, 1910-1952.

20. — *Aristotle De Anima.* With translation, introduction and notes. ed. R. D. Hicks. Cambridge, University Press, 1907.

21. Averroes. *Aristotelis Stagiritae Opera Omnia cum Averrois Cordubensis variis in eadem Commentariis.* Venice, Juntas, 11 vol., 1550.

22. Boethius. *In Topica Ciceronis Commentaria.* PL 64, 909-1169.

23. St. Bonaventure. *Opera Omnia.* Ad Claras Aquas (Quaracchi), 10 vol., 1882-1902.

24. — *Opera Theologica Selecta.* Ad Claras Aquas (Quaracchi) 4 vol., 1934-1949.

25. Clarenbaldus of Arras. *Der Kommentar des Clarenbaldus su Boethius De Trinitate.* ed. Wilhelm Jansen. Breslau, 1926.

26. Gilbert de la Porrée. *Commentaria in Librum de Trinitate.* PL 64, 1247-1256.

27. John of Salisbury. *Metalogicon,* Libri IV. ed. G.C.I. Webb. Oxford, Clarendon Press, 1929.

28. Nemesius. *Nemesii Episcopi Premnon Physicon sive περὶ φύσεως ἀνθρώπου Liber a.* *N. Alfano Archiepiscopo Salerni in Latinum Translatum.* ed. C. Burkhard. Leipsig, Teubner, 1917.

29. — *Gregorii Nyeseni (Nemesii Emeseni) περὶ φύσεως ἀνθρώπου Liber a Burgundione in Latinum Translatus.* ed. C. Burkhard. Vienna, 5 fascicles, 1891-1902.

30. Peter Cantor. *Verbum Abbreviatum.* PL 205, 23-370.

31. Robert of Melun. *Oeuvres de Robert de Melun,* Tome I, *Questiones de Divina Pagina,* *Texte In edit.* ed. R. Martin. (Spicilegium Sacrum Lovaniense, 13) Louvain, 1932.

Secondary Sources

The list which follows contains the works cited in the study and a few additional titles immediately connected with the topics treated. The list is divided into two sections: 1) Textual, Literary, Historical Section and 2) Doctrinal Section. In assigning an article or a book to one of these two sections, I have been guided solely by the *use I have made of the work.* For that reason, some works which are almost purely doctrinal are included in the first section. This indicates that I was concerned only with textual or historical indications or notes which they contained.

For complete bibliographies on St. Thomas, the following works may be consulted:

1. P. Mandonnet and J. Destrez, *Bibliographie Thomiste* (Bibl. Thom. 1) Le Saulchoir, Kain (Belgique) 1921.

2. Vernon J. Bourke, *Thomistic Bibliography, 1920-1940.* St. Louis, Modern Schoolman, 1945.

For more recent bibliographical listings, cf. the following periodicals:

1. *Bulletin Thomiste.* Organe de la Societe Thomists. Le Saulchoir.

2. *Revue des sciences philosophiques et théologiques.* Paris, Vrin.

3. *Tijdschrift voor Philosophie;* cf. section: "Bibliographisch Repertorium." Utrecht.

4. *Repertoire bibliographique de la philosophie. Louvain.*

I. Textual, Literary, Historical Section:

32. *Actes De Leon XIII.* Paris, Maison de la Bonne Press, 7 vol. No date.

33. *Acta Sanctorum, Boll.* Martius, I. Paris and Rome, 1865.

34. Axters, Etienne. "Pour l'état des manuscrits des Questions Disputées de Saint Thomas d'Aquin," in *Divus Thomas* (Piacenza) 38 (1935) p. 129-159.

35. Birkenmajer, A. "Ueber die Reihenfolge und die Entstehungszeit der Quaestiones disputatae des hl. Thomas von Aquin," in *Phil. Jahrbuch,* 34 (1921) p. 31-49.

36. Blanche, F. A. "Le vocabulaire de l'argumentation et la structure de l'article dans les oeuvres de saint Thomas," in *Revue des sc. phil. et théol.,* 14 (1925) p. 167-187.

37. Bochenski, I. M. "Sancti Thomae Aquinatis De Modalibus Opusculum et Doctrina," in *Angelicum,* 17 (1940) p. 180-218.

38. Bouyges, Maurice. "L'idée génératrice du De Potentia de saint Thomas," in *Revue de philosophie,* 2 (1931) p. 120 ff.

39. *Bullarum Privilegiorum ac Diplomatum Romanorum Pentificum Amplissima Collectio.* ed. C. Cocquelines. Rome, Hieronymus Mainardus, 14 vol., 1739-44.

40. Chenu, M.-D. *Introduction a l'étude de saint Thomas d'Aquin.* Montreal-Paris, 1950.

41. Coxe, H., *et al. Catalogi codicum mss. Bibliothecae Bodleianae.* Oxford, 9 parts, 1853-1883.

42. Coxe, H. *Catalogus codicum mss. qui in collegiis aulisque Oxoniensibus hodie adservantur.* Oxford, 2 vol., 1852.

43. Coyecque, E. *Catalogue général des manuscrits des bibliothèques publiques de France.* Departments, Tome 19: Amiens. Paris, Plon, 1893.

44. De Heredia, Vincente Beltran. "Cronica del movimiento tomista," in *La Ciencia Tomista,* 37 (1928) p. 58-76.

45. — "Los manuscritos de Santo Tomás en la Bibliotheca del Cabildo de Toledo," in *La Ciencia Tomista,* 33 (1926) p. 398-412.

46. — "Los manuscritos de Santo Tomás de la Bibliotheca Nacional de Madrid," in *La Ciencia Tomista,* 34 (1926) p. 88-111.

47. — "Los manuscritos de Santo Tomás en la Biblioteca Real de Madrid," in *La Ciencia Tomista,* 34 (1926) p. 196-216.

48. Denifle, H. "Quellen sur Gelehrtengeschichte des Predigerordens in 13. and 14. Jahrhundert," in *Archiv fur Litteratur-und Kirchen-Geschichte des Mittelalters.* Zweiter Band. Berlin, 1886.

49. Denifle, H. and Chatelain, A. *Chartularium Universitatis Parisiensis.* Paris, 4 vol., 1889-1897.

50. Destrez, Jean. *Études critiques sur les oeuvres de saint Thomas d'Aquin d'apres la tradition manuscrite.* (Bibl. thom. 17) I. Paris, Vrin, 1933.

51. Glorieux, P. *La Littérature Quodlibétique de 1260 à 1320.* (Bibl. thom. 5) Le Saulchoir, Kain (Belgique) 1925.

52. — *La Littérature Quodlibétique II* (Bibl. thom. 21) Paris, Vrin, 1935.

53. — "Les questions disputées de saint Thomas et leur suite chronologique," in *Recherches de théol. anc. et med.,* 4 (1932) p. 5-33.

54. — "Pour la chronolgie de la Somme," in *Mélanges de science religieuse,* 2 (1945) p. 59-98.

55. — "Repertoire des maîtres en théologie de Paris au XIIIe siècle. Paris, Vrin, 2 vol., 1933.

56. —"Une élection priorale à Gand en 1309," in *Archivum Fratrum Praedicatorum,* 7 (1937) p. 246-267.

57. Grabmann, Martin. *Die Aristoteleskommentare des Simon von Faversham.* (Sitz. der Bayerischen Akad. der Wissenschaften phil.-hist. abteilung, 1933, heft 3) Munchen, 1933.

58. —*Die Werke des hl. Thomas von Aquin.* 3rd ed. in *Beitrage* . . . Band XII, Heft 1/2. Münster, Westfalen, 1949.

59. —*I Papi del Duecento e l'Aristotelismo.* 2 vol. Vol. I, *I divieti ecclesiastici di Aristotele sotto Innocenzo III e Gregorio IX.* Rome, 1941. Vol. II, *Guglielmo di Moerbeke O.P. il traduttore delle opere di Aristotele.* Rome, 1946.

60. —"Les commentaires de saint Thomas d'Aquin sur les ouvrages d'Aristote," in *Annales de l'Institut Superieur de Philosophie,* 3 (1914) p. 231-281.

61. Grech, Gundisalvus M. "The Leonine Edition of the Works of St. Thomas Aquinas, Its Origin, Method and Published Works," in *From an Abundant Spring.* ed. The *Thomist* staff. New York, Kenedy, 1952.

62. Haskins, Charles Homer. *Studies in the History of Mediaeval Science.* Cambridge, Harvard, 1924.

63. Henquinet, F. M. "Descriptio Codicis 158 Assisii in Bibliotheca Communali," in *Archivum Franciscanum Historicum,* 24 (1931) p. 91-108.

64. Keeler, Lee W. "Editions and critical editions," in *Gregorianum,* 18 (1937) p. 432-439.

65. —"History of the editions of St. Thomas's 'De Unitate Intellectus' ", in *Gregorianum,* 17 (1936) p. 53-81.

66. —"The vulgate text of St. Thomas' Commentary on the Ethics," in *Gregorianum,* 17 (1936) p. 413-436.

67. Klibansky, R. *The Continuity of the Platonic Tradition.* London, Warburg Institute, 1939.

68. Koch, J. "Ueber die Reihenfolge der Quaestiones disputatae des hl. Thomas von Aquin," in *Phil. Jahrbuch,* 37 (1924) p. 359-367.

69. Lacombe, G. *et al. Aristoteles Latinus.* Pars Prior. Rome, 1939.

70. Little, A. G., and Pelster, F. *Oxford Theology and Theologians.* Oxford, Hist. Soc. Vol 96, 1934.

71. Lottin, O. "La date de la question disputée "de malo" de saint Thomas d'Aquin," in *Revue d'histoire ecclésiastique,* 24 (1928) p. 373-388.

72. Mandonnet, P. "Chronologie des écrits scripturaires de saint Thomas d'Aquin," in *Revue Thomiste,* 33 (1928) p. 27-45, 116-155, 211-245; 34 (1929), p. 53-69, 132-145, 489-519.

73. —"Chronologie des questions disputées de saint Thomas d'Aquin," in *Revue Thomiste,* 23 (1918) p. 266-287, 340-371.

74. —"Chronologie sommaire de la vie et des écrits de saint Thomas," in *Revue des sc. phil. et théol.* 9 (1920) p. 142-152.

75. —*Des écrits authentiques de S. Thomas d'Aquin.* 2nd ed. Fribourg, 1910.

76. —"Les questions disputées de saint Thomas", intro. to his ed. of *Quaestiones Disputatae.* Paris, Lethielleux, 1925. Vol. I, p. 1-24.

77. —"Saint Thomas d'Aquin createur de la dispute quodlibetique," in *Revue des sc. phil. et théol.,* 15 (1926) p. 477-506; 16 (1927) p. 5-38.

78. Mascarucci, P. "Le edizioni della Somma Teologica e l'edizione Leonina", in *Sapienza,* 1 (1948) p. 259-271.

79. Michelitsch, A. *Thomas-Schriften,* I, Graz und Wien, 1913.

80. Moos, M.-F. "Une nouvelle édition de l'écrit de saint Thomas sur les Sentences," in *Revue Thomiste,* 38 (1933) p. 576-602.

81. Muckle, J. T. "Greek Works Translated Directly into Latin before 1350," in *Mediaeval Studies,* 4 (1942) p. 33-42; 5 (1943) p. 102-114.

82. Muratori. *Scriptores Rerum Italicarum.* Tome XI. *Ptolomaei Lucensis Historica Ecclesiastica.* pp. 754-1242.

83. O'Rahilly, Alfred. "Notes on St. Thomas," in *The Irish Ecclesiastical Record,* 43 (1927) p. 481-490.

84. Pare, G., *et al. La Renaissance du XIIe siécle. Les écoles et l'enseignement.* Ottawa-Paris, 1933.

85. Pelster, F. "Beiträge sur Chronologie der Quodlibeta des hl. Thomas von Aquin," in *Gregorianum,* 8 (1927) p. 508-538; 10 (1929) p. 52-71, 387-403.

86. — "Die Uebersetsungen der aristotelischen Metaphysic in den Werken des hl. Thomas von Aquin," in *Gregorianum,* 16 (1935) p. 325-348, 531-561; 17 (1936) p. 377-406.

87. — "La quaestio disputata de S. Thomas 'de Unione Verbi Incarnati," in *Archives de philosophie,* 3 (1925) p. 198-245.

88. — "Zur Datierung der Quaestio disputata De spiritualibus creaturis," in *Gregorianum,* 6 (1925) p. 231-247.

89. Pelzer, Augustus. *Codices Vaticani Latini.* Tomus II, Pars Prior. In Bibliotheca Vaticana, 1931.

90. Quetif, J. and Echard, J. *Scriptores Ordinis Praedicatorum.* Lutetiae Parisiorum, apud Ballard et Simart, 2 vol., 1719, 1721.

91. Rashdall, H. *The Universities of Europe in the Middle Ages.* Rev. ed. F. M. Powicke and A. B. Emden. Oxford, Clarendon Press, 3 vol., 1936.

92. Salman, D. Review of Keeler's *De Unitate Intellectus,* in *Bulletin Thomiste,* 5 (1937) p. 63-65.

93. Sarton, George. *Introduction to the History of Science.* Carnegie Inst. of Washington, 3 vol., 5 parts, 1927-1948.

94. Stegmüller, Fridericus. *Repertorium Commentariorum in Sententias Petri Lombardi.* Würzburg, 2 vol., 1947.

95. Suermondt, Clemens. "Il contributo dell'edizione Leonina per la conoscensa di S. Tomasso," in *Scholastica Ratione Historico-Critica Instauranda.* (Bibl. Pont. Athen. Anton. 7) Rome, 1951, p. 235-282.

96. Synave, P. "La révélation des verités divines naturelles d'apres saint Thomas," in *Mélanges Mandonnet,* I (1930), p. 353-365.

97. — "Le problème chronologique des question disputées de saint Thomas d'Aquin," in *Revue Thomiste,* 31 (1926) p. 154-159.

98. Wals, Angelus. *Saint Thomas Aquinas.* tr. by Sebastian Bullough. Westminster, Md., Newman, 1951.

99. Zedler, Beatrice H. "The inner unity of the *De Potentia,"* in *The Modern Schoolman,* 25 (1948) p. 91-106.

100. — "Saint Thomas and Avicenna in the 'De Potentia Dei' ", in *Traditio,* 6 (1948) p. 105-159.

II. Doctrinal Section

101. Amann, E. "Némésius d'Èmèse" in *Dict. de théol. cath.* Tome 11, p. I, 1931, p. 62-67.

102. Bardy, Gustave. "Les sources patristiques grecques de S. Thomas," in *Revue des sc. phil. et théol.,* 12 (1923) p. 493-502.

103. Berube, C., *La connaissance de l'individuel au moyen age,* Paris, Presses Universitaires De France, 1964.

104. Bledsoe, J. P., "Aquinas on the Soul," *Laval Theologique et Philosophique,* 29 (1973) pp. 273-289.

105. Gadiou, R. *La Jeunesse d'Origene.* Paris, Beauchesne, 1935.

106. Callus, D., "The Problem of the Plurality of Forms in the 13th Century. The Thomist Innovation," in *L'Homme et son destin,* pp. 577-585.

107. Chossat, Marcel, "Saint Thomas d'Aquin et Siger de Brabant," in *Revue de philosophie,* 24 (1914) p. 552-575; 25 (1914) p. 25-52.

108. — "L'Averroïsme de saint Thomas," in *Archives de philosophie,* 9 (1932) p. 129-177.

109. Congar, Y., "L'historicité de l'homme selon Thomas d'Aquin," *Doctor Communis,* 22 (1969) pp. 297-304.

110. Delhaye, P., "A Propos de 'Persona Humana'," *Esprit et Vie* 86 (1976) pp. 177-186; 193-204; 225-234.

111. Etzwiler, J. P., "Man as Embodied Spirit," *New Scholastism,* 54 (1980) pp. 358-377.

112. Forest, A., et al. *Le mouvement doctrinal du IXe au XIVe siecle.* (Histoire de l'église, 13. ed. Fliche and Jarry) Bloud and Gay, 1951.

113. Gaul, Leopold. *Albert des Grossen Verhältnis zu Plato,* in *Beiträge . . .* Band XII, Heft 1. Münster i. W., 1913.

114. Geyer, B. (ed.) *Friedrich Ueberwegs Grundriss der Geschichte der Philosophie,* II, *Die Patristische und Scholastische Philosophie.* Berlin, 1928.

115. Étienne Gilson. "L'âme raisonnable chez Albert le Grand," in *Arch. d'hist. doct. et litt. du moyen âge,* 14 (1945) p. 5-72.

116. — "Doctrinal history and its interpretation," in *Speculum,* 24 (1949) p. 483-492.

117. — Review of F. Van Steenberghen's *Siger de Brabant,* Vol. II. In *Comptes Rendues, Bulletin Thomiste,* 6 (1940-42) p. 5-22.

118. — *L'ésprit de la philosophie médiévale.* 2 vol. Paris, 1932. Trans. as *The Spirit of Mediaeval Philosophy* by A. H. C. Downes. London, Sheed and Ward, 1936.

119. — *La philosophie au moyen âge.* 2nd ed. Paris, Payot, 1947.

120. — "Pourquoi saint Thomas a critiqué saint Augustin," in *Archives,* 1 (1926-27) p. 5-127.

121. — "Les sources greco-arabes de l'augustinisme avicennisant," in *Archives* 2 (1927) p. 89-149.

122. — *Le Thomisme,* Intro. à la philosophie de saint Thomas d'Aquin. 5th ed. Paris, Vrin, 1948.

123. Girodat, C.R., "The Thomistic Theory of Personal Growth and Development," *Angelicum,* 58 (1981) pp. 137-150.

124. Glorieux, P., "L'Université de Paris au XIIIe siecle," *Nouvelles de l'inst. Cath. de Paris,* 1957, no. 3, pp. 2-7; no. 4, pp. 1-10.

125. Greenen, G., "Les 'Sentences' de Pierre Lombard dans la 'Somme' de Saint Thomas," in *Miscellanea Lombardiana,* Novara, Instituto Geografico De Agostini, 1957, pp. 295-304.

126. Henle, R., *St. Thomas and Platonism,* The Hague, Nijhoff, 1956.

127. Hess, C.R., "Aquinas' Organic Synthesis of Plato and Aristotle," *Angelicum* 58 (1981) pp. 339-350.

128. Knowles, D., *The historical context of the philosophical works of St. Thomas Aquinas,* London, Blackfriars, 1958.

129. Mandonnet, P. *Siger de Brabant. L'Averroïsme latin au XIIIe siecle.* 2nd ed. 2 vol. Louvain, 1911.

130. Mazzarella, Pasquale. *Il "De Unitate" di Alberto Magno e di Tommaso d'Aquino in Rapporto alla Teoria Averroistica; Concordanze, Divergense, Sviluppi.* Naples, 1949.

131. McCormick, J. F. "Quaestiones Disputandae," in *New Scholasticism,* 13 (1939) pp. 368-374.

132. Moreau, J., "L'homme et son Âme selon S. Thomas d'Aquin," *Revue Philosophique de Louvain,* 74 (1976) pp. 5-29.

133. Muller-Thym, B. J. *The Establishment of the University of Being in the Doctrine of Meister Eckhart of Hochheim.* New York, Sheed and Ward, 1939.

134. O'Neil, Charles J. "Plotinus as critic of the Aristotelian soul," in *Proceedings* of the American Cath. Phil. Association, 23 (1949) pp. 156-166.

135. — "St. Thomas and the Nature of Man," in *Proceedings* of the Amer. Cath. Phil. Assoc., 25 (1951) pp. 41-66.

136. Pace, E. A. "The soul in the system of St. Thomas," in *Cath. U. Bulletin,* 4 (1898), pp. 50-61.

137. Pegis, A. C. "In umbra intelligentiae," in *New Scholasticism,* 14 (1940) pp. 146-180.

138. — *St. Thomas and the Problem of the Soul in the Thirteenth Century.* Toronto, St. Michael's College, 1934.

139. — "Some permanent contributions of medieval philosophy to the notion of man," in *Transactions* of the Royal Society of Canada. 3rd series, Sec. II, Vol. 46 (1952) pp. 67-78.

140. Reyna, R., "On the Soul: A Philosophical Exploration on the Active Intellect in Averroes, Aristotle and Aquinas," *The Thomist,* 36 (1972) pp. 131-149.

141. Robb, James H., *Man as Infinite Spirit.* Milwaukee, Marquette University Press, 1974.

142. Reilly, G. C. *The Psychology of St. Albert the Great Compared with that of St. Thomas.* (Diss.) Washington, Cath. U., 1934.

143. Roland-Gosselin, M.-D. "Sur les relations de l'âme et du corps d'ápres Avicenne," in *Mélanges Mandonnet,* 2 (Bibl. Thomiste, 14) Paris, 1930, pp. 47-54.

144. Sertillanges, A.-D. *S. Thomas d'Aquin.* 4th ed. 2 vol., Paris, 1925.

145. de Solages, Bruno. "La cohérence de la métaphysique de l'âme d'Albert le Grand," in *Mélanges Cavallera.* Toulouse, 1948.

146. van Steenberghen, Fernand. *Aristote en Occident, Les origines de l'aristotelisme Parisien.* Louvain, 1946.

147. — *Siger de Brabant,* Vol. II, *Siger dans l'histoire de l'aristotelisme."* Louvain, 1942.

148. Verberle, G., "Man as a 'Frontier' according to Aquinas," in *Aquinas and Problems of his Time.* Leuven, University Press. The Hague, Martinus Nijhoff, 1976, pp. 195-223.

149. Zedler, B., "Averroes and Immortality," *New Scholasticism,* 1954, pp. 436-453.

150. — "St. Thomas, interpreter of Avicenna," *Modern Schoolman,* 1955, pp. 1-18.

GLOSSARY OF TERMS

These reciprocal word lists are intended as an aid to the reader without access to the Latin text who wishes to compare the terminology of the translation with the Latin terms used by St. Thomas. The lists are not a complete index, but are restricted to terms which seem of greater importance or interest.

The following conventions are observed.

1. Where no references are given, the term has this sense throughout.

2. Where the verbal equivalence is obvious, a term is not listed; e.g., *modus* — mode.

3. By way of exception to the above, a term is listed when the translator has assigned to it both its obvious verbal equivalent and other meanings. Thus "*ratio* — reason *pass.*" indicates that 'reason' is the usual translation of *ratio;* while the other meanings assigned by the translator are then given.

4. To facilitate the use of both lists, paginal references are in most cases given with both the English and the Latin term.

English - Latin

achieve fullness of being	perfici 121
acted on, be	pati 242, 244
action	actio *pass.* actus 145
activity	actus 167, 207
actual, actually	actu, in actu
actualization	reductio 201
affected, be	pati *pass.* adfici 238
affection	affectus 245
affectivity	pati (Sbst.) 98
air	aer 113, 245
alike	conformis 157
alteration	mutatio 55

analogically, analogously   per (secundum) analogiam 233,
                                        239
analogous   proportionatus 229
appropriate   conveniens 129, 169
                                     proprius 115
aptitude   habilitas 180
argument   probatio 122
                                     ratio 94, 104, 109, 198, 218
arranged   dispositus 115, 117
assembling   compositio 139
assert   ponere 234
atmosphere   aer 49

balanced proportion   complexio 135
being   ens (q.v.)
beings   entia, res
bereft of   alienatus 190
blending   complexio 116, 120
boundary line   confinium 48
brain   cerebrum 116
by nature   natus est

capability   capacitas 59, 111
capable of knowledge   cognoscitivus 48
cause   causa pass.
                                     agens 97, 106
                                     movens 71
change   mutatio pass.
                                     alteratio 168
change, to   mutare, transmutare
choice   electio pass.
                                     arbitrium 102, 103
circumscribed   comprehensus 49
coalesce   colligari 130
coarse   grossus 114
cogitative power   virtus, vis, cogitativa 116, 167
cognitive power   potentia cognoscitiva
combination   complexio 111, 117
combine   commiscere 116
compact   densus 48
complete   perfectus 140, 141
complete, to   perficere 47, 95
composed   compositus pass.
                                     commixtus 117
composite, the   compositum
composite being   conjunctum 98, 131
composition   compositio pass.
                                     complexio 89
compound   mixtum 126, 133
compounded   commixtus 117

compounds — corpora mixta 48, 106
conceived, be (in the mind) — attendi 154
condition — habitudo 116
confined, be — includi 55
constant state — habitus 88
constituted — reductus 116
contained — comprehensus 59
contemplating — consideratio 200
'continuation' — continuatio Q 16 *pass.*

decision — electio 179
decomposition — putrefactio 86
definition — definitio *pass.*
    ratio 46
deliberation, by — conferendo 167
deluded — varius 73
dense — grossus 245
deprived — denudatus 116
desire — appetitus 178
desire, to — appetere
desires — concupiscentiae
devoid of — denudatus 57
digest — resolvere 171
directed toward — inclinatus 200
discriminate — dijudicare 167
disposition — dispositio *pass.*
    complexio 84
dispersion — resolutio 168
dissolution — corruptio 113

efficacious — virtuosus 107
elemental, elementary, body — corpus elementare 113, 120
elevated, be — assumi 101
embryo — animal conceptum 61
    embryo 145
empty, be — denudari 65
entity — hoc aliquid
essence — essentia *pass.*
    quod quid est 163
    quod quid erat esse 68
    quod est 96
essential — essentialis *pass.*
    proprius (q.v.)
essential predicaiton — praedicatio per se 149
essentially — de se, per se, secundum se,
    proprie
estimative power — [vis] aestimativa 122, 167
evidence — signum 178

exact   certus 115
exact same   uniformis 138
excellence   bonitas 115
                                           nobilitas 51
excess   excellentia 115
existence, act of existence   esse (q.v.)
experience   experientia 187
experience, to   pati 97
experiences   experimenta 84
extrinsic principle   ab extrinseco 146

faculty   potentia 71
failure   inefficacia 61
fetus   conceptum 145
fickle   varius 73
fiery   calidus 112
figure   figura *pass.*
                                           forma 79
first efficient cause   primum agens 106
first heaven   caelum primum 67
fit   habilis 115
fitted   dispositus 120
force   vis 154
formal difference   differentia formae,
                                           formalis 72, 104
formal object   ratio objecti 170
                                           (cp. 191, 192)
formal principle   principium formale 95
formality   ratio 170
formally distinct   non unius rationis 218
formed   reductus 111
free of   absolutus 207
                                           denudatus 177
from without   ab extrinseco
fulfillment   complementum 48
                                           completio 106
fullness   perfectio 141
                                           totalitas 141
functionless   otiosus 174

gaze   aspectus 220
gaze on   intueri 207
grounded   fundatus 59
grounded, be   radicari *pass.*
                                           fundari 102, 110
                                           inesse 59

habitual knowledge	scientia in habitu 219
habitual scientific knowledge	habitus scientiarum 70
hardened	congellabilis 120
hierarchy	hierarchia *pass.*
	ordo 105, 127, 148, 150
hindered, be	pati 62
ideal reasons	rationes ideales 233, 239
imagination	imaginatio, phantasia
immediately cognized	speculata Q 16 *pass.*
implanted	inditus 184
in a qualified sense	secundum quid
in reality	in rerum natura 78, 79, 94
	in rebus 66
incapacitated	orbatus 199
independent	absolutus 47
influence	compassio 79
	impressio 87
influx	influxus *pass.*
	influentia 215, 217
informed	formatus 51
infusion	influentia 218
	influxus 233
	infusio 146
inhere	inhaerere *pass.*
	inesse 128
innate	inditus 115
	innatus 107, 184
	insitus 88
inorganic	inanimatus 105
	mineralis 106
intense	excellens 247
intermediary	medium
intermingled	permixtus 57
intermingled, be	misceri 124
intrinsic principle of action	intrinsecum agens 166
intuition	intuitus 109
investigation	inquirendo, inquisitio *pass.*
	inventio 191
its own	proprius (q.v.)
joined	conjunctus
joined, conjoined, to be	continuari 58, 196
judgment	aestimatio 247
keenness	acumen 218, 247
keep in existence	conservare 171

knowledge

cognitio, scientia *pass.*
apprehensio 131
notitia (Aug.) 159

level (Sbst.)
light of glory
likeness

gradus
illustratio gloriae 107
similitudo *pass.*
species 122

limit
limited, be
lofty

mensura 120
determinari 239
altus 163, 164, 168
nobilis 112, 113
sublimis 111, 117

lowly
luminous

ignobilis 111
fulgidus 115
lucidus 77, 119

manifold
mean
meaning
median, middle, state
medium of sight
mixture

multiplicatus 163
medium 116
ratio 61
medium 102, 120
diaphanum 76
commixtio 118
complexio 46
mixtio 133
mixtum 94

moist, the
moist element
moisture

humor 96
humidum 120
humectatio 168
humidum 126

natural

naturalis *pass.*
proprius (q.v.)

natural unit
naturally, by nature

unum quid naturale 140
naturaliter *pass.*
natus est

nature

natura *pass.*
ratio 71, 107, 244
species 48, 98

negative judgment
noble
notion

negatio 109
honorabilis 85
notio *pass.*
ratio 176, 178, 237

obliterated, be
oneness
ordered
ordering

tolli 175
unitas 69, 70
dispositus 112, 121
dispositio 116

part	pars *pass.*
	complementum 71
participate	participare *pass.*
	communico 62
particular phenomena	particularia 114
particular reason	ratio particularis 167
particularized	particulatus 114
patient, the	patiens
permeated	absorptus 186
philosopher of nature	naturalis 109
philosophy of nature	naturalis consideratio 178
pliant	mollis 115
positive indication	notificatio 109
power	possibilitas 201
	potentia (q.v.)
	potestas 140
	virtus, vis *pass.*
power of sense	sensus 59, 126
predicated of, be	praedicari *pass.*
	denominari 137
preservation	conservatio 164
prime mover	primum movens 173
primary faculty of sensation	sensitivum primum 165, 172
principle, principles	principium, principia *pass.*
	rationes 90
principle of sensibility	principium sensitivum 56
privilege	beneficium 117
product	operatum 55
proper sense	sensus proprius 167, 168
property	proprietas, proprium
proportion	proportio *pass.*
	convenientia 248
qualified entity	quale quid 46
quick in motion	agilis 113
rank	gradus 106
reasoning process	discursus 100, 107
reflective activity	consideratio 200
related	ordinatus 148
related to, be	comparari ad *pass.*
	se habere ad *pass.*
	se extendere ad 170
relation	comparatio 47
	habitudo 74, 127, 249
	proportio 60, 211
replacement	alteratio 157
restricted	definitus 66
	specialis 128

restricted, be   determinari 60
retained, be   conservari 167
retentive   conservativus 167
revealed, be   indicari 107
rooted, be   radicari 205

section   signum 137
sensation   sensus 88, 115
separate *and* separated   separatus
shape   figura 56
                              forma 79
share in   communico 46
sight   aspectus 200, 206
single   unus 76, 106, 134
specific difference   differentia *pass.*
                              differentia secundum
                              speciem 67
specific nature   species
spirit   spiritus *pass.*
                              animus (cit.) 154
structured   determinatus 86
subject to, be   pati 201
substantial unit   unum per se 124
suffer   pati 238
suffering   passio
suitable   conveniens 114, 115, 116, 117
superior   excellens 200

tendency   inclinatio 167, 247, 248
thinking, act of   considerare 155
'to be,' the   esse 47, 91, 96
traces   vestigia 238
transmission, by   transmutando 234
transmitter   vehiculum 119
transparency   diaphanum 49, 96
                              diaphaneitas 96
turn to   converti, se convertere, ad

undergo   pati 94
unifying sense   sensus communis 167, 235
unit   unum *pass.*
                              unitas 72, 105, 128
understanding, act of   intelligere
union   unio *pass.*
                              concretio 53
                              conjunctio 86
                              continuatio 58
united   concretus 53

universal	universalis *pass.*
	communis 170
universe of things	rerum natura 49
unusually strong	intensus 150
vigorously	intensive 79
virtually	virtute 133, 223
vision	aspectus 217
without form	informis 51
without qualification	simpliciter

Latin - English

ab extrinseco	from without *pass.*
	extrinsic principle 146
absolutus	free of body 207
	independent 47
absorptus	permeated 186
actu, in actu	actual, actually
actus	act *pass.*
	action 145
	activity 167, 207
acumen	keenness 218, 247
adfici	be affected 238
aer	air 113, 245
	atmosphere 49
aestimatio	judgment 247
affectus	affection 245
agens	agent *pass.*
	cause 95, 106
agens intrinsecum	intrinsic principle of action 166
agilis	quick in motion 113
alienatus	bereft of 190
alteratio	alteration 247
	change 168
	replacement 157
animal conceptum	embryo 61
animus	spirit (cit.) 154
appetere	desire *pass.*
	seek 171
appetitus	appetite *pass.*
	desire 178
apprehensio	apprehension *pass.*
	knowledge 131
aptus	endowed, suitable 115

arbitrium
aspectus

assumi
attendi

beneficium
bonitas

caelum primum
calidus
capacitas

cerebrum
certus
cognoscitivus
colligari
commiscere
commixtio
commixtus
communico

communis

comparari ad
comparatio
compassio
complementum

completio
complexio

compositio

compositum

comprehensus

conceptum
concretio
concretus
concupiscentia
concupiscentiae

choice 102, 103
gaze 220
sight 200, 206
vision 217
be elevated 101
be conceived (in mind) 154

privilege 117
goodness *pass.*
excellence 115

first heaven 67
fiery 112
capacity *pass.*
capability 59, 111
brain 116
exact 115
capable of knowledge 48
coalesce 130
combine 116
mixture 118
composed, compounded 117
participate 62
share in 46
common, general *pass.*
universal 170
be related to
relation 47
influence 79
fulfillment 48
part 71
fulfillment 106
blending 116, 120
combination 111, 117
composition 89
disposition 84
balanced proportion 84
composition *pass.*
assembling 139
the composite *pass.*
something made up of parts 140
contained 59
circumscribed 49
fetus 145
union 53
united 53
concupiscence, lust
desires

conferendo	by deliberation 167
confinium	boundary line 48
conformis	alike 157
congellabilis	hardened 120
conjunctio	union 86
conjunctum	composite being, the composite 98, 131
conjunctus	joined
conservare	conserve 158, 166
	keep in existence 171
conservari	be retained 167
conservatio	conservation 164
	preservation 120
conservativus	retentive 167
considerare	act of thinking 155
consideratio	reflective activity 200
continuari	be joined, conjoined 58, 196
continuatio	conjoining 58
	union 58
	'continuation' (Averr.) Q 16 *pass.*
conveniens	appropriate 129, 169
	suitable 114, 115, 116, 117
convenientia	proportion 248
convertere se, converti, ad	turn to
corpora mixta	compound bodies 118, 126
	compounds 48, 106
	mixed bodies 105
corpus elementare	elemental, elementary, body 113, 120
corruptio	corruption *pass.*
	dissolution 113
definitus	restricted 66
denominare	give its name 227
denominari	be predicated of 137
densus	compact 48
denudari	be empty 65
denudatus	deprived 116
	free of 177
	devoid 57
determinari	be determined *pass.*
	be restricted, limited 60, 239
determinatus	determined *pass.*
	structured 86
diaphaneitas	transparency 96

diaphanum

transparency, the
transparent *pass.*
medium of sight 76

differentia

specific difference

differentia formae, formalis

formal difference 72, 104

differentia secundum speciem

specific difference

dijudicare

discriminate 167

discursus

discursiveness 108
reasoning process 100, 107

dispositio

disposition *pass.*
ordering 116

dispositus

arranged 115, 117
fitted 120
ordered 112, 121

electio

choice *pass.*
decision 179

ens

(a) being, beings (entia) *pass.*,
    e.g. 130: secundum quod est
    e. est unum
being, e.g. 102: e. nec est genus
    nec differentia

esse

existence, act of existence *pass.*
an existent 174
being, e.g. 176: e. consequitur
    formam. Cp. triplex e. rerum
    216; e. reale 58; e. sensibile,
    intelligibile 237
the 'to be' 47, 91, 96

excellens

excellent 239
in the highest degree 195
intense 247
superior 200

excellentia

excess 115

experientia

experience 187

experimenta

experiences 83

figura

figure *pass.*
shape 56

forma

form *pass.*
shape, figure 79

formae elementares

forms of the elements

formatus

informed 51

fulgidus

luminous 115

fundari

be grounded 102, 110
be located 59

fundatus

grounded 59

gradus	grade, level *pass.*
	rank 106
grossus	coarse 114
	dense 245
habilis	fit 115
habilitas	aptitude 180
habitudo	condition 116
	relation 74, 127, 249
habitus	habit *pass.*
	constant state 88
habitus scientiarum	habitual scientific
	knowledge 70, 196
hoc aliquid	entity
honorabilis	noble 85
humectatio	moisture 168
humidum	the moist element 120
	moisture 126
ignobilis	lowly 111
illustratio gloriae	light of glory 107
impressio	impression *pass.*
	influence 87
in rerum natura, in rebus	in reality 66, 78, 79, 94
inanimatus	inorganic 105
inclinatio	inclination 180, 238
	tendency 167, 247, 248
inclinatus	directed toward 200
includi	be confined 55
indicari	be revealed 107
inditus	implanted 184
	innate 115
inefficacia	failure 61
inesse	be grounded 59
	inhere 128
influentia	influx 215, 217
	infusion 218
influxus (PPP)	infused 208, 212, 232
informis	without form 51
insitus	innate 88
intelligere	act of understanding
intensive	vigorously 79
intensus	unusually strong 150
intueri	gaze on 207
intuitus	intuition 109
inventio	investigation 191

lucidus — luminous 77, 119

medians — through the medium of *pass.*
by means of 124
medium — medium *pass.*
intermediary Q 9 *pass.* 237
mean 116
median, middle, state 102, 120
mensura — limit 120
mineralis — mineral 106
inanimate 105
misceri — be intermingled 124
mixtio — compound, mixture 133
mixtum — compound 126, 133
mixture 94
mollis — pliant 115
movens — cause 71
multiplicatus — manifold 163
mutatio — change, mutation *pass.*
alteration 55

natura — nature *pass.*
species 48, 98
naturalis — philosopher of nature 109
naturalis consideratio — philosophy of nature 178
natus est — by nature, naturally 48, 57, 185,
234, 249; cp. 166
negatio — negative judgment 109
nobilis — high, lofty, noble
nobilitas — excellence 51
notificatio — positive indication 109
notitia — knowledge (Aug.) 159

operatum — product 55
orbatus — incapacitated 199
ordinari — be oriented 207
ordinatus — related 148
ordo — order *pass.*
hierarchy 105, 127, 148, 150
rank 115
otiosus — functionless 174

particularia — particular phenomena 114
particulatus — particularized 114
passio — passion *pass.*
suffering 117 Q 21 *pass.*

pati	be affected *pass.*
	be acted on 242, 244
	be hindered 62
	be subject to 201
	experience 97
	suffer 238
	undergo 94
pati (Sbst.)	affectivity 98
patiens	the patient
perfectio	perfection *pass.*
	fullness 141
perfectus	perfect, complete
perficere	to perfect *pass.*
	to complete 47, 95
perfici	achieve fullness of being 121
permixtus	intermingled 57
phantasia	imagination
ponere	assert 234
possibilitas	power 201
potentia	potency *pass.*
	faculty 71
	power (= principia operandi 155, 156) 225 Qq 12, 13 *pass.*
potestas	power 140
primum agens	first efficient cause 106
primum movens	prime mover 173
principia constitutiva	principles which constitute the essence 139
principium, principia	principle, principles *pass.*
	beginning, starting point 103, 250
probatio	argument 122
proportio	proportion *pass.*
	relation 60, 211
proportionatus	proportioned *pass.*
	analogous 229
proprius	This term, of frequent occurrence, is given both as 'proper' and as 'essential' *pass.* Thus accidentia p. — 'proper accidents;' operatio p. — 'essential operation.' Also 'natural' (114, 116, 127) and 'its own' (173, 216, 249, 250).
putrefactio	decomposition 86
quale quid	qualified entity 46

quod quid est, erat esse,
    quod est   essence 68, 163, 96

radicari   be grounded *pass.*
                                     be rooted 205
ratio   reason *pass.*
                                     argument 94, 104, 109, 198, 218
                                     definition 46, 105, 116, 208
                                     formality 170 (cp. 218)
                                     meaning 61
                                     nature 71, 107, 244
                                     notion 176, 178, 237
                                     principle 90
ratio formalis objecti   formality as an object 191, 192
ratio objecti   formal object 170
ratio particularis   particular reason 167
reduci   be brought (to) *pass.*
                                     become actualized 77
reductio   actualization 201
reductus   constituted 116
                                     formed 111
rerum natura   nature as a whole 117
                                     reality 78
                                     universe of things 49
res   things, beings
resolutio   dispersion 168
resolvere   digest 171

scientia in habitu   habitual knowledge 219
secundum quid   in a qualified sense
sensitivum primum   primary faculty of sensation 165,
                                         172
sensus   sense, senses *pass.*
                                     sense power 59, 126
                                     sensation 88, 115
sensus communis   unifying sense 167, 235
sensus proprius   proper sense 167, 168
separatus   separate, separated
signum   evidence 178
                                     section 137
similitudo   likeness
simpliciter   without qualification, in the
                                         absolute sense
species   species, specific nature *pass.*
                                     likeness 122
                                     nature 48, 98
specialis   restricted 128

speculata	'speculated,' immediately cognized Q 16 *pass.*
spiritus (Pl.)	['animal'] spirts 116, 119 Q 8 *pass.*
sublimis	lofty 111, 117
tolli	be obliterated 175
totalitas	totality *pass.*
	fullness 141
transmutare	change *pass.*
	transmit 234
transmutatio	transformation 158
uniformis	exact same 138
uniformius	more unifiedly 237
unitas	oneness 69, 70
	unit 72, 105, 128
unum	unit
unum per se	substantial unit 124
unum quid naturale	natural unit 140
unus	one *pass.*
	single 76, 106, 134
varius	deluded, fickle 73
vehiculum	transmitter 119
vestigia	traces 238
virtuosus	efficacious 107
	powerful 155
virtus	power, virtue *pass.*
	capability 140
virtute	virtually 133, 223
vis	power *pass.*
	force 154
vis collativa	power which compares 167

MEDIAEVAL PHILOSOPHICAL TEXTS IN TRANSLATION

Translation #1: "Grosseteste: On Light"
by Clare Riedl-Trans.
This treatise is significant as an introduction to an influential thinker and man of science of the Middle Ages.

Translation #2: "St. Augustine: Against the Academicians"
by Sister Mary Patricia, R.S.M.-Trans.
Augustine aims to prove that man need not be content with mere probability in the realm of knowledge.

Translation #3: "Pico Della Mirandola: Of Being and Unity"
by Victor M. Hamm-Trans.
In this work Pico tried to discover the genuine thought of Plato and Aristotle on being and unity.

Translation #4: "Francis Suarez: On the Various Kinds of Distinction"
by Cyril Vollert, S.J.-Trans.
Suarez propounds his theory on distinctions, a point of capital importance for a grasp of Suarezian metaphysics.

Translation #5: "St. Thomas Aquinas: On Spiritual Creatures"
by Mary C. Fitzpatrick-Trans.
This book falls into two general divisions: an introduction and the translation from the Latin.

Translation #6: "Meditations of Guigo"
by John J. Jolin, S.J.-Trans.
A series of reflections by Guigo, 12th century Prior of the hermitage Charterhouse.

Translation #7: "Giles of Rome: Theorems on Existence and Essence"
by Michael V. Murray, S.J.-Trans.
An essay dealing with the a priori deductions of being and its conditions.

Translation #8: "John of St. Thomas: Outlines of Formal Logic"
by Francis C. Wade, S.J.-Trans.
A standard English translation of the Logic of John of St. Thomas.

Translation #9: "Hugh of St. Victor: Soliloquy in the Earnest Money of the Soul"
Kevin Herbert-Trans.
The purpose of the work is to direct the soul toward a true love of self, an attitude which is identical with a love of God.

Translation #10: "St. Thomas Aquinas: On Charity"
by Lottie Kendzierski-Trans.
This treatise is significant as an expression of St. Thomas' discussion on the virtue of charity in itself, its object, subject, order, precepts, and principal act.

Translation #11: "Aristotle: On Interpretation-Commentary by St. Thomas and Cajetan"
Jean T. Oesterle-Trans.
This translation will be of particular value to teachers and students of logic.

Translation #12: "Desiderius Erasmus of Rotterdam: On Copia of Words and Ideas"
by Donald B. King and H. David Rix-Trans.
One of the most popular and influential books of the 16th century is made available here for the first time in English.

Translation #13: "Peter of Spain: Tractatus Syncategorematum and Selected Anonymous Treatises"
by Joseph P. Mullally and Roland Houde-Trans.
The first English translation of these tracts now makes it possible for scholars of logic to better appreciate the continuity of Formal Logic.

Translation #14: "Cajetan: Commentary on St. Thomas Aquinas' On Being and Essence"
by Lottie Kendzierski and Francis C. Wade, S.J.-Trans.
A basic understanding of the relation between Cajetan and St. Thomas.

Translation #15: "Suarez: Disputation VI, On Formal and Universal Unity"
by James F. Ross-Trans.
The study of late mediaeval philosophy and the decline of scholasticism.

Translation #16: "St. Thomas, Sieger de Brabant, St. Bonaventure: On the Eternity of the World"
by Cyril Vollert, S.J., Lottie Kendzierski, Paul Byrne-Trans.
A combined work bringing together the writings of three great scholars on the philosophical problem of the eternity of the world.

Translation #17: "Geoffrey of Vinsauf: Instruction in the Method and Art of Speaking and Versifying"
by Roger P. Parr–Trans.
This text, of one of the most important mediaeval literary theorists, is here for
the first time translated into English.

Translation #18: "Liber De Pomo: The Apple, or Aristotle's Death"
by Mary F. Rousseau–Trans.
A significant item in the history of mediaeval thought, never previously translated
into English from the Latin.

Translation #19: "St. Thomas Aquinas: On the Unity of the Intellect Against the Averroists"
by Beatrice H. Zedler–Trans.
This is a polemical treatise that St. Thomas wrote to answer a difficult problem
confronting his times.

Translation #20: "The Universal Treatise of Nicholas of Autrecourt"
by Leonard L. Kennedy C.S.B., Richard E. Arnold, S.J. and Arthur E.
Millward, A.M.
This treatise gives an indication of the deep philosophical skepticism at the
University of Paris in the mid-fourteenth century.

Translation #21 "Pseudo-Dionysius Aeropagite: The Divine Names and Mystical Theology"
by John D. Jones–Trans.
Among the most important works in the transition from later Greek to Medieval
thought.

Translation #22 "Matthew of Vendôme: Ars Versificatoria (The Art of the Versemaker)"
by Roger P. Parr–Trans.
The Text of this, the earliest of the major treatises of the *Artest Poetical* is here
translated in toto with special emphasis given to maintaining the full nature of
the complete original text.

Translation #23 "Suarez on Individuation, Metaphysical Disputation V: Individual Unity and
its Principle",
by Jorge J.E. Gracia–Trans.
Gracia discusses in masterful detail the main positions on the problem of individuation developed in the Middle Ages and offers his own original view.

Translation #24 Francis Suarez: On the Essence of the Finite Being as Such, on the Existence
of That Essence and Their Distinction.
by Norman J. Wells–Trans.
From the Latin "De Essentia Entis Ut Tale Est, Et De Illius Esse, Eorumque
Distinctione, by Francisco Suarez, S.J. in the 16th Century.

Translation #25 "The Book of Causes (Liber De Causis)"
by Dennis Brand–Trans.
One of the central documents in the dossier on Neo-Platonism in the Middle
Ages. Translated from the 13th Century Latin.

Translation #26 "Giles of Rome: Errores Philosophorum"
by John O. Riedl–Trans.
A previously little-known work that bears new attention due to revived interest
in mediaeval studies. Author makes compilation of exact source references of the
Errores philosophorum, Aristotelis, Averrois, Avicennae, Algazelis, Alinkdi,
Rabbi Moysis, which were contrary to the Christian Faith.

Translation #27 "St. Thomas Aquinas: Questions on the Soul"
by James H. Robb–Trans.
The last major text of St. Thomas on Man as Incarnate spirit. In this last of his
major texts on what it means to be a human being, St. Thomas develops a new
and unique approach to the question. The introduction discusses and summarizes
the key themes of St. Thomas' philosophical anthropology.

James H. Robb, Ph.D. is editor of the Mediaeval Philosophical Texts in Translation.

Copies of this translation and the others in the series are obtainable from:
Marquette University Press
Marquette University
Milwaukee, Wisconsin 53233, U.S.A.

Publishers of:

• Mediaeval Philosophical   • Père Marquette   • St. Thomas
Texts in Translation   Theology Lectures   Aquinas Lectures